The Suzuki® Violinist

a guide for teachers and parents

William Starr

Revised Edition

© 2000, 1976 Summy-Birchard Music
division of Summy-Birchard, Inc.
Exclusive print rights administered by Alfred Music
All rights reserved.   Produced in USA.

ISBN 0-87487-605-2

Summy-Birchard Inc.
Exclusively distributed by
Alfred Music

CONTENTS

Acknowledgements

Many words of tribute, admiration and gratitude have been given to Shinichi Suzuki over the years. I should like to add my boundless appreciation for the new vistas which he opened for me—the ideals which he set before all teachers of children which make teaching and learning an exciting endeavor full of personal and professional challenge. For this and his personal help in making this book fulfill its purpose of spreading his philosophy and methodology, I say a deeply felt 'thank you'. Also for his gracious permission given to me for the use of the following: a reproduction of one of his shikishi for the front cover, quotations from his autobiography, "Nurtured by Love", excerpts of a talk given to the Japan Institute of Educational Psychology, numerous quotations from our conversations over the years, quotations from the Suzuki-Starr videotapes, and pictures of him demonstrating facets of his Talent Education program.

In addition I should like to extend my warm appreciation to Waltraud Suzuki for her assistance and encouragement, a n d to numerous Japanese teachers, especially Denda-sensei, Hirose-sensei, Kataoka-sensei, Mori-sensei, Yamamura-sensei, and Yamashite-sensei, to Japanese parents and children, and the staff of Suzuki's Talent Education Institute in Matsumoto, particularly Mitsuko Miasaka.

I wish to thank Hiroko Iritani Driver and Susan Shields, who have been teachers in our University of Tennessee Suzuki program, for the interview on Japanese-American differences.

For photographs, recognition is due Susan Shields for the picture on page 18, Art Montzka for pictures on pages 1, 23, and 29, and Stephen Driver for pictures on pages 23, 55, and 69. All the rest of the pictures were taken by the author.

Lastly, I should like to thank my dearest wife, Connie, and my children for suggestions, proof-reading, typing, and above all, encouragement and forbearance.

Shinichi and Waltraud Suzuki with the author.

Preface

I face publication of this book with a little uneasiness because I am setting down in immovable type words which describe something living and evolving, the Talent Education program of Shinichi Suzuki. I thought that the best way to force myself to complete this book was to keep announcing my intentions publicly. I would like to apologize here to all those who, over the last seven years, thought these announcements indicated that publication was imminent. The seven-year delay, however, was not just the result of abulia or procrastination in the face of a difficult task but also necessary to provide for ample time to assess needs, problems, and successes on the Western scene.

This book was written for those least informed about Suzuki philosophy and methodology. Specifically, I had in mind the non-musical parent, the novice teacher, and the experienced teacher who had had little contact with the Suzuki approach. I hope it will also prove of value to the eclectic inquiring teacher who has no intention of becoming a Suzuki disciple.

These words cannot defend themselves. They lie helpless, subject to all kinds of misinterpretations. How I wish they were able to rise and say, "But that isn't what we mean!". I have tried for clarity, but I'm sure there must be for some readers many examples of over-simplification.

My desire to aid the written word has given rise to extensive use of the photograph. It has been called the thousand-word substitute, yet here it has its limitations in that the photograph is arrested motion, a still picture from only one angle. This calls for another picture, and yet another. Hopefully, the photographs will serve an instructive role for parent and teacher, and may catch the observant eye of the youngster who comprehends without analysis.

This manual deals primarily with personal observation of Suzuki over a ten-year period, 1965-1975, as described elsewhere in this book. I hope the reader realizes that Suzuki's own statement, "We must continue to search for new and better ways to teach," may lead him or his followers to new means of aiding the development of musical talent. This should not lessen the importance of this material which reflects the thirty-year development of the empirical method of the man whose eminently successful work has attracted worldwide attention.

I have repeatedly made use of phrases such as "Suzuki's idea is . . . .", "Suzuki thinks . . .", "Suzuki's observation is . . . .", etc. I didn't mean to exclude these ideas from the province of others. Newcomers to the Suzuki approach are heard upon occasion to protest, "But I've been doing some of these things for years!" The Suzuki package contains all kinds of ideas others have used in whole or in part. I suppose it is the package itself that is unique, although one might be hard pressed to find a pre-Suzuki teacher who accompanied a three-year-old onto the stage, fixed her violin and bow properly, then remained close to her on bended knee as she played her first recital solo, a six-note rhythmic figure on the open E string!

The suggested exercises were inserted after a request by an old friend and Suzuki colleague, Betty Newell. They should be taken for what they are called, SUGGESTED EXERCISES. While writing them, I envisioned a parent needing help in daily practice. My advice to those of you not liking the suggested exercises because they usurp your realm of creativity: ignore them or read them and then do your own thing if you feel it would be better for your student.

Someone has said that no two Suzuki teachers teach alike. Who disputes this? Suzuki doesn't always teach alike himself. After all, both the teacher and the student are unique. To be applied successfully, the Suzuki approach, even with a well laid out plan to follow, requires a great deal of creativity from the teacher. "I thought it was all programmed" bewailed a new Suzuki teacher, "and now I find that I have to think harder than ever!"

Marvin Rabin once said that anyone following a method or leading pedagogue should be encouraged to list his or her own name after that of the leader, indicating the individual's interpretive or creative role. Then Mrs. Jones would not say, "I am teaching the Suzuki method", but rather, "I am teaching the Suzuki-Jones method". This would not be vanity. It would be stating a reality.

Why is this book not entitled "the Suzuki method"? Suzuki himself doesn't like the term, because he regards it as more than a method. He thought if the word "method" were to be used, it should be called the "mother-tongue" method.

The Suzuki approach, based on what he calls the "mother-tongue method", differs from traditional methods of teaching instrumental music because it involves the student at a very early age which necessitates much participation on the part of the parent. This necessary involvement of the parent creates problems arising from additional relationships. Normally, the Western parent's involvement in the child's study has been minimal. The parent took the child to the lessons, or saw that he went on time, and urged or insisted that he practice. Both parents usually attended the annual recitals and orchestral programs.

The relationship is much more complicated when the parent accepts the role of home-teacher. And so, a book on Suzuki study needs to contain a step-by-step methodology presented with an eye on the fact that the student is most often quite young. Psychological aspects of this early training need to be covered.

Suzuki is the first to realize how difficult it is to describe quality verbally, especially the ever-shifting standard of quality in this approach. Asked why he hadn't written a detailed exposition of his way of teaching, he answered that he preferred to work with his teachers in person. His annual refresher course for teachers gives him a chance to impart new ideas and to reinforce the established ideas. He believes in a great deal of repetition to ensure that they all understand. Since he listens to all the tapes submitted for graduation to all levels, he has a good idea how all of the teachers are teaching.

It is common to witness three different reactions to anything new: those who reject it automatically, those who embrace it without question, and the majority who look at the new with skepticism but are ready to adopt it as they are convinced of its validity, as they see its success. "Does it work?" they ask. Adherents flocked to the Suzuki banner after the young Japanese players began to tour. "Suzuki" as one critic said, "spread not only widely but wildly". Might not a powerful reason for this have been that countless teachers and parents were unhappy with the status quo and remembered vividly how unhappy they had been with their training as children?

It's impossible to recall every person who engaged in the pioneer efforts to introduce Suzuki's way to the West, but I would like to acknowledge several individuals who did play an important role in those early years: Kenji Mochizuki, who as an Oberlin student showed a film of Suzuki children to the Ohio String Teachers Association; Clifford Cook, who arranged that demonstration and John Kendall, who was in the audience, both of whom brought so much attention to Suzuki throughout America in spoken word and print; and Robert Klotman, 1964 president of the American String Teachers Association, and the ASTA leadership, including Cook and Kendall, who were instrumental in bringing Suzuki and a small group of Japanese children for that historic appearance at the Music Educators National Conference in Philadelphia in 1964.

Suzuki's application of the mother tongue method to music continues to spread, not only in the Americas, but throughout Europe, Australia, Africa, a n d Asia.

Among the many different reasons teachers and parents cite for their continuation in Suzuki programs are these: fewer dropouts, growing evidence of a higher rate of success with those who continue, more enjoyment in teaching, happier and more enthusiastic students, and promotion of family togetherness with music. Watching changing attitudes of parents and teachers toward children as they study as Suzuki violinists, I wonder if Suzuki might not have had an ulterior motive besides "for the happiness of all children", that is, "for the character formation of parents and teachers"!

About the Author

William Starr, with bachelor's and master's degrees and a Performer's Certificate in Violin from the Eastman School of Music, made his debut with the Kansas City Philharmonic at the age of 17. After performing in the Rochester Philharmonic, he continued study with Paul Stassevitch before coming to the University of Tennessee as first violinist of the University String Quartet and concertmaster of the Knoxville Symphony Orchestra. He is presently professor of music, conductor of the symphony and director of the Suzuki program at the University of Tennessee. He has written several college texts that are in wide use throughout the country.

Starr, now internationally recognized as a leading authority on Suzuki violin study, began teaching with the Suzuki approach in 1964 after hearing Suzuki and the first tour group of Japanese children at the Music Educators National Conference in Philadelphia. The Suzuki program at U-T, now in its twelfth year, is one of the most highly developed programs in the U.S. Children from the U-T program have appeared with great acclaim in two tours of Venezuela, at the 1972 Music Educators National Conference in Atlanta, at the international conference of the World Organization For Human Potential in Philadelphia in 1973, and at the 1974 national conference of the American Symphony Orchestra League in Memphis.

After attending Suzuki workshops in 1965, 1966, and 1968, and visiting Japan for a month in 1967, Starr returned to Japan for fourteen months in 1968-1969 with his wife Constance and their eight children.

In Matsumoto he observed Suzuki and his teachers at close hand in week-by-week instruction. Five of the Starr children studied in the Talent Education program in Japan, two with Suzuki. Starr conducted Suzuki's string orchestra in Matsumoto, and taught Suzuki's teacher-trainee classes in basic theory, sight-reading, and chamber music. In the summer of 1969 he taught Suzuki's students for six weeks, and also appeared as guest instructor in Tokyo, Nagoya, and Nagano.

At the same time Mrs. Starr, a graduate in piano from the Eastman School of Music, was in close observation of the Suzuki approach to piano study. She was able to work with Haruko Kataoka, the now internationally known Suzuki piano teacher who is in residence at the Talent Education Institute in Matsumoto.

Starr returned to Japan in the summer of 1973 to observe Suzuki again, and attended the First International Suzuki Conference in Hawaii in the summer of 1975. His daughter, Judith, spent the year 1974-1975 studying with Suzuki in Japan.

During the last six years he has given a great number of workshops and speeches at national and state conventions and at universities and colleges throughout the U.S. He has also taught in Canada, Venezuela, England and Switzerland.

In addition to making the Suzuki-Starr videotapes, on his visits to Japan Starr compiled an extensive notebook of observations. These and the videotapes are the sources for most of the material of this book.

The "Mother Tongue Method" of Education and the Law of Ability

by

SHIN-ICHI SUZUKI

*Excerpts of a talk given to
the Japan Institute of Educational Psychology*

October 16, 1973

Every child can be educated by the "Mother Tongue" method. It was forty years ago when this astonishing fact occurred to me. Children everywhere in the world were speaking in their own language; moreover, they did this fluently, which required a very high level of proficiency. "What was this all about?" I asked myself. People generally have believed that a child that makes poor grades in school was just born that way. "Brainless and dull witted" was the common and unthinking reproof. And yet these same children, unless born with brain damage, found no difficulty in speaking such a complicated language as Japanese fluently. If they really had been brainless they would not have had the ability to speak as they did. What did it signify? Why did it appear that the 'mother tongue' ability could be taught with the greatest of ease to every child (that is the ability to speak, to make the necessary sounds in the correct context, and not the ability to handle the intricacies of grammar), and yet why did they not do well in various subjects at school, acquiring this learning just as they did their language? What is this ability? Can it be acquired, or is it in-born? To enquire further, what does in-born mean? Is it really true that talent for such things as music, literature, painting or any of the other arts is in-born? Like everyone else, I believed at that time, forty years ago, that if a child did badly at school, he was either lazy, dull-witted, or brainless. And I also believed that talent was in-born.

* * *

From that very day I started to study this problem and observe the practicability of the "Mother Tongue" method:

—The environmental conditions and their influence on the new-born baby as it accustoms itself to the sounds of the 'mother tongue'.

—Teaching the child by constant repetition to utter its first sound. Usually 'mama mama mama' and so on.

—Everyday attitude of the parents after the baby starts to talk.

—Natural progress through daily practice.

—The skillfulness with which the parents build up enthusiasm in the child, and the happiness the child finds in acquiring its new-found ability.

As a result I learned that the natural method of teaching a child its mother tongue is a marvelous educational process. It fills the child with enthusiasm. It

Shinichi Suzuki.

is a natural process in which practice continues from morning till night. The child feels none of the anguish that so often accompanies learning by conventional methods which are applied to other forms of education. What child would refuse to learn its 'mother tongue', that is, quit this means of communication, because they found the routine dull? Every child in such an environment grows steadily and without mishap toward an involvement in this delightful ability, and responds according to the stimuli supplied it by the parents.

With this method, what human abilities might be developed! Superior environment; skill to build up enthusiasm; joy in practice and more practice. Surely the "Mother Tongue" method is the most outstanding example of the development of human ability.

Sometime later I tried to adapt this method to music education for young children. I accepted a number of children without first auditioning them, and began to teach them violin experimentally, convinced that every child would develop. The children did show great progress and enjoyed the process. What has happened to those children of forty years ago, and how active they are now in all parts of the world, will be reported in a later chapter. Anyhow, the "Mother Tongue" method was capable of being adapted to music education as well as other lines of learning, and I felt more and more confident that this concept would stand the test of time.

— Experimental Class at Regular School —

Twenty-five years ago, I very eagerly wanted to have a school experiment conducted, using my "Mother Tongue" method in their daily routine, and I asked Principal Kamijo of a primary school in Matsumoto if he might try it out. He graciously acceded to my request and the experiment in education was launched. The school had four groups in first grade, and one was chosen as the experimental group. I suggested that no one should be 'failed', no drop-outs allowed, and one of the teachers, a Mr. Tanaka, was put in charge and the experiment was under way. There was one child who could not even count up to three; she seemed to be somewhat retarded, but I did observe that she was speaking her native tongue with ease. I asked Mr. Tanaka not to fail her and I explained my method to him. He understood very well and saw this child through her difficulties so that by the time she reached fourth grade she was no different from any of the other children in a class of forty. Later she passed her entrance examination for high school, which presents no small challenge in Japan, where high school entrance examinations are highly competitive. This experiment, carried out in a regular primary school in Matsumoto, by regular teachers, certainly proved that it is possible to educate in primary school in such a way that no child need be dropped from a class. It was clear that each child could develop his own abilities very successfully by the use of this method. In this class the following things were observed: No homework was assigned; the knowledge was absorbed to the degree that it became an unconscious effort, (each child 'made it his own' so to speak); the lessons were performed in an enjoyable atmosphere, and, most important of all, no child was ever made to feel inferior. Unfortunately this class had to be abandoned after some four years; for Principal Kamijo died, and his successor had no belief in, or sympathy with the experiment, despite the urgent pleas of the parents and the children alike. The group was broken up and spread among the other classes, reverting to what was, in the eyes of the new Principal, I have no doubt, a more conventional approach to education.

— Talent Education at Yoji Gakuen —

Next I would like to report on the experimental pre-school (that is, pre-primary school) methods we conduct at the Talent Institute for the purpose of applying educational methods that develop children's individual abilities so that the ability becomes an in-tegral part of the child. Twenty-five years ago I founded in Matsumoto the Talent Education Institute for pre-school children, called in Japanese 'Yoji Gakuen', and invited Miss Yano, an educator in this part of the country, to start the project in this method of learning so that every child might develop his ability to the point where it becomes a part of him. The children were, and are, accepted without any tests. This school has been continuing for twenty-five years. There are sixty children in the class, comprising in age those of three, four and five years. We do not separate them according to age, which normally is done in regular schools, because we know very well that the three year olds grow up steadily under the stimulating environment afforded by the older children. In one year, they usually acquire the ability to memorize one hundred and seventy to one hundred and eighty *haiku,* and they are able to repeat any one of them clearly upon demand. A *haiku* is a short Japanese poem of five, seven and five syllables in three lines. Of course, we train them to develop many other abilities, such as physical education and the development of quick reflexes, writing numbers correctly, and reading *kanji.* Drawing and calligraphy are taught as is English conversation. They are also taught to speak their mother tongue, Japanese, clearly and correctly. To do this we use the same training methods as are used to train T.V. announcers. To observe the enthusiasm and happiness of these tiny children is the deepest source of satisfaction for those who work with them. During the last seven years we have tested the I.Q. (Tanaka-Binet system) for the five year olds who graduate from pre-school to primary first grade. The average I.Q. has been near 160. In 1973 the average was 158.

Michael and Keiko enjoying Suzuki's Yoji-Gakuen.

The many parents who have heard about this school are flocking to enter their children, until, at this moment, we are fully loaded for the next four years. The children who will be enrolled four years from now are as yet unborn.

To sum up: The "Mother Tongue" method leads the child, by repeated stimulation, to develop an ability and make it his own. If a young child is taken to Alaska where he is raised in the cold climate, the stimulation of the cold environment over a period of years will develop his ability to endure on his skin and over his whole body the frigid temperature. On the other hand, if the child's experience of the cold weather in Alaska is brief, then the child, on returning to Tokyo, will have only learned about a cold experience and will have not been able to make the ability to endure cold as a part of his own makeup. The child, educated to use this method of learning, will find that it can be brought into play in building other abilities as well. It is somewhat similar to the theory of principal and interest. Interest produces more money and more money produces more interest which, in turn, produces still more interest.

Now comes the physical side of it all. In the example of the child and his experience in Alaska, it is realized that this experience of building the ability to withstand the cold actually was a physiological one. I would like to think that the "Mother Tongue" method can also be regarded as physiological, the only difference in the experience being the difference between air and sound, on the one hand developing, through constant experience the ability to endure cold and, on the other, through constant experience of sound the ability to speak one's mother tongue. It seems to me that the interaction between parent and baby, the sharing of their lives, the parent's mind, senses, and the functions which the baby instinctively learns and makes its own, are also entirely physiological. I do not know whether this subject is in the field of physiology of the brain or not; but from my experience I am disposed to think so.

— Why So Many Dropouts? —

The method and the aim of education must become different from that which the child regularly experiences in primary school to-day. And it cannot be repeated too often that the several abilities of the children must be developed to the degree that they form a part of their makeup. What is happening in primary schools is that a set curriculum is adhered to at any cost without regard to the human equation. Increasingly difficult material is forced on the children as a routine matter, and some children, unable to keep up the pace, become deeply discouraged, give the impression of being retarded, and eventually drop out. And too often, the parent, not being in the close relationship with the child which we stress at the Talent Education Institute, is apt to dismiss this distressing situation, saying, "Well, he was born that way and I can't help it." Unfortunately this attitude is all too prevalent throughout the world,

and it accounts, I am sure, for the number of underdeveloped children we encounter. This underdevelopment is due to the failure of education at home, starting from the baby's first cry. If young plants are damaged, we know quite well what the result will be. If we damage young lives we should also know what the result will be. I look for the day when nations will give much more attention to this most important subject, so important to national well-being, and implement a national policy that ensures proper development. As I have pointed out in this section dealing with the serious matter of 'drops-outs', the differing abilities of first graders is a very serious matter. Under our present system the children, varied in abilities, including the capacity for learning, are thrown together in one class and, as pointed out before, advanced without regard to their capacity for developing an ability and making it a part of themselves. This method produces many difficulties and frustrations for the teachers also. They sense that what is taking place is bound to produce a lack of enthusiasm in the child, a feeling of disappointment leading to complete indifference and, eventually, to dropping out. In our Talent Education Institute we teachers have a warning phrase; To force the 'manuals' (the curriculum) is to produce the 'drop-out'. In Japanese the word for 'education' is *kyoiku*. *Kyo* means to teach, and *iku* means to bring up. There is considerable subtlety here when we become aware that *teaching* produces drop-outs and *bringing up* produces the well balanced child, and that the two combine to make the child's ability his very own. We must realize that the "Mother Tongue" method is what this is all about.

* * *

Let us return to Mr. Tanaka and his first grade at the primary school mentioned before in the experimental class, which was guaranteed not to produce or allow drop-outs. The initial lessons of the first graders were recognized as of vast importance. Just as in the beginning of learning the mother tongue, the start was kept very slow. Extremely easy material was chosen at the start, and all the children accomplished what was set with no mistakes and full marks. This was a start in building confidence and enthusiasm. He made sure that *every* child understood the material and made no mistakes. He stressed, trained and practiced this theory of 'no mistakes'. Further he realized, as we all know, that small children have a short attention span. Some children become bored or inattentive after five or six minutes. When this happened, say in the math lesson he would immediately switch to language, and when the attention of a child appeared on the wane in this subject, still another was chosen. At the end of a year these young children had developed the ability to concentrate on any one subject for some forty-five minutes!

In language he would repeat the training five times a day for periods of five to ten minutes. He would first give them eight words to learn (with no mistakes), and when each child had learned them and made them his own, he would add two more. Thus they would practice the original eight along with two new ones. Additions were made in such fashion during the learning of their first book. When I was informed that this was accomplished, I went to the school to observe the class at work. The children sat with their books in front of them, but *closed*. Mr. Tanaka called on a child to read Lesson 12. The child stood up and recited clearly and correctly without any mistakes and without recourse to the book. Then another one did the same with Lesson 17. During the time they had been engaged with learning their first book they had, of course, learned not only to read but to write. So he directed the whole class to write Lesson 18, which they did easily and well, and at a remarkably fast tempo. If this method, with which I had asked Mr. Tanaka to experiment, is used, every child will grow, full of enthusiasm, encouraged and fired with the joy of study, which will grow like a snowball of discovered abilities. I used exactly the same method in the teaching of music, producing no drop-outs. Every child can be developed.

— A Report on My Experiment —

I started to study the "Mother Tongue" method and began applying it to teaching the violin some forty years ago, convinced that every child could be developed if taught in this way. I accepted children without first auditioning them and trained them along the lines of the "Mother Tongue" method or, as it is called in Western Countries, the "Suzuki Method". The first pupil I worked with was the four-year-old Toshiya Eto. Next was the three-year-old Koji Toyoda followed by the Kobayashi brothers, Hidetaro Suzuki, Takaya Urakawa, and many others, all accompanied by their enthusiastic and cooperative parents. They all made rewarding progress. At eleven years of age Toshiya Eto won the prestigious Mainichi Shimbun award. I have never pressed any of my young charges to enter the professional field. That is not my aim in education, but, at the same time, I have never deterred those who felt the urge, and many of the original students went abroad to study professionally with distinguished teachers in the United States, France, Belgium and Germany. They have gained high positions in the realm of string instruments. Toshiya Eto is known throughout the world as an outstanding soloist. Koji Toyoda is now concertmaster of the Berlin Radio Symphony orchestra. Takeshi Kobayashi is concertmaster of the Czechoslovakian Symphony; Kenji Kobayashi concertmaster of the Oklahoma Symphony; Hidetaro Suzuki of the Quebec Symphony, and Takaya Urakawa of the Bamberg Symphony. There was a time when the Japanese people were assumed by Westerners to be most unmusical, and indeed, from the Western point of view this was once true. Never having been exposed to Western music they knew nothing of it. However, no one had looked into the fact that the average Japanese child is able to speak his mother tongue long before he can read it. As I have explained at length, this was the truth which gave me the clue to the so-called "Mother Tongue" method of education, not just in music education, but

in all branches of training. My story of the preliminary experiment in the Primary School in Matsumoto makes this clear. Applying the "Mother Tongue" method to musical education of the aforementioned group, among the first to be so exposed, I found further evidence of the effectiveness of the method. Realizing that every child born into this world has ability of one sort or another (that is, of course, with the exception of those tragically retarded) and that the "Mother Tongue" method can be used in their education, I have often pondered whether or not if all nations and races were to concern themselves much more with this type of education, a much better atmosphere of understanding and peace among men might be the end product.

We all know how strongly my very close friend, the late Pablo Casals, believed in this ideal of brotherhood and the great part that music could play in it.

— The Law of Ability —

In conducting observations, I have thought about what the source of ability might be, and have come to the conclusion that it is the great power of life itself. This great power of life governs physical growth. It imparts ability during the growth process, which responds to outside stimulation so that life can be sustained. This stimulation enables the child to develop his ability as a part of his make-up. This great power of life which governs every function of the body, is centered in the brain, an organ with capabilities far beyond any computer. I can no longer bring myself to believe in what is commonly referred to as an inborn talent, be it musical, literary or any other form. My forty years of experiments in child education have persuaded me against such a belief. I have no doubt that people are born with hereditary physiological differences, but I believe that a person's abilities grow and develop depending on stimulation from the outside. Babies, whether born in primitive times or in contemporary times, start at the same point and receive environmental stimulation according to their respective periods, growing up as adults suited to the era in which they live.

It would be true therefore, to say that a a baby born in the twentieth century, but nurtured and raised by stone age people in a stone age environment, would develop abilities that would correspond with that age. I am often asked what I consider to be the limits of growth in a child's ability. I do not know what the limits are, but I am persuaded that the child's ability can grow to the level mankind can reach, by the time man's history terminates. As a practical answer, I would say that a child can, at the very least, develop all his various abilities to the high level of his ability in using his mother tongue. And this level is very high.

* * *

I have learned that musical ability is not in-born, and that it is possible to raise a child to be tone deaf or to raise the child to have superior musical ability. Imagine, if you will, a Mozart or a Beethoven brought

4

up from birth to cacaphony, to every variety of unmusical sound. My own observations tell me that we would not have had a Ninth or a Jupiter Symphony. Thus any child similarly exposed would grow up tone deaf. Children raised in Osaka, hearing their parents talking every day, grow up with all the delicate differences of the Osaka dialect, and those in Tokyo acquire a Tokyo dialect. There are only human beings in the human family, and the word 'genius' is a term of respect we apply to those who have made an outstanding success of the abilities they have acquired as they grew up under good fostering.

Some claim that, as a result of heredity, a person has it in him to be a musician, an artist, a writer; that the talent is in-born, and, in some cases, amounts to a 'natural genius'. I just do not believe this. When one considers all the babies that are given the miracle of life and the power to live, it is saddening to see those who are improperly brought up, where their kind of education has failed them from the age of zero years old, without beneficial environmental stimulation, and who are judged by unthinking people to have been *born* that way.

It is an ancient Japanese custom to catch a wild baby nightingale in the mountains and place it in association with a domesticated bird, one with a particularly beautiful song. The wild creature from the mountains hears this excellent singing every day and in due time it, too, is giving forth the sounds it has been listening to. On the other hand, if the bird has for too long heard the croaking of the mother bird, then the capture of the little creature will prove to be too late, and the subsequent attempt to train it as described above will end in failure. This is another example of the Law of Ability. In Japan there are hundreds of babies who listen daily to a recording of the first movement of the Mozart Serenade for string orchestra. The parents report to me that it is not very long before a very strong and deeply pleasurable reaction is observed, and by the time the child is some four or five months old, it is responding to the music with joyous movement. In the same way, and at the same time, the baby is absorbing every emotion the parents display to it: 'The fate of children is in the parents' hands.' It is at once a wonderful and critical responsibility, since children absorb into their make-up everything from their environment.

Some children are brought up by parents who seem to believe that the proper way to raise them is by a regime of persistent scolding and bullying. In accordance with the Law of Ability, the children develop their own *ability* to be scolded and therefore resistance. It is a frightening thing, and the eventual outcome causes the parents to wonder why their child was *born* so obstinate. Of course the child is not *born* so. It has developed its own ability to be obstinate.

— An Appeal for a World Policy of Child Development —

In October of 1968 at the Assembly Hall of the United Nations in New York I appealed to those gathered there to consider the necessity of a world-wide policy of proper child development, education and care. I explained that every child is influenced from the moment of birth by its environment and that every child can be *developed*. But there is only one way.

In every country in the world today there are countless parents who, in ignorance of proper child training, are raising miserable, twisted personalities. It is one of the most urgent problems of our time, and appears to be mankind's major blind spot. When one considers the important part for good or evil that this future citizen of the world will play, I am unable to understand why the nations forsake such a critical task. I wish the countries of the entire world would establish and carry out national policies for child training and care as quickly as possible. When you contemplate a carefully cultivated green field and think of the care taken in the raising and cultivation of it, you cannot help but wonder that all that went into that project should be denied to children; whereas if they, too, received the care that the field had received, they would grow up to be good human beings with their respective abilities highly developed, who would build a good society. But the raising and educating of children must be founded on a proper knowledge of how all this is to be accomplished. If the situation is left as it is now, and we fail to raise the 'young plants' as they should be raised, then I do not see how one can expect to have good nations in this world. Without good people you cannot have good nations. As a national policy it is the first imperative that instructors should be stationed throughout the country in the cities, towns and villages, and that as soon as a new baby is registered at the appropriate office, the instructor should visit the family and teach the parents the best way to bring up the child both in matters of health and in the developing of its abilities from the very beginning. The parents should be taught how to do all this on their own and have a deep personal involvement with the child. The instructor would then visit his territory regularly, give further guidance and assistance to the parents, and watch the child's development. If such a system were to be established, and if the children of the world were accorded such care, guidance, parental relationship and sense of responsibility, then, I am convinced, the world would start to change very greatly. I ended by urging my listeners to give this very important matter their earnest consideration for the sake of children all over the world. I was accorded a warmhearted ovation, but I could not help wondering which country would be the first to take a step in this direction. I wish it were possible to believe it might happen at least by the Twenty-first Century!

Some four years ago I, along with Mr. Masaru Ibuka, Chairman of Sony Corporation and a strong believer, visited the then Prime Minister Sato at his official residence and discussed with him for about an hour the need for a national policy of child development. Although he displayed considerable interest, it is sad to relate that nothing came of it. If such a national policy could be carried out in as many countries as possible (and, of course, I would like to see Japan in the lead) I think that in twenty to thirty years a great change in the world would be seen. The love that parents have for their children would be awakened to proper child development through the guidance of trained instructors, and good character and ability would be promoted in every home. By these means I am certain that many children on this earth would be saved. When it is realized that babies can be raised in many different ways, it is clear that the manner of bringing up children is the responsibility of all adults in the world.

I would like to ask that scholars and educators clarify the concept that ability is not in-born, and dismiss the common error of assuming that failure in a child is due to its being born that way. Failure is not in-born and ability is not in-born. There is the story of the two little savage girls, three and four years of age, who were raised in the wilds by wolves and, of course, behaved like wolves. There was nothing in-born there; they absorbed the outside stimulation, developed a wolf-like ability and made it their own!

One more request I would make is that educators study the "Mother Tongue" method and develop ways for the abilities of children to grow in the same manner as all children acquire the complex ability to speak their mother tongue, thereby ushering in as early as possible the age when the tragedy of the 'drop out' will have been abolished from our system of education.

I have already spent forty years exerting efforts in this direction, but as a layman, I can do very little. Scholars and professional educators with their great influence, can exercise great leadership in changing the world.

Role of Listening in Talent Education

As is evident from everything Suzuki has written or said about Talent Education, an underlying principle is that the child's musical education, insofar as the development of his ear is concerned, should parallel the manner in which he acquired his mother tongue. All normal children learn to speak the mother tongue fluently, without benefit of formal schooling, text or classroom. Young children have an uncanny aptitude for recognizing and later reproducing delicate nuances of spoken languages. Suzuki believes and has demonstrated through his teaching that a young child can develop, in the same manner, a highly discriminating musical ear. Much repetitive listening is necessary, just as it is in in the acquisition of the mother tongue.

Suzuki feels that the child's musical education should start shortly after birth, with the baby being exposed to repeated playings of a single selection of music. Many parents feel that they are already training the child if they leave the classical music FM radio station on all day, or if they play various recordings throughout the day. It is true that the baby will assimilate some of the general characteristics of the music, but not nearly so effectively as he would with repeated exposures to a limited repertoire.

In his *Outline of Talent Education Method,* Suzuki writes: "If I let a newborn baby listen to classical music, for example, a Brandenburg Concerto or Tschaikowsky Serenade or a Beethoven quartet, I choose one movement from such classics and let the baby listen to the same tune every day. In about five months time the baby will memorize this melody. If you do not believe this, please try it yourself.

It is very easy to test whether the infant has memorized the melody or not. To relate one of my experiences: A certain friend of ours had a baby. At that time its sister was six years old and she would practice the first movement of Vivaldi's G Minor Concerto every day. I visited their home when the baby was five months old. The baby was in a good mood and in its mother's arms. So I decided on the test. I played Bach's Minuetto. The baby looked happy. In between I switched to the first movement of Vivaldi, which the baby was always hearing. At the first three notes, the baby moved his whole body in time with the music and looked much happier. He clearly distinguished these two melodies.

We should try to let babies listen to good music and to nurture a good music sense as early as possible.

Let me here explain how a nightingale is trained to sing well. If we catch a very young, wild nightingale in the spring and put a good-voiced nightingale beside it for about 30 days, the throat of the baby nightingale changes so that it will be able to sing like its teacher. By changing the surroundings, the wild bird will change in order to fit the new situation. If we use a gramophone to train a nightingale, the bird will sing accordingly—even imitating the sound of the needle going over the surface of the record.

Almost the same may be said of human beings. Children listen to the pronouncing of words by their parents and their vocal chords adjust themselves physiologically to make the same kind of pronunciation as their parents. The pronunciation of English by a Japanese child and an American child is different. This is because the physical adjustment has not been made by the Japanese child.

To give a bad example: If a nightingale that sings poorly is kept close to a young nightingale for some time, the young bird will learn to sing poorly. This is one basic rule.

From my tests of twenty years, I have found that young children who have been given a chance to listen to good music acquire a good sense of music—just like naturally being accustomed to their mother tongue. We should realize that even a child of six has been receiving education for six years. From a musical point of view, the child can be educated by good music, bad music, or no music at all."

Before the child begins his study of the violin, the mother should see that he listens daily to the recording of Twinkle and the first pieces of Book I. This should continue as he learns the basic posture and bow hold so that by the time he begins to learn to play Twinkle, he has the music thoroughly memorized. None of his energy or attention should be diverted into recalling the notes as he begins to play. Suzuki stresses that this listening also motivates the child to want to play the music.

Listening should be established as a daily habit. The child need not be forced to sit down and listen to the recording. He can listen while doing something else. The child easily absorbs the sounds without seeming to be paying any attention to the music. In spite of the fact that Suzuki constantly preaches the importance of much listening, he still finds it difficult to convince some mothers. He remarks that the most effective statement he can make and one that does seem to impress mothers, is that the young child's rate of progress is directly dependent upon the amount of listening he does.

Some Japanese mothers combine music listening with daily breakfast, and others play recordings as the child lies in bed before going to sleep. Mothers who find that mechanical problems are often the biggest hindrance to the establishment of a daily routine make tape recordings of the songs with several repetitions on the tape. Thus they can play a single tape without having the interminable changes that call them from their work. Some use "endless" cassette tapes that repeat continuously. One ingenious mother made a cassette tape recording, then strapped a small cassette recorder to the back of her little girl who then was able to listen while playing in the sandbox in the garden!

Adults should understand, Suzuki warns, that the child will not tire of the recording as an adult might. The small child loves familiar sounds, but if he hears a parent complain about the repetitions of the recording, he may adopt the attitude of the parent and his musical training will be stunted. The child should not only listen to recordings of the pieces that he is studying, but also to recordings of the pieces that he will study in the future. Some parents make tapes of a whole book of selections which include future works and review. An advanced student may enjoy listening to the earlier pieces for review to help him keep them in his memory for group lessons and concerts.

Listening to the recordings of the literature remains important throughout the training of the child. The advanced student may have to listen quite carefully to distinguish the delicate nuances in a performance of a selection such as the second movement of the Bach Concerto in A Minor. Some children listen to such recordings with the music before them. Concentrated listening is necessary for the advanced student to determine the correct pitches in rapid passages.

It is very important that the more advanced student listen to the new pieces well in advance of his study of these pieces. This will save him and the teacher much time as he learns new pieces. One Talent Education teacher asked his students to listen to the Seitz Concerto #5, in Book IV, for six monhts before starting to learn to play the piece. These same students then played this Seitz movement well after only two weeks of practice.

Many of the Japanese homes are quite small, and so the mother hears the recording as often as the child. This makes her role as assistant teacher easier as she is well equipped to help the child because she knows exactly how the piece should sound, and can easily tell when her child is playing a wrong note or playing out of tune.

In summation, Suzuki believes that not only will the child's ear be well trained by listening, but that he will be motivated to want to play the music he hears. Also, the student who has all the music memorized will be able to give all of his attention to the problems of playing the instrument. He will not be distracted by reading notes or trying to recall the next note. Suzuki thinks it is invaluable for the child to develop his musical memory, and to become accustomed to performing without notes.

Motivation

"How do you help mothers awaken in their children the desire to play violin?" "How do you help the child to enjoy practicing the violin?" These are questions frequently asked Suzuki in Japan and America. After more than thirty years of experience teaching small children, Suzuki still regards the problem of motivation as *the* principal problem for parents and teachers.

An often overlooked aspect of the mother-tongue education is the awakening of the desire to speak as a result of the environment of the young child. The importance of the role of listening to records for the development of musical sensitivity oftentimes overshadows the effect of listening on motivation. "The baby cannot speak at birth, but in his everyday environment he hears his mother and father speak, and gradually begins his desire to speak," says Suzuki, who tries to follow the same path of motivation in his violin instruction program.

In his book, *Nurtured by Love,* Suzuki describes what he feels is the ideal way to begin instruction:

"Although we accept infants, at first we do not have them play the violin. First, we teach the mother to play one piece so that she will be a good teacher at home. As for the child, we first have him simply listen at home to a record of the piece he will be learning. Children are really educated in the home, so in order that the child will have good posture and practice properly at home, it is necessary for the parent to have first-hand experience. The correct education of the child depends on this. Until the parent can play one piece, the child does not play at all. This principle is very important indeed, because although the parent may want him to do so, the three or four year old child has no desire to learn the violin. The idea is to get the child to say, "I want to play, too", so the first piece is played every day on the phonograph, and in the studio he just watches the other children (and his mother) having their lessons. The proper environment is created for the child. The mother, moreover, both at home and in the studio, plays on a small violin more suited to the child. The child will naturally before long take the violin away from his mother, thinking, "I want to play too". He knows the tune already. The other children are having fun; he wants to join in the fun. We have caused him to acquire this desire.

This situation having been created, lessons are led up to in the following order. First the parent asks, "Would you like to play the violin too?" The answer is "Yes!" "You will practice hard?" "Yes". "All right, let's ask the teacher if you can join in next time". This always succeeds. What a thrill the first private lesson always is! "I did it too," the child boasts. "Now I can play with the other children". Parents who understand children make fine teachers. In the studio there are private lessons and group lessons. Parents who do not understand children think they are paying for the private lessons and that the group lessons are just recreation periods. So although they make sure that their children attend the private lessons, they often fail to bring them to the group lessons. But the fact is that what the children enjoy most is the group playing. They play with children who are more advanced than they are; the influence is enormous, and is marvelous for their training. This is real talent education".

Suzuki feels that the three-year-old is most desirous of pleasing the mother and therefore regards this as the best starting age. However, by no means all of the mothers wanting to register their children for lessons bring three-year-olds as beginners. "Do you turn older children away?" "What is the oldest child you accept as a beginner?" These questions are often directed to Suzuki. "No age limit", he replies. "I say to mothers of older children, 'Let us start today before the child is older!' "

Although teaching the mother first is generally accepted as being the ideal way for a beginner to start in Talent Education, for one reason or another not all Talent Education teachers do this. Some are content that the mother knows how to teach the child at home. If the child is older than three, the desire to imitate the mother may be overshadowed by the desire to be independent. At any age, Suzuki has found it normal that the child wants to please the parents and teacher. The child expects his parents to be vitally interested in what he is doing, and wants praise for his successful development. In Japan often the whole family shows great interest in the child's violin playing.

Praise

In a lesson for a beginning three-year-old, Suzuki was heard to say 'umai' (good) after every effort the child made. He never said, "No, that is not good", but only "Good. Can you do this better? Let's try again." He urges the mother also to praise the child at every step. Many mothers withhold praise if the child does badly thinking that if they then praise the child, he will not know when he is doing well and when he isn't. Suzuki explains that there can be degrees of praise and that it is better to be silent than to be critical. In most cases, the ingenious mother can find something worthwhile to call to the child's attention. "That tone was better". "You remembered all the notes." "You held your violin higher". "Your bow hold was good". If the teacher and mother are guiding the child properly they need not worry about a little undeserved praise. "Very good. Can you do better?" is the basic Suzuki formula.

Suzuki is quoted from a videotape interview:

"In Japan, some mothers never say 'very good'. I say to mother, "Please say 'Very good. You can play well, but can you play much better?' 'Yes, I can'. With pieces that are already known, mother and teacher must ask for them again and again asking for better tone, better intonation, and better tempo. Gradually we can make ability from repetition of pieces that are known by the child".

Attitude of Parent and Teacher

Suzuki was asked about patient perseverance in the mother and teacher. "Patience is not necessary. We don't need patience. While the child is learning to speak his mother-tongue the parent doesn't feel he needs patience. Everyone enjoys the child's learning. My teaching is my leisure time. Children play at lessons. Nice time for children and nice time for mother and teacher. I watch what point I can bring to the child's attention. Patience is not necessary. Mothers should enjoy each step as children learn. Beginners grow so slowly, same as mother-tongue education".

Suzuki is by no means the only teacher in Talent Education who thoroughly enjoys teaching small children. I felt the spirit of enjoyment while watching a number of teachers at work. This spirit was contagious. Many of the children and mothers seemed to be enjoying themselves. Mothers often moved to the rhythm of the music. I was surprised to find mothers of advanced children enjoying the behavior and actions of very small beginners learning 'Twinkle'.

Home Concerts

Suzuki urges each mother to stage weekly 'home concerts' for the father to be shown the child's progress. These concerts can be scheduled at the beginning of instruction even before the child can perform anything. Many mothers have made this a real event, making small stages or platforms out of boxes for these concerts. At first, the child walks up onto the 'stage' with his violin tucked under his arm and his bow in his hand. After facing the father, he bows solemnly and then leaves the stage. He has shown the father how well he can· hold the violin 'at rest'. In the early months when the progress is very slow as the teacher and mother are trying to prepare the child's posture and bow hold properly, the weekly home concert can be quite an incentive for the child. Every small step forward is noticed and applauded.

Private Lessons

Suzuki finds that the private lessons provide a great deal of motivation if the teacher really loves children and enjoys teaching them. The private lesson is always a public affair in Talent Education. Suzuki says that the child should always watch lessons of other children. He considers this environment essential, observing that the child learns from the advanced students possibly more than he does directly from his teacher.

Suzuki expresses considerable sympathy for the teacher just starting a program. "This is so difficult, without the environment of the advanced children to inspire the beginners. When I started in Matsumoto 24 years ago, it was very difficult because of the limited environment of the private lessons. We had at first only six children playing 'Twinkle', taking turns playing on our only small violin! Beginning teachers should expect the beginning year of their program to be the most difficult. Even the second year, their older students will help them teach the new beginners."

In a typical Talent Education private lesson the studio is filled with mothers and children who wait patiently watching private lessons of other students.

"I saw in America", Suzuki commented, "sometimes only one child and one mother alone with the teacher in the studio. This is a very bad environment. Perhaps the child's progress is very slow and the desire to play is very weak. If the mother says, 'You must study', then the child plays only for the mother, not for himself, but if the child sees other children play every week in lessons, he will want to play as they do. Mother and child must stay and watch other children. Advanced children also play in the room. Mothers watch everything. Children enjoy playing for others and enjoy watching others play."

Early Participation in Concerts

Early participation in concerts is a fine motivating force for beginners, Suzuki believes, not only in the home concert, but also in public recitals and concerts. I witnessed a charming demonstration of this idea of early participation at a prefectural concert performed by over four hundred students. Immediately after intermission, members of the audience hurried quickly to their seats to see the beginners bow. The children came on stage solemnly, violins under their right arms and bows clutched in their fingers. After they had been lined up, a chord was played on the piano, and they bowed, staring out at the audience which responded with resounding applause. They then ran happily off the stage. Some had come sixty miles by train for this event!

Concerts and Recitals

Beginners are always taken to concerts and recitals of the more advanced children. They are much more stimulated by the playing of their peers than by adult performances. "In Matsumoto now we have many advanced small children," says Suzuki. "When beginners attend concerts, we find they learn more rapidly than children of the same age years ago before we had such a favorable environment."

Concert deportment is important. The Talent Education concerts in Japan are rather relaxed affairs, obviously given primarily for the children on the stage and in the audience. Children are not kept absolutely quiet throughout the performance. If the mother is always scolding a child, insisting that he not move or make a sound, he will regard the concerts as unpleasant affairs. Naturally, there must be a happy medium. The children cannot be allowed free rein but the atmosphere should not be too repressive. If most of the members of the audience are reasonably attentive, the majority of the children will conform fairly well. Of course, concert behavior is a problem but not one to be solved by the parents forcing 'adult' attention and behavior on a small child. If the child is sufficiently praised for reasonable behavior and attends concerts with some regularity, his deportment will most likely become satisfactory.

Parents should always realize that even a seemingly indifferent child is absorbing more than seems possible. Eiko Suzuki, (no relation to Mr. Suzuki) is one of Suzuki's fine adult students and now a teacher in Talent Education. She began her study of violin at the age of two. Once in her fourth year her parents took her to a violin recital given by a visiting soloist. The little girl did not sit still one minute, but constantly annoyed her father by climbing all over the seat and watching the audience throughout much of the program. The father thought the evening a total loss until several months later when Eiko recognized a sonata being played over the radio as having been on that recital program months earlier. Her incredulous father had to find a concert program to verify her statement before he believed his little daughter who had seemed so inattentive that evening.

Graduation Tapes

To increase motivation in the young children, Suzuki has created a system of "graduations" throughout Talent Education in Japan. Presently there are five levels. The graduation pieces are: 1) Gavotte: Gossec, Book 1. 2) Bourree: Bach, Book III. 3) Concerto in G Minor, 1st movement: Vivaldi, Book V. 4) Concerto in A minor, 1st movement: Bach, Book VII. 5) Concerto in D Major: Mozart, Book X.

Talent Education youngsters from all over Japan send tapes of these selections to Suzuki to qualify for "graduation" from one level of difficulty to the next. This means that Suzuki listens to approximately one thousand tapes every year. All of the children graduate, and all are rated "excellent" or better by Suzuki!

At the end of the student's selection, Suzuki records comments and advice for improvement. Not all of these remarks deal with technique, tone, or musical sensitivity. For instance, graduates progressing on to the Bach Concerto in A Minor have been given words of advice that must have received warm welcomes in Japanese households.

"Now you are going to play great concertos of Mozart and Bach, and you must try to catch the heart of Bach and Mozart in their music. You must practice every day to catch the feelings of others without words. Look at your mother and father. Can you see how they feel? Try to see when your mother needs your help—before she asks. Then it is too late. If you practice every day, watching not to harm anyone by what you say, and also trying to catch how they feel, then you will develop sensitivity toward the feelings of others. Perhaps later you will also catch the heart of Bach and Mozart in their music."

Suzuki receives many letters from mothers expressing their gratitude to him for these words of advice to their children.

Some Suzuki teachers in the West give pins or certificates to students in recognition of their graduation to another level. These are usually presented at the recital at which the children have performed their graduation pieces.

Teacher-Parent Cooperation

The teacher and mother should discuss the problem of motivation together frequently, suggests Suzuki, considering ways to influence the child. The mother and teacher should be very sensitive to the state of mind of the child. Suzuki does not believe that the correct way is to force the child to practice every day. The highest degree of ingenuity and creative imagination must be brought into play to create the most favorable environment for the child.

Children enjoy playing together. Suzuki's Summer School.

The Private Lesson. Points for Teachers

Suzuki teaching a private lesson.

Another private lesson with Suzuki.

Some observers who have heard groups of Suzuki-trained Japanese youngsters playing in unison have mistakenly come to think of the Suzuki method as being principally group instruction. Although Suzuki does advocate a special kind of group lesson, it is the private lesson that is the heart of this method. In Talent Education in Japan the private lesson is a social affair with often three or four children and their mothers in the studio at the same time. Suzuki wants the mothers and children to observe the lessons of others. The teacher teaches each child individually, although he may occasionally ask several children to play together.

Lessons vary in length according to the need and capability of the child. Sometimes the lessons of beginners are only five minutes in length. Since mothers and children watch lessons of other students, however, the educative process continues while they are in the room observing. Many Japanese mothers observe lessons for an hour in addition to their own children's lessons. I attended one Sunday afternoon of lessons at which many of the mothers and fathers remained for over two hours. At times the adults were intent upon observation, applauding occasionally for some particularly good playing. At other times they carried on very quiet social conversation. In the middle of the afternoon they served tea and cakes to the teacher and others in attendance. The whole atmosphere was extremely relaxed.

In Talent Education in Japan it is understood that the lessons of beginners will necessarily be shorter than those of the more advanced students. There is accordingly a sliding scale of payment. In 1969 parents paid 1800 yen ($5) monthly until the student completed Book III; and finally 3200 yen ($9) per month.

Lesson Deportment

Mention must be made of the child's deportment in the private lesson. Occasional visitors often think the Japanese child is perfectly behaved and wholly attentive during the lessons. Japanese teachers say that this is not always so. Often a beginner may be quite difficult. He may not pay attention nor do what the teacher asks. This is another case where Suzuki says environment is so important. If the recalcitrant child sees the other children behaving properly, he will tend toward their behavior. At the first lessons, the four-year-old may complain that he is "so tired", and that he cannot hold the violin up for more than a minute. The teacher keeps working with him, trying to help him hold the instrument properly. I noticed that some of the Japanese teachers quite frequently started talking to the child immediately after he had finished playing a piece or an excerpt from one. Quite often the child kept the violin at the chin while listening, and then proceeded to repeat or play something new without taking the violin down. Many, many four-year-old children were seen to take fifteen minute lessons without once saying a word or lowering the violin from playing position. After observing six months of training, I was treated to the unbelievable experience of seeing my own four-year-old, an often "too tired" little one, hold the violin up in the same way for an entire lesson of fifteen minutes.

The children are usually a model of attention when they are being given private instruction. They never speak to the teacher unless addressed. Social amenities come before or after the lesson.

At the beginning of each private lesson, the child bows to the teacher and the teacher returns the bow of respect. Many of the children say, as they bow, "Onegaishimasu", or "Please help me". At the close of the lesson, child and teacher again bow, the child saying, "Domo arigato gozaimashita", or "Thank you very much for what you have done". Within the time limits of these two bows, the child gives the teacher his undivided attention.

However, this is not necessarily the case when the child is observing other children's lessons. Some children may be rapt in attention, and others are seemingly oblivious to what is going on. They are not noisy. They may talk in whispers, and shift around incessantly. They may go out to the bathroom two or three times in one hour. The attitudes of the teacher and parent are not repressive. The children are treated as children and are not expected to sit perfectly quietly and attentively for an hour. It seems that the parents and teachers have been convinced that Suzuki is right when he says that the child is absorbing a great deal even when he seems to be completely inattentive.

I observed a four-year-old who did not glance at the teacher or the student who was playing for at least ten minutes, and yet when the performing student played a passage staccato instead of legato, the four-year-old suddenly burst into song, singing the piece with the correct articulation, and still not looking at the performer. It may be that since the child is not forced or urged to pay close attention to others while they are taking lessons, but only expected to be reasonably quiet, he is then able to focus complete attention on the teacher when he himself is being instructed.

At each lesson the teacher should allow the child to perform one piece through without interruption. The child should be encouraged to go on playing even though he makes a mistake. This is excellent training for public performance. It helps the child develop concentration. Often children who feel they are going to be interrupted after making a mistake call out, "Wait!" to the teacher, wanting to go on by themselves. Some teachers ask children to "sing along" internally as they perform in order to help develop the sense of continuity.

After the child has learned the notes of a piece, then he is ready for intensive work refining his intonation, his phrasing, and overall technique. When Suzuki adds new pieces, he keeps the child playing the previous pieces also so that the child always has material available for cultivating his performance ability to a high degree. He learns notes of a new piece at the same time he is refining his playing of the old pieces.

Most teachers know the situation that usually exists after a child has played in a recital and is busy learning a new piece. If he does not review the older selections, he will forget them, and until he learns the new piece, he can play nothing. In contrast to this common occurrence, Suzuki's 'pyramid' approach keeps the children's repertoire in good shape. They are almost always ready for an 'instant' concert for public or family. As an example, Suzuki keeps the beginner playing the Twinkle variations every day until he has completed 'Perpetual Motion'.

Characteristics of a Good Teacher

Suzuki feels that the teacher should know how to play the violin very well, at least on the elementary level. In addition, he should, of course, know how to teach the child step by step in the intricacies of violin technique. His mind should be open and receptive to new ideas. He should always be striving to find new and better ways to introduce the material to the child. He should be relaxed and enjoy the lessons in themselves and not only as part of the development of his pupil's abilities. "Above all", says Suzuki, "the teacher should have a passion for true education, a deep understanding of children, and the love of a mother". He should always work with the mother to help motivate the child properly so that he will enjoy practicing correctly at home. If the private lesson is an enjoyable affair for all, he will have contributed greatly to the successful motivation of the child.

Naturally the teacher is expected to follow Suzuki in the frequent expression of praise. He should strive to correct with as little criticism as possible. The child should feel that the teacher enjoys teaching the child and is happy when he does well. Teachers can be more relaxed when they don't have to keep a sharp eye on the clock. They need not stop if the lesson is highly productive, nor need they struggle to stretch the lesson of an inattentive child to thirty minutes. If the mothers are aware that both performance and observation are

Mr. Yamamura's private lesson.

Mr. Hirose's private lesson.

valuable then they will be less likely to measure the time of the lessons given to their own children and compare with that given others.

The following anecdote of Suzuki's own teaching serves well to illustrate his use of praise to encourage the child.

"One day a teacher brought me a student who played very badly. The teacher said he did not think he could teach the child any longer since the child would not concentrate in the lessons. He asked me if I would try to teach him a lesson. When the child came to me, I said, 'I would like to hear something. Would you please play for me?' The child then played very badly. I said, 'Thank you. You can play'. The child was very glad. I added, 'You play so, but I play this way. Can you play as I play? Can you? Maybe you cannot.' 'Yes, I can', replied the child. 'Please try now'. He played then a little better. For the next measure I asked the same question, 'Can you play so?' 'Yes, I can'. Gradually measure by measure we played the piece and the lesson was finished. After the lesson, the teacher said, 'Wonderful! But, what did you mean when you said, "You can play very well?" It is not true.' 'No, I did not say that. When some children are brought to me to play, teachers ask, 'Please play for Mr. Suzuki'. Some refuse, saying, 'No, I don't want to!' But this child played. And so I said, 'Thank you. You can play'. 'Very well, I did not say. The child was very glad to hear me say 'You can play'. When I saw that he was glad, I tried to have him play better. If I had said, 'What piece is this? I cannot recognize it. You must play better', he would not have wanted to play for me any more. So also at home mothers must say, 'Good. Now can you play much better?' "

Suzuki firmly believes that the teacher should dwell on only one technical problem at a time. American visitors who watched Suzuki teach an American child in Matsumoto were surprised at his not mentioning the child's bad intonation. He spent the entire lesson adjusting the bow hold. Those of us who saw the next lesson heard nothing about the bow hold which had improved reasonably. He did reset the bow hold several times but without comment. Suzuki spent that next lesson on intonation. "If I had tried to deal with both problems at the same lesson," he said later, "the boy would probably have done neither well. Teachers and parents should remember this. They should be trying to help the child."

Suzuki doesn't believe that it is helpful to recite to a student all of his errors. This might impress an observer, showing how watchful the teacher was, but it most likely would depress the child. Most students would also be unable to remember all of a great number of suggestions for improvement. Confusion and frustration would follow. An older student would be expected to remember more, but even with them Suzuki feels the teacher must be very careful.

Suzuki uses a lively wit to entertain the youngsters as he instructs them. They love his humorous expressions and his picturesque speech which stimulate their imaginations and stir them to do as he asks. Careful observation of each of his witticisms, however, shows a direct relationship to the solving of a technical problem. Teachers trying to imitate Suzuki should keep this in mind.

Parts of Private Lesson

The private lesson should fall into three parts, as should home practice sessions: 1) work on the current piece, 2) review for reinforcement, 3) "preview" work on problems to come. Not all of these need representation in each lesson or practice session, but if any are missing over a period of time, the student's education is being slighted.

Everyone expects to work on the current piece. This is traditional. Suzuki parents also expect the teacher to ask for some review work for reinforcement, but they don't know when new technical problems should be introduced. If the child is practicing three hours a day, the time at which new technical problems are introduced is not critical. It is best for the average child, however, to be given new technical problems before he arrives at the piece containing these problems. "Children like what they can do," says Suzuki. If new problems are introduced in fragments ahead of time, the child will feel more comfortable when he arrives at the piece because he has already encountered the most difficult parts.

For example, Twinkle can be played on the D string before the D string level is encountered in a new piece. Another example: the difficult group of eight 16th notes in the Gossec 'Gavotte' can be presented in advance. The fragment is so short, it won't tire the youngster. He will be excited to know that he is already working on the Gavotte, even though he has two or three more pieces to go before he studies the entire piece.

One clever Japanese teacher introduced several of the difficult passages of the Gossec Gavotte in advance to a five-year-old, then taught the whole piece, but went on to Book II as the child continued to practice the Gavotte daily. She didn't want to demoralize the little boy who was experiencing considerable difficulty with the selection. His study of the Gavotte actually overlapped the study of three pieces before and three afterwards.

This is an example of the importance of sensitivity to the child's temperament. Some teachers are adamant with all children. "You cannot go on until this is mastered." Other teachers take a different position and allow the child to drop the piece without learning it nearly as well as he could have at that point. The attitude of the Japanese teacher cited above is superior to either of these. The child should be taught not to flee from challenges, yet the teacher should not allow the child's spirit to be crushed by them.

In the private lesson, it is good for the children of different levels to play together occasionally. A child may be asked to play with a more advanced student who can produce a bigger tone or play the piece more rapidly. Suzuki finds this to be a good stimulation provided no unhealthy spirit of competition enters. The teacher should merely say, "Let's play together". The younger child will try to equal the tone and technique of the more advanced player.

Music reading is not introduced in Talent Education until the pupil reaches Book IV. By this time the child's memory, musical sensitivity and playing skill should have been sufficiently trained. Problems of posture and the bow hold should have been solved and his attention freed from them. However, even after the child has acquired the ability to read musical notation, he is expected to play without music at all lessons. This provides continual training for his musical memory, and will help him when he performs in public without music. If he practices continually with music and uses the music at his lessons, he will feel very insecure when he plays from memory in public and will not be able to demonstrate his best ability.

Parent Training

The teacher's training of the parent is very important. New parents should be instructed in parental behavior at lessons. They should be asked to avoid talking to the children during the lessons. The child needs only one teacher at a time. Expressions of praise or disapproval are equally out of place, as is the sharp, audible intake of breath, or the sigh.

Parents should be encouraged to take notes, not only to refresh their memories during the week, but also to have a valuable record of growth of their children's skills.

The teacher should make sure that the parent understands what is to be practiced and how it is to be done. One experienced Japanese teacher stated that he felt many novice teachers presented new material clearly but didn't ask for enough repetitions of the correct practice procedure in the lesson. "I learned long ago that mothers and children often forgot just how I wanted it done, so I make them repeat new problems again and again in the lesson." Teachers must guide the home practice as well as possible. Their assignments should be clear, and yet allow for creativity on the part of parent or child.

Suzuki has eliminated the thousands of dry exercises children used to practice, feeling that the child would practice his technique if he knew that it was directly drawn from pieces that he was looking forward to playing. It is up to the teacher to create the necessary exercises. Very short excerpts can be practiced many times by the student without his tiring of them. This instills good practice habits, accustoming the student to this kind of work rather than playing through the new piece over and over until somehow he can get through it.

It is good for the teacher to point out to the parent and child in advance the errors he may fall into "naturally". "You will feel like holding the violin directly in front of you because you can see it more easily that way, but you can't play it well that way". "You may want to hold the violin in the palm of your left hand because you don't want to drop it, but it will be hard to play that way."

Suzuki's Vital Points

"What piece is your child studying?" is a question teachers often hear in parent's conversations at group lessons. No one ever asks the next question, "And how well does she play it?" Parents should be reminded constantly of the qualitative aspect of performance.

In order to deemphasize the importance of the speedy acquisition of new repertoire, Suzuki prepared a progress report (reproduced below) to call attention to vital points for study other than the pieces themselves.

At each lesson the teacher fills out a whole bar for each entry if the development is adequate. The graph covers sixteen weeks of lessons. Spaces are provided for work exceeding expectations. After the chart is complete, the parent and child have a good profile of the growth for the four months of study.

One imaginative teacher personified Suzuki's Vital Points, saying to the child "Posture is far ahead of Tone! Do you think we can help Tone to catch up?"

Suzuki's Vital Points change, of course, as the child advances.

Abilities of Children

Suzuki does not believe that talent is inborn. He believes that every child can be educated. He came to realize this after thirty years of experience teaching small children and witnessing so many who excelled, given the proper instruction and environment. These well-known statements of Suzuki bother many people who feel that he has closed his eyes to the 'slow-learner'. Two statements of Suzuki's are given here to show that this is not so: 1) "The only superior ability that a child might have at birth is the speed and sensitivity with which he absorbs his environment"; 2) "I have no doubt that people are born with hereditary physiological differences, but I believe that a person's abilities grow and develop depending on stimulation from the outside".

Child's Rate of Growth

Suzuki stresses that the main point for the teacher and parent to keep in mind is that all children do not mature or learn at the same rate. Everyone accepts this when the children learn to talk and walk, but many forget this point when they expect all children who study music to progress at the same rate. However, Suzuki also has said that it should not be assumed that the slow beginner will always progress slowly. He tells his famous Peeko Miyazawa story to illustrate his statement that 'Ability breeds ability'. This is the story of the slow-learning parakeet who hears the name 'Peeko'

VITAL POINTS

1 TONALIZATION Ability to produce a beautiful big tone.

2 Ability to maintain good posture.

3 Ability to hold the bow properly.

4 Ability to change strings and use correct form.

5 Ability to play music with sensitivity.

6 Ability to play with right intonation.

7 Eagerness for study.

8 Ability to play fine and clear trill.

9 Ability to use correct movement of right arm (elbow).

10 Ability to play with good quick movement of right hand.

PROGRESS REPORT

Weeks	1	2	3	4	5	6	7	8	9	10	11	12	13	14	15	16		
1 Tone																		
2 Posture																		
3 Holding Bow																		
4 Change Strings																		
5 Musical Sensitivity																		
6 Intonation																		
7 Eager to Study																		
8 Trill																		
9 Motion of Right Arm																		
10 Quick Motion of Right Hand																		

three thousand times before responding and speaking that name. The persistent owner, a Suzuki Talent Education teacher, found that the parakeet needed only two hundred repetitions of the next word, his surname Miyazawa, before he repeated it. After that, his learning rate further escalated until he could repeat words after one hearing.

Each child, says Suzuki, is born with a wonderful living soul that responds to his environment. He learns everything from his environment. However, one child may respond after only fifty repetitions of a stimulus. Another may have to absorb a hundred repetitions before responding. Teachers and parents should repeat this fact to themselves every day. Absorption and learning rates vary with each individual and also vary within the learning period.

Suzuki feels that the world must be full of children who are 'drops-outs' in some endeavor or other because they were not given enough repetitions at the beginning or were made to move too rapidly at the beginning. It is only when the child learns to walk, talk, and learns to use his hands for holding, grasping, and manipulating that he dictates how and when he is ready to produce, that is, when he is ready to walk, talk and use his hands.

One would never hear a mother say to a small child learning the mother tongue, "You've said 'mama' fifty times. That's enough. Next word." And yet that's what is done in school and at the music lesson when the teacher thinks the child has done enough and should go on to the next problem. However, in these endeavors the child cannot help as well. He knows when he is walking well, but he does not know definitely that his bow hold is a good one. The teacher must watch very carefully to determine when he feels the child is ready to move on to the next problem.

Suzuki's approach to musical education has been hailed as the most effective way yet devised to teach many small children, yet its very success depends upon its adaptability for each child's needs, since each child has his own growth rate. Throughout this book there are suggested exercises extracted from the music. Some children may need all of these, plus additional ones concocted by the individual teacher and parent. A fine teacher, explaining her attitude toward teaching, said, "I try to think of as many as ten small steps for one technical point. For some children I may use all ten and wish I could think of more, with others I may need only three or four, and occasionally a child may move from step one to step ten at once. How do I know how many steps to use? Every once in a while, I try the final step. If the child can do it, fine. If not, I back up to use more graduated preliminary steps." If the teacher moves too rapidly and sees her error, it is not difficult to back-track immediately. The teacher should tell the student that he is not quite ready to move on.

The teacher should use every available aid to encourage the slow beginner through difficult periods. All kinds of reinforcement should be employed by parent and teacher particularly when the student is on a plateau and feels no perceptible growth.

The Suzuki books have been called a well-graded series of compositions for the development of the child's technique and musical sensitivity. This does not mean each selection presents a new problem or even a different version of an old one. Some selections repeat nearly the same versions of the same problems in order that the point may be mastered at that level. Other selections are 'breathers' in that they are easier than the preceding ones. This gives the child a real sense of accomplishment in that he can learn a 'new' piece so easily. Suzuki arrived at this selection by trial and error in the early years. He has admitted that some pieces are there because "the children love to play them". They are great morale boosters and motivate the child to practice so that he can play them.

The teacher should strive to develop the child's concentration span in the lesson, although giving the child moments of relaxation. The teacher should be very sensitive to signs, however small, of exhaustion. One young Japanese teacher told of a student who was improving a particular skill so well through many repetitions of a single passage that she forgot just how many repetitions she had asked for. "Suddenly", she exclaimed, "he lowered his violin quickly and gave out a piercing scream. I felt badly that I had pushed the little fellow so far."

Creative parents often find new ways to aid their children. One Japanese mother was so creative with her two children that the teacher remarked how easy it was to teach them. "I merely have to point out what's to be done, and this mother figures out how to do it. She loved the challenge of accomplishing this on her own."

The mother is continually referred to as the assistant teacher. We should not overlook the fact that the child should eventually become independent in his musical study. This should be encouraged little by little. Some teachers tell their students from the beginning that they want them to become good self-teachers. A child is encouraged in this if the teacher occasionally plays for the child asking the child to correct the teacher when necessary. By the time the child is advanced, if he is old enough and reads the music well, he can be given a new piece without any previous instruction from the teacher. He should be asked to find the most difficult passages and show his teacher how they should be practiced.

Within the structure of a well-graded list of compositions as found in the Suzuki books, there is still the need for creative work to be done by each teacher as he approaches each child with his own particular problems. Two principles should be constantly before the Suzuki teacher: 1) EVERY CHILD CAN BE EDUCATED, 2) EACH CHILD HAS HIS OWN GROWTH RATE.

Ten Points for Teachers

(Dr. Suzuki compiled a list of "Ten Points" which he circulated among all his Suzuki-trained teachers in Japan and also made available to us. He said to us, "Teachers of the 'Suzuki' approach must strive to attend to these ten points. During lessons, the teachers must be able to recognize at once which of the points needs most attention.")

1. It is of utmost importance that parents and children understand the value of listening to recordings at home. Listening is central to the development of musical sensitivity.

2. The teacher must understand and be able to illustrate "tonalization" for his students. This involves producing a beautiful tone by finding the "Sound point", or the perfect pitch of each note at which sympathetic vibrations of the other strings will occur. It is at this point that the sound will have the greatest resonance.

3. A nice vibrato should be encouraged and taught, but only after the "sound point" has been located.

4. A feeling for rhythm must be taught. Teachers must remember to maintain a *musical* tempo by avoiding rushing or playing too fast.

5. Excellent intonation should be mastered in this first position. Take time to tune each note.

6. Develop a brilliant trill by beginning with slow, one-note trills. These may be gradually speeded up, and more notes may be added as soon as the quick one-note trill is clear. Every note must sound regardless of the speed being used.

7. From the very first pieces, expression and temperament should be taught. This is more effectively accomplished through demonstration than through explanation.

8. Emphasize the value of "E string posture" for the right hand.

9. Special attention should be given to preparation at home. Be sure to discuss and demonstrate practice procedures with mothers.

10. The teacher must be able to teach *every* child. It is the teacher's responsibility to motivate his students sufficiently that he will never be able to find an excuse ("This child does not practice.") for a poor student.

These are weighty responsibilities, but in the words of John Kendall, "Good teaching is everywhere the same; it involves patience, constant encouragement, enthusiasm, psychological insight, technical and musical proficiency, use of good materials and methodology, and above all, imagination."

Parent as Teacher. Home Practice.

A Japanese mother acts as teacher as she works in the rice field. The little girl was a student of Susan Shields in Omachi, Japan.

(The term 'mother' is used more frequently than 'parent' throughout this chapter solely because more mothers than fathers seem to have the opportunity to attend lessons and practice with their children. The impression must not be given that fathers cannot assume this role. The author wishes to acknowledge the growing number of fathers who, having the opportunity, do work with their children.)

The mother who wishes to be a good home teacher for her child must constantly remind herself that she has entered her child in the Talent Education program for the happiness of the child. One of the most common errors in attitude is that of the mother who keeps thinking about how she is suffering through all of the child's struggle to learn to play so that he may get the best seat in the school orchestra, or win prizes and fame in contests, or simply enjoy playing well when he becomes an adult. It is Suzuki's oft expressed wish that all, parents, teachers, and children, enjoy the whole process of musical instruction for the child as it unfolds, not merely endure it as a sacrifice to attain some worthy future goal. Of course parents should be goal-oriented in that they want their children to learn to play as well as possible, yet at the same time they should not concentrate on progress to distant goals without enjoying the everyday signs of growth in each child's spirit, love and enjoyment of music, and musical skill.

Always Suzuki urges mothers to wait, relax, and enjoy each step as the child learns. "Beginners grow so slowly, same as mother-tongue. Do you mothers say, 'Yesterday our baby was born. One week later, he says "ma-ma" '? No! He must live a long time in his environment. Mother waits for the child to speak. Also, with the violin, the mother gives good environment, then waits as the child learns to play."

In particular, the mother should learn to relax at the lessons, putting aside other cares to take delight in the lessons themselves. If something is worrying us Westerners, it is difficult for us to enjoy anything else, the worry so covers our pleasures. Shakespeare stated it clearly when Bushy speaks to his queen after Richard II is taken away: "Each substance of a grief hath twenty shadows, which show like grief itself. . . ." Contrast the queen's attitude with the moral given Easterners in the tale of Buddha wherein a certain man, being chased by a tiger, found himself at the edge of a cliff. Grabbing a vine and lowering himself over the edge, he looked down to see two tigers pacing the beach below. Suddenly becoming aware of a strong vibration through the vine he looked up to see two rats chewing the vine stem. After this assessment of his position, he came to notice a bush near his face, a bush laden with succulent-looking berries. Freeing one hand, he took a berry and tasted it. "Delicious!" he exclaimed aloud. Buddha's tale ends here.

Japanese Mothers at Lessons

American visitors to Talent Education studios in Japan are often intent upon the attitudes of the mothers at lessons. First noticed is their obvious enthusiasm for the music and for the children's playing. If they have tired of the Twinkle Variations, one would never suspect it from their behavior. Some move in rhythm to the music. Some tap their feet to the beat, and most are always ready to smile or laugh at the cute antics of the children. It is also obvious by the attitudes of the children that they have had respect for the teacher previously instilled in them.

In the observation of hundreds of lessons I never noticed any manifestations of boredom on the part of mothers attending private lessons. No mothers were seen reading magazines, writing letters, or taking short naps. The mothers did not talk to the children during the lessons, or make any audible expressions of approval or disapproval. They were not only very attentive during their own children's instruction but they also watched other children's lessons carefully.

Teacher Must Guide Mother

The teacher and the mother are both well aware of the fact that the teacher must help the mother to be a good home teacher. The mother feels this responsibility very strongly. Suzuki often tells the mothers that six days of poor, misguided practice at home can cancel out the best teaching in the private lessons. The teachers instruct the mothers carefully in practice procedures. They show the mothers what should be done and how to work with the children. Many mothers carry notebooks in which they record the teacher's instruction at each lesson. Some mothers of advanced students watch the music during the lessons, making notes on the music pages.

The mothers who are most effective as home teachers have been diligent about playing the recordings for the children, and have incidentally memorized all of the music themselves through this intensive listening. Some of them teach themselves musical notation long before Suzuki asks it of the child. One mother told of having much difficulty with learning notation. She made brackets with colored pencils over passages in other than first position.

At times Suzuki has to contend with over-ambitious mothers often called "Kyoiku" (education) mothers, who repeatedly train the child past the teacher's assignment. "Where are you going?" Suzuki asks the mothers gently. "Please wait and follow me. I'll lead you there." The mother should follow the teacher. If she feels that her child is not being challenged or is being pushed too rapidly, she should discuss this with the teacher privately.

Suzuki advises regular meetings of mothers and teachers. In Matsumoto they are held about once a month. Here the mothers share their common problems. The most frequently discussed problem was that of getting the children to do an adequate amount of practice.

Home Practice

Suzuki points out that practice periods should grow in length along with the span of concentration. "At home two or three minutes of practice may be enough for a beginner. Perhaps this can be done four or five itmes a day. Gradually each practice period can be longer as the child begins to play the Twinkle Variations. If he can play all the variations of Twinkle, which may take four minutes, his ability to concentrate is also developed to that length of time. As other pieces are added, the period of concentration lengthens naturally."

Parents should expect the child to function at different levels of concentration, much as they use different levels in their daily life. Intense cortical activity cannot be maintained by small children for long periods of time. Practice periods should contain many pauses for physical and mental rest. If technical goals are changed often during the practice session, the child can maintain a higher level of concentration for longer periods of time.

During the practice periods at home, the mother should make it clear to the child that she is his friend and helper. She should avoid negative criticism. Her instructions might include such as these: "Let's see how you can play that better. Remember how sensei (teacher) asked us to practice this way every day." "Oh, we haven't practiced bowing at the frog today. You promised sensei that you would try to get it better this week." "Why don't you play May Song straight through without any stops? Just like a concert!" "Can you play Allegro for me, remembering to move your elbow up and down?"

Suzuki says, "The child's practice is easier for him and much more effective if the mother calls attention to only one point at a time. Sometimes mothers give too many instructions at one time. 'Your elbow is too high; please raise the violin; your bow is crooked; your third finger is too low, etc.' This is very bad. The child feels that he cannot change all of these things at once and becomes discouraged."

Each parent working with a child should be sensitive to those aspects of the child's personality that relate to practice. In this regard it is useless to compare one's child with other children. Some children become very frustrated when they are unable to learn quickly. Others are much more patient with themselves. A few actually like repetitive practice.

Repetitions for certain children cannot be done one after another. If the teacher has requested that a certain passage be practiced ten times daily, the parent might ask the child how many repetitions he or she would like to play at one time.

For those perfectionists who despair of learning at each new step, the parent should point out skills that have already been acquired. "Remember when you couldn't hold the violin at all, or when you couldn't move your right arm in rhythm? Look how easy those things are for you now!"

Most parents know about the "impossible" days. Rather than omit practice on these days, why not have a short review concert, with the parent requesting particular attention to only one detail as each piece is played?

In his book, *Nurtured by Love*, Suzuki discusses practice and the development of ability as follows: "My child doesn't like to practice at home", complain quite a few parents. It is because they do not understand the mind of a child who thinks that the violin is for fun. Parents of this sort resent paying good money just to have the child think it is a mere game. In other words, they are calculating about education, and their attitude discourages the children. Starting children off with the fun of playing a game, letting their spirit of fun lead them in the right direction, is the way all education of children should be started.

Hitomi Kasuya was three and would play the violin for three hours every day. How could a three-year-old do that, many people think. Hitomi's mother bought her a violin instead of a doll and played a record of the piece to be studied over and over again as a kind of background music. Hitomi played with the violin all day, as if it were a toy. Her mother would now and then show her the correct way to play, according to our instructions, letting Hitomi think she was having a game with her. This is the art of education at its best. The thing that matters is the result: that the child acquires the skill. If you are formal and strict and have a 'This is education' attitude, you will immediately warp the child. First you must educate the mind then inculcate the skill. This is the correct, natural method. Hitomi Kasuya developed rapidly with this method, and in 1964, when she was five, she took her little violin and went to America with us.

In contrast to the children who do not like to practice at home, there are plenty of examples in which, because of the wise leading of the mothers, violin practice becomes a natural event of the day.

One year at summer school I noticed a six-year-old playing the Vivaldi concerto in a minor with fine style and tone. I asked the mother how long the child had been playing. "One year and a half." "How well she plays! How long does she practice every day?" "About three hours." That was what I had thought. A child who practices well shows it in his playing. You can tell immediately. Practicing according to the correct method and practicing as much as possible is the way to acquire ability. If one is faithful to this principle, superior skill develops without fail. If you compare a person who practices five minutes a day with one who practices three hours a day, the difference, even though they both practice daily, is enormous. Those who fail to practice suf-

ficiently fail to acquire ability. Only the effort that is actually expended will bear results. There is no short cut. If the five-minute-a-day person wants to accomplish what the three-hour-a-day person does, it will take him nine years to accomplish what the other accomplishes in three months. There is no reason why it should be otherwise. Hitomi Kasuya, Toshiya Eto, Koji Toyoda, Kenji Kobayashi and others all practiced three hours a day and more.

For someone to complain, "But I studied for five years" means nothing. It all depends on how much he did each day. "I spent five years on it", someone says, But five minutes a day for five years is only 150 hours. What a person should have said is, "I did it for a hundred and fifty hours, and I'm still no better." To put your talent up on the shelf and then say you were born without any is utter nonsense.

The development of ability is straightforward. This can be absolutely relied upon. People either become experts at doing the right thing, which is seen as a fine talent, or they become experts at doing something wrong and unacceptable, which is seen as lack of talent. So it behooves everyone to become expert in the right things, and the more training he receives, the better. Depending upon these two things—practice and the practice of the right things—superior ability can be produced in anyone. For twenty years I have watched with my own eyes the education of thousands of children, as well as the effect on them of the superiority or inferiority of their parents and teachers, and I can say without any hesitation whatsoever that this is true."

Formation of Good Habits

Suzuki says that children who play badly usually play the same way all the time. If they have bad posture, it is always the same bad posture, not a different one each day. "This means the child has learned well to play badly", says Suzuki. Since they couldn't play at all at the beginning, why didn't they learn proper posture at the outset? And yet teachers see the same bad habits in ill-trained students the world over. It's safe to assume that these very common bad habits are most often the result of "natural" errors. For example: it is "natural" for a person to hold an object he examines directly in front of him, yet he cannot play the violin well if it is held directly in front of him. He must learn to hold the violin to the left, even though it is not "natural" for one to keep one's head turned to the left to look at anything for any length of time. Another example: it is "natural" for one to hold a fragile object securely in the hand. The beginner who cannot hold the violin securely between chin and shoulder will grasp the violin tightly in his left hand, preferably in the palm, to lessen the danger of dropping it. A third example: it is "natural" to hold a slender object such as a bow strongly, with the hand clenched or with the tips of the fingers. The correct bow hold seems awkward and risky to most beginners. What is "bad" may feel "good" to the child relying on "natural" guidelines. The teacher should take pains to demonstrate this to parent and child.

What may seem at the beginning to be an insignificant error may, if not corrected, loom as a major obstacle to growth as the child progresses. I like to use the analogy of a ship's navigator to drive home this point to teachers and parents. Navigators are always sensitive to errors in initial course headings. I was the navigator of a small ship during World War II. After the war ended, two of our small LCSs left Shanghai for the States with scheduled stops at Wake Island and Hawaii. Lacking the sophisticated radar equipment of larger ships, we kept close watch on our course, knowing that Wake was only a tiny dot in the vast Pacific Ocean. Even if we had calculated a direct course at the beginning of the journey, we knew that we would have to correct the course daily as the ship was affected by wind, current, and possible compass error. So the violin teacher, after planning a very careful beginning for the child's development, must watch constantly for changes in the child's basic posture and hand positions as he encounters new technical problems, much as the navigator watches for deviations from the ship's true course. Would that this were not so! How happy all would be if the student always retained what he had learned. In the early years, however, the left hand may slip out of position when the student begins to learn new finger patterns, vibrato, or shifting. The bow hold may also deteriorate as more complex music is studied. Some teachers tell parents that if the child is started correctly everything will be all right. Of course parents like to hear this. We should be more candid. We should admit that the posture and hand positions may be in a state of flux for several years but assure parents that careful watching should keep the child on the right track.

Suzuki asks teachers to try their very best to avoid the necessity of the child's doing remedial work, since it is so frustrating for all concerned—child, teacher, and parent. Certainly the most painful kind of practice seems to be that during which the child is trying to correct an error that is well implanted. All assistance, sympathy, and encouragement possible should be given the child by both teacher and parent.

One father used a stop watch to play a game with his little boy to lighten the load of remedial practice. The child had fallen into the habit of pushing the tip of the left thumb into the neck of the violin. The father was told by the teacher to ask the child to play only review pieces that week, with careful attention to be given to the offending thumb. At each practice period the father timed the boy, watching to see when the thumb would change from the correct position. After each try, they looked at the stop watch together. "Seven seconds the first time!" exclaimed the father. "Let's see how much longer you can do it next time!"

A Japanese teacher suggested a game to a little boy who had trouble playing through any piece without forgetting, no matter how long he had listened. "At the next lesson, please give me a list of the pieces you played

straight through each day without forgetting. If you forget, you must go back to the very beginning and play it over without forgetting if you wish to count that piece." This challenged the little boy, although he didn't do very well the first week. His mother kept encouraging him, and the teacher kept repeating the same request each week. Six weeks later the little fellow announced proudly that he had played fourteen pieces without forgetting. He had developed considerable power of concentration through this game.

Tuning the Violin

Keeping the violin strings in tune can be a real problem for some parents. The parent should ask the teacher for help in this matter. Tuners on the A and E strings are almost necessary for the parent to tune the very small violins. Parents who do not have pianos should purchase pitch pipes for tuning. They should practice tuning with the teacher at the lesson so that he can determine whether or not they are tuning reasonably correctly. One teacher encouraged her parents to phone her if they were having trouble tuning, saying that she could help them adjust the pitch over the phone. "An out-of-tune violin can ruin a week's practice!" she exclaimed.

Accompaniment tapes are now being made available for home practice. These are invaluable for parents who cannot accompany their children at the piano. These tapes assist the child in preparing for solo recitals and group concerts.

Practice, How Much and When?

Many teachers and mothers in Japan were asked to give an estimate of the average amount of daily practice. There were such extremes that it would be an oversimplification to quote one figure. One teacher was quoted as saying his very youngest beginners probably only practiced five minutes a day for several months. However, these same children were most likely spending 60 to 90 minutes a day after they began to study pieces. Many children were found to be practicing between 45 to 90 minutes daily up through their years in elementary school. Of course, there were a number of exceptions found where little ones practiced two to three hours daily. These children were always easy to identify in group concerts. They were the youngest children performing the very difficult pieces. Japanese public school education, with its emphasis on testing for entrance into prestige high schools and universities, takes its toll on children in middle school and high school. In Japan, children do not automatically attend a regional high school. They must pass tests for entrance into school, and all of the children in an area can qualify by high scores for admittance into the elite high school of the area which sends many of its graduates to prestige universities. Many teachers admit that their violin students who are not interested in music as a profession, and they are in the majority in Talent Education, are hard pressed to find time for practice in middle and high school. Forty-five minutes to an hour a day seemed to be quoted many, many times as the average amount of daily practice time for these children.

American children and parents seem to have less time for practice than their Japanese counterparts. Among American families there seems to be great variety in the practice schedules. Some successful parents schedule practice periods at the same time each day. Some children practice early in the morning each day before they go to school. A complex home routine prevents others from such regularity. Their practice periods occur at different times on different days. The principle that must guide parents is that the acquisition of a skill flourishes best with daily practice. Suzuki jokingly advises, "Children don't have to practice every day—only those days on which they eat!"

Everyone knows there are days in busy American households in which no practice time seems available. Parents should realize however, that even five or ten minutes is better than none. They should ask the teacher, "If we have only five minutes some days, what is the best way we can use those minutes?"

Some parents keep a record of the weekly practice schedule to show to the teacher at each lesson. Others keep a list of the pieces to be reviewed and the dates they are practiced. If the list is long, the child reviews different ones each day. The parent's record prevents a piece being forgotten. This systematic review keeps the child prepared for group lessons.

Child as Self-Instructor

The parent guiding the child's practice must not lose sight of the ultimate aim to make the child independent of parental help. This can be effected by degrees, beginning even during the early stages of study. The parent should try, as should the teacher in the private lesson, to involve the child in judgments and decisions regarding his own playing and practice. This helps the child to concentrate on his playing. "What would you like to do first?" "How many times do you want to repeat that exercise now?" "How does that need to be improved?" In this way the parent as helper withdraws imperceptibly as the child assumes more and more his role as self-instructor, a role he will need as he reaches maturity.

And finally, parents should never forget these words of Shinichi Suzuki: "The greatest duty and joy given to us adults is the privilege of developing our children's potentialities and of educating desirable human beings with beautiful harmonious minds and high sensitivity. I believe sensitivity and love toward music and art are very important things to all people whether they are politicians, scientists, businessmen or laborers. They are the things that make our lives rich."

Questionnaire for Suzuki Parents

Do you see that your child listens regularly to the recordings?

Do you take good notes during lessons so that you can be a good home teacher?

Do you shout, scream, or make sarcastic remarks?

Are you positive about home practice, or does your attitude suggest it as a chore?

Do you plan practice as a daily habit, even if only a minimum can be done?

Do you arrange home concerts for family and/or friends?

Are your child's practice sessions too often just play-along times with the tape?

What is the ratio of praise to criticism in your comments to your child?

Do you show enthusiasm consistently?

Does your child always listen in advance to pieces he is about to study?

Do you practice after lessons, or discuss the lesson in the car afterwards?

Do you observe other lessons?

Do you take your child to concerts?

In practice periods, do you ask for too much at one time?

Are both parents involved in this phase of the child's development?

Practicing Can Be Fun!

Suzuki said on many occasions that teachers and parents should do everything possible to make practice enjoyable, urging mothers not to scold their children to get them to practice. In drawing up his method of teaching violin based on the mother-tongue principles, he tried everything he could think of to make practice a pleasant experience.

Focusing on the music the children were to study, he chose music that he found attractive to his small students. He admitted that certain pieces were in his books not always to present or reinforce a certain technique, but simply because he found them to be great favorites of the children. They loved to play them. Handel's "Bourrée" in Book 2 was one of these pieces.

Suzuki realized that if a child listened repeatedly to music she was to study, that listening would whet her appetite to play it. He knew, too, that seeing and hearing other children play that same piece would prove motivational. Instituting group lessons and choosing a common repertoire for all the children was Suzuki's way of filling these needs.

His private lessons were designed to be enjoyable. Pupils looked forward to playing for him what they had learned. Lessons were a social affair, with students and their parents present to watch other lessons. Suzuki urged every mother to build in her child's heart a desire to do well for the teacher. He wanted the child to look forward to the teacher's pleasure at the child's accomplishment.

In spite of all of his efforts to make practice enjoyable, Suzuki found that whenever he talked to mothers, they always wanted to hear good ideas for making practice periods at home more pleasant.

Over and over again Suzuki said, "We must all work together, teachers and parents, to continue to develop new ideas to help children learn to play more easily, and to enjoy their learning." Many teachers and parents have taken this very seriously and have developed fine ideas for motivating the children to practice well.

The Child as Her Own Teacher

As often happens when many individuals are trying to solve the same problem, some of them will come up with similar solutions. So, an idea that I discovered to be extremely beneficial, and that I have spoken of to parents and teachers in many places, and that Connie and I wrote about in *To Learn With Love*, may have also arisen elsewhere at about the same time.

This idea was to make the child her own teacher by using metaphors to stimulate the child's imagination. I have always thought that the "Suzuki triangle" should be changed to a square. The child should be moved over with the teacher and parent. The attention of all three—parent, teacher and child—should be directed to the fourth point of the square: the child's arms, hands and fingers.

The child should believe this fundamental truth: She is the most important of these three in training her fingers and arms. The teacher should be the guide with the parent as helper, but the child trains herself to hold the violin and bow, put the fingers down and draw the bow. If she's a good teacher, she plays well; if not, she plays badly. At various times I have called the child "Teacher, Captain of the Ship, Pilot, Boss, General, even Policeman."

A Talk to 100 Teachers (Students) Ages 8–14

I gave my first talk on this subject at the Suzuki Institute at Stanford in 1975, not to an audience of parents or teachers but of children! Almost all the parents, living in the area around Stanford, had dropped off their children for morning classes and were returning to have lunch with them at noon.

This was the first day of the Institute and a student recital of four advanced children chosen from audition tapes was scheduled for 11 a.m. At 10:45, Jackie Corina, the director, received a call that the car bringing the soloists had broken down some miles away. There was no way they could get there in time to play a recital, but Jackie was not going to let one hundred unchaperoned children loose in Stanford's new music building, so she came up to me, begging, "Please go in and talk to the children until lunch break!" "About what?" "Anything, but please keep them in that auditorium till noon!"

People often say that their most creative ideas come under stress. So it was with me. I had ten minutes, some three-by-five cards, and a mind racing to prepare a talk to a crowd of children from 8 to 14 years of age now noisily gathering in the hall. Aha! Practice! At two minutes to eleven, I hit upon two stories I would tell them about practice and tossed away my cards: the first story, "Training Your Crew," and the second, "The Smart, Fat Baby."

Training Your Crew

I began with this story of my first experience in training to be a Naval officer in World War ll:

Our first training on a ship dealt with bringing a ship along the side of another ship. You'd probably call it "parking" a ship. It's like your mom or dad parking a car in a parking space. But it's a lot harder to "park" a ship. When your mom turns the wheel, the car turns. When she steps on the brake, the car stops quickly, unless she's speeding!

When the captain of a ship wants to turn a ship, he calls down to the seaman on the wheel to turn the ship right or left, sharply or gradually. The seaman turns the wheel, which turns the rudder underneath the back (in Navy terms, the stern) of the ship. The turn takes time. A medium-sized ship will take several hundred feet to complete the turn. And stopping a ship! That's a problem! You call down to the engine room, "All engines back full!" and they have to adjust the propellers underneath the stern of the ship so that they will make the ship go backward instead of going forward. Even when the propellers—we called them screws—were reversed, the ship would keep gliding ahead until the engines could not only stop the ship but make it go backward. Stopping a ship would often take more than half the length of a football field!

Shiphandlers have two more problems: one, the current of the water carries the ship forward, backward or sideways; two, the wind blows the ship to one side or the other. We had to figure out all of these things on the spot when we tried to come alongside another ship. It took practice to do it well in a reasonable amount of time.

To train us, they took a group of us officers out in a ship and showed us how to come alongside a ship that was anchored out in the bay. An experienced officer did it first and then gave each of us a chance to do it, one by one.

It looked easy when he did it. First, he brought the ship in close, slowed it down almost to a stop and then ordered the crew to throw the ropes—we called them lines—over to the crew on the other ship. The guys on the other ship wrapped the lines around some posts on their ship, and gradually we came alongside as they pulled on the lines and our officer gave instructions to the men in the engine room how to set the engines.

They took us alphabetically so, since my name began with "S," I was put near the bottom of the list. Most of the officers got books to read from the ship's library and found a place to sit on deck and read while they waited for their turn to practice. Instead, I decided to watch the other men so I would know what to do when my turn came. Guess what? By watching them, I learned more what not to do! Some of the timid ones stayed so far away from the other ship that the crew couldn't throw the lines over that far. Others came up so close and so fast that we would have hit the other ship if the teacher hadn't changed the orders.

I watched them for four days, six hours a day! By the time my turn came up, I was confident I knew what to do. I brought our ship alongside so closely that our men were able to hand the lines over to the other ship. Still, we weren't in any danger of hitting the other ship because we were parallel to it, and moving very slowly.

It felt good when everybody clapped and the teacher said I was the best student. Why? I had learned by watching, and in the same way you can learn by watching other students' performances and lessons.

Three months later I did a dumb thing when I was captain of my own ship! I was bringing my ship alongside another at Pearl Harbor in Hawaii. As we got close, I called down to the engine room, "Starboard engine (that's the one on the right) back two-thirds (that's two-thirds of the top speed)!" That meant I wanted to slow the ship down as the starboard engine started to move the ship back.

What happened shocked me! Instead of slowing down, we went faster and hit the other ship, knocking down everybody standing on both ships! Fortunately we didn't do any serious damage to either ship. After we recovered and tied up to the other ship, I raced down to the engine room.

"Didn't I send down orders to go back? Why did you go forward? Weren't you paying attention to my orders?!"

"Sorry, sir," said one of the men, "we were all laughing at a joke and we weren't paying careful attention to your signals. If we could see outside, we wouldn't have made such a dumb mistake. We flew all over the place when we hit that ship!"

That's when I realized I had made a big mistake. When I was in training, they were using a well-trained crew that was used to following orders. But I hadn't trained my crew to be alert and follow orders exactly as given. Also, they hadn't been given the opportunity to practice enough. After that embarrassing accident (in the Navy if anything goes wrong on a ship, they always blame the captain), I started a training program that made our crew one of the best in the Navy! We drilled and drilled and drilled until everything ran smoothly, almost automatically.

And that, my dear boys and girls, is what you're doing when you practice. You're the captain who's training your crew! Who's in your crew? Your fingers, your hands and your arms! And they don't know whether they're doing it right or not! They're like the men in the engine room who couldn't see out! You need to train your crew very well or they'll make big mistakes—like playing with bad tone, wrong notes, wrong rhythms, crooked bowing or playing out of tune.

Imagine your eyes and ears are up in a control tower in your head, where they can see and hear everything going on below. You can call down to your bow hand's pinkie, "I see you. You're supposed to be on top of the frog!" or to your left wrist, "Don't slump!" or to your bow arm's elbow, "You're up too high for the E string! Get down!" or to your first finger, "You're not on the tape!"

Don't be too hard on them, though. Remember: You're always learning new pieces and your crew is always having to learn to do something new. Would you like to overhear them talking together about how lousy a teacher you are? Remember that just as in the Navy everybody blames the captain if something goes wrong, people will blame you for bad playing, not your fingers, hands or arms.

You'll be surprised how much faster you'll learn if you start thinking of yourselves as trainers, or teachers. Your mothers will love it if they hear you practice, without being reminded, new music slowly and carefully in small chunks!

Perhaps some of you give your moms or dads a lot of trouble when they try to help you practice. Right? If you took the responsibility of training your own crew, they wouldn't need to say much at all. And you and your parents would both be happier about practice!

The Smart, Fat Baby

Now I'm going to tell you a story about a smart, fat baby named Miranda. She was not fat when she was born, but she was very, very smart although nobody knew that when she was born. In fact, she was so smart that she was probably the smartest baby that had ever been born. When she was one month old, just a tiny baby, she was as smart as an eight-year-old! You eight-year-olds know that's pretty smart. You know how much more you know than a little baby.

When Miranda was only a few months old, she could figure out what her mom and dad were saying! She used to think, "Are my parents idiots? They talk sensibly to each other, but when they talk to me all they say is 'ma-ma' or 'da-da' or 'kitchie-koo' over and over again. I'd like to learn different words, but I can't hear what they are saying when they're not near me. When they lean over the crib, it's always that baby-talk nonsense."

Miranda also noticed that when they talked to her they always talked very slowly and clearly, but when they talked to each other they talked very quickly.

She said to herself, "I'm going to watch how they talk, and then I'm going to say 'Mama' just like they do."

Anyway, after the fat baby, who wasn't fat then, had listened to her parents enough, she decided not only to say "Ma-ma," but also to add, "How does that sound? Are you surprised?"

Miranda Refuses to Practice Talking

As her mommy leaned over her and said, "Say 'Ma-ma,' Miranda," Miranda smiled, opened her mouth and said something like, "Meh, meh, meh, meh, meh" very quickly.

"Daddy, come here! Miranda's starting to talk!" her mom called excitedly.

"Did she say 'Mama'?" he asked as he ran into the room.

"I'm not sure what she was trying to say. Sounded like baby-talk. You know how those first words always sound."

At the same time, Miranda, the fat baby, who was not fat yet, was saying to herself, "That didn't come out the way I wanted. I guess I shouldn't try to imitate Mommy but just talk the way I feel it should sound."

Miranda then said, "I'm sorry that I didn't speak clearly," but that's not what the parents heard. You know what they heard coming out of Miranda's mouth? "Meh, meh, meh,

meh, meh, meh, meh!"

"Isn't that cute?" Mommy said. "Meh, meh, meh, meh, you are a darling baby."

That made Miranda angry, and she said, "I'm not trying to talk baby-talk", but this also came out: "meh, meh, meh, meh."

Miranda was disgusted. "How am I supposed to make these people understand? They should be able to figure out what I'm saying."

In the next few days, Miranda tried to say several different things to her mommy: "I can understand you perfectly; why can't you understand me?" "Has Daddy gone to the office already?" and "I don't like that food," but all of these came out as 'meh, meh, meh's of different lengths.

Miranda decided to stop trying to talk for a while, and just listen. "I refuse to be like these other dumb babies they talk about that just say 'ma-ma' over and over again. That's probably all they understand anyway." Miranda, now sitting in a high chair at the table, became more and more interested in listening to all the talk around her.

Miranda Refuses to Practice Using a Spoon

She enjoyed sitting in her high chair at the table stuffing food into her mouth with both hands between spoonfuls given by her mommy and daddy. They finally handed her a spoon. "Don't bother holding on to it. I know how to use it" she "meh, meh, meh"ed. Grabbing it from her mommy, Miranda poked the spoon into her food and then jabbed it into her eye. Disgusted, she threw the spoon on the floor, wiped her face with her hand and then proceeded to stuff her mouth with both hands. Did all the food go into her mouth? What do you think? No, much of it was smeared on her face, but she did get enough to fill her tummy.

After that, every time her mommy handed her a spoon or left it on the high chair tray, she threw it on the floor. Miranda thought hands were the best for eating anyway. She wondered who dreamed up the idea of a spoon.

Her parents gave up trying to get her to talk or to use a spoon, but Miranda heard her mom say, "I know she's smart and understands much more than she lets on. Watch her eyes and expressions. I even think she knows what I'm saying right now. See her nod? Okay, Miranda, are you playing games with us?" Miranda just smiled.

Miranda Refuses to Practice Walking

Shortly after this, Miranda made her first attempts at walking. She would pull herself up, try to balance without holding on and then sit down with a plunk. One day she let go of the chair with both hands and took one step. She fell flat on her face and her head hit the edge of the table as she fell. She cried and cried and cried, and that was her last step. She sat most of the time, crawling only when something she wanted was out of reach.

Miranda loved to eat and eat and eat. Then she just sat and sat and sat. This is when she became a fat baby because she didn't do any exercise. She just became fatter, and fatter and fatter.

Her parents took her to doctors for all kinds of tests. The tests showed she was very smart. Since none of the doctors had ever met a smart, fat baby like Miranda, they didn't have any good advice to give her parents.

Francine Refuses to Practice Her Violin

One day, a day that would turn out to be the most important day in Miranda's young life, Miranda overheard her mommy telling her daddy about a friend of hers who had a little girl named Francine. Francine, four years old, was taking violin lessons and was driving her mother crazy. She learned her pieces very quickly, but she played all of them very sloppily. Her bow slid all over the place, her fingers went down anywhere, she still held the violin with a slumped hand and she held the bow like a bat.

"Georgette says Francine refuses to practice. She learns all the notes from the recording and then just plays through the pieces from beginning to end, never stopping to correct her mistakes. She never slows down when she reaches a hard spot. She never plays the pieces more than once. 'I know that piece already,' Francine always says. 'Why should I have to play it over and over? That's for dummies. I want to play a new piece every day.'

"Francine's mother hopes that, after Francine falls further and further behind the other students, she'll wake up and realize that her teacher is serious about practice, good practice. Practice is a word Francine hates. She hates the way her teacher wants her to play pieces slowly and work on the hard parts. Francine's mom is too ashamed to tell the teacher that she never really practices at home, but only plays straight through each piece, telling her mother not to interrupt her.

"I feel so sorry for Francine's mom and for Francine, too," she continued. "I told her that many music teachers have trouble with smart kids who think they don't need to practice. Once they know the notes, they can't understand that their arms and fingers have to be taught by playing things many times. It's just like a baby learns to speak, to walk and to use her hands."

Miranda Finally Decides She Needs to Practice

Right at that moment, Miranda's mom's eyes widened. She looked straight at Miranda and didn't say anything for a long, long time. Finally she spoke, slowly and quietly, to that smart, fat baby Miranda.

"You heard that, Miranda. I know you're smart, but every baby, smart or not, has to practice. I want you to think about that word 'practice,' Miranda. It means doing things carefully, each in small steps, over and over again until arms, legs, fingers, hands and mouth can do what they are able to. Then you can talk, walk and feed yourself.

"The first thing I'm going to do is say 'mama' over and over again to you. When you say 'mama' back to me clearly and easily, then I'll add another word. And Daddy and I will stop saying anything except 'mama' at the dinner table until you join us. Won't that be fun?

"And many times every day I'm going to help you to your feet, and hold on with one hand as you try your first steps. I'll never give up until you are walking. Once you start running around, you'll see all that fat disappear, too.

"Don't forget the spoon either, Miranda. What would you think if you could eat only the food you put in your mouth with the spoon?"

Miranda sighed a long, slow sigh. "Oh me, I guess she's right," Miranda said to herself. Then out loud, Miranda said slowly and carefully, "Meh, meh....ma—ma." Her very first practice!

Miranda is no longer the smart, fat baby. She's just a smart little girl who runs around, feeds herself and tells everybody, "I guess we all have to practice before we can do anything, don't we? Knowing how to do things isn't enough. Anyway, I'm having fun being my own teacher!

And it's a lot of fun being able to do things for myself, like eating, talking, walking and running!"

Now I would like to ask you two questions. What would Miranda say to all of you boys and girls who are learning to play violin? And what answer would you give if I asked you how you are going to train your crews? Both of these questions have the same one-word answer, don't they? Let's hear you yell it out, okay? "Practice!" rang out loud and clear. It filled the auditorium!

Another Talk To 80 Teachers (Students) Ages 8–14

During a summer institute in Montana, I was asked to talk about practice to children playing Book 3 and up (ages about 8–14). My greeting surprised the children. "I'm happy to be here talking this afternoon to this wonderful group of teachers."

A number of them immediately yelled out, "We're not teachers! We're students!"

"Oh, but you *are* teachers! How do I know that?

"I just came from the lunch room. I saw some of you eating lunch. I also saw some babies in there eating. You know how babies feeding themselves get food all over their faces.

"But I don't see food on any of your faces!" I added as I walked across the front row of children, peering closely at them. "You must have taught your hands how to hold a spoon so you could hit your mouths without spilling the food and getting it all over your faces."

They burst out laughing, thinking of themselves with food all over their faces. Some of them pantomimed the action of bringing a spoon up to their mouths and missing.

"How did you learn to hit your mouth every time? You practiced, right?" "Right!" "Did you practice holding the spoon upside down?" "No!" "So you not only practiced, but you practiced the right way!"

"Let me show you another wonderful thing you did when you came in here, something that told me you were good teachers. All of you just walked, or ran, into the room. Nobody crawled in on their knees!" More laughter. "Why does that make us teachers?" one boy yelled.

"Because *you* taught yourselves to walk. Who put your right foot in front of your left one? You did, not your mom or your dad. One of them might have kept you from falling, but sooner or later you went off on your own. And you kept trying, even if you fell down—plunk!

"It's too bad you can't remember your first step. You had to hold on to somebody's hand, or a chair. You also don't remember how many times you sat down suddenly—plunk—when you thought you were going to fall. Can you see yourself, standing there wobbling back and forth and then trying to walk? You didn't teach yourself to walk in one day, even though you saw many people walking around, and it looked so easy. But when you tried, it didn't seem easy.

"How did you teach yourself to walk?" "We practiced!" they all yelled. "Did you try to walk by standing on your heels?" "No!" "So you practiced the right way!"

"Guess what else you taught yourself to do as a baby. You've already showed me what it is here today."

"We learned to talk!" some yelled.

"Please say, 'We taught ourselves to talk.' And how did you teach yourselves to talk?"

"We practiced!" came the chorus.

"So, when you were babies, you practiced and practiced and practiced! You taught yourselves to..." (here I pantomimed eating) "Hit our mouths with the spoon! Stop being so messy! Feed ourselves!" came in the answers shouted out.

"You also taught yourselves to..." (here I started walking) "Walk!" "How did you do that?" "By practicing!"

"So you've done a lot of practicing in your lives, right?!" "Right!"

"What kind of practice?" "Good practice!"

"You see why I said I was glad to have this meeting with all of you young teachers. Now you know why I called you teachers, don't you?" "Yes!"

"Now I'm going to tell you a story about a smart, fat baby." (Here I repeated the story of Miranda that I had first used at Stanford.)

"Poor Miranda! Just think of all that time she wasted because she wouldn't practice! And I wonder about Francine, the smart girl who thought she could learn to play the violin without practicing. Miranda could really give her some good advice, don't you think?"

If Fingers Could Talk

"I wish your fingers, hands, and arms could talk to you when you practiced! Sounds crazy, but just think how wonderful that would be! Your teachers and your mothers would think so! What do you think your fingers might say? How about this: 'Slow down! You're going so fast we haven't time to know if we're doing it right' or this: 'You'd better let us play that over and over slowly before you go on to something else' or this: 'You do too much at once. We can't remember what to do!'....or this.... 'Take it easy! We've never done this before!'

"Okay. Hold your left hand in front of you. Please repeat after me as though your fingers were talking: 'Please practice slowly!'"

(I could hardly hear their responses, there was so much wild laughter. Some wiggled their fingers as they talked.)

'Please practice hard parts in small chunks!'

'Please give us good directions what to do AHEAD OF TIME!'

'We can do wonderful things if you teach us right.'

'Remember that we don't know if what you teach us is right or wrong.'

'We promise to do it right—if you teach us right—and help us practice enough!'

(I waited for the shouting and laughter to die down.)

"Did you hear what the fingers said about practicing in small chunks? Let's play a little game."

Learning Weird Names in Small Chunks

"Repeat after me these names: Smith, Jones, Davis, Brown, Black.

Good! Now repeat after me these names: Stolarevsky, Ussachevsky, Bach, Yatsugatake, Kirigamine."

(The only clear answer I got of course was Bach.)

"What's the matter with you? Didn't you hear what I said? I thought I spoke clearly!"

(Here they all began to shout protests. Among them I could hear: 'You went too fast,' 'those were weird names.')

"Okay. I'll say them again, slower. Listen carefully."

(A few got part of the first name and Bach, but the response was weak. Before I had a chance to say anything, a boy yelled out, 'Say them slowly one by one')

"Aha, you want them in small chunks since they're weird names. That's a good idea. You know, that sounds like what your fingers asked you to do, doesn't it—tell you to practice in small chunks?"

(When I slowed down, broke the long names into two-syllable chunks and repeated each until they all knew it, they were delighted to find they could repeat the names easily.)

"So, you see, you learned all of those weird names easily when I broke them up into small chunks. Your new pieces that seem so long and difficult can be learned easily the same way. In spite of what your teachers say, most of you practice straight through new pieces, don't you? Now you know that wastes a lot of time!"

The Boy Who Ate His Bicycle

"Here is another example of how a big problem can be solved by breaking it into small chunks. This is a true story of a boy who got his name in the *Guinness Book of World Records* by eating his bicycle."

'Eating his bicycle?' 'Ugh!' 'Crazy boy!' 'I'll bet he had a stomach ache!'

"How'd he do it? It took him a long, long time. First he broke it into small chunks and then ground them into pow-

der. He ate a little of the bicycle powder each day with his cereal, sometimes with salad and sometimes in his spaghetti sauce. You see how a big problem can be solved if it's broken down into small chunks. But please don't try to eat your bicycles! Just practice your new music in small chunks!"

"Boys and girls, our time is up. I enjoyed talking to you teachers. You understand now that you are able to teach yourselves many new things. Don't forget Miranda, the smart, fat baby, and Francine, the smart, sloppy violin student. They'd have been better off if they did what you're going to do now. And what is that?"

'Practice!' was shouted in unison, followed by a wonderful jumble of remarks: "Slowly, in small chunks," "Not like Francine," "Stolarevky, Ussachevsky, Bach," "Miranda wasn't really that smart!" "I can't wait to tell my little sister about Miranda!" "I wouldn't want my fingers to talk to me!" "Yatsugatake, Yatsugatake, Yatsugatake! I remember it!" "That was a weird talk, but it was funny," and so on, and so on.

At least I knew they had listened!

Little Susie's Lesson

After a morning session with a lively group of enthusiastic new teachers, I was scheduled to teach several demonstration lessons. A cute, blond five-year-old we'll name Susie, dressed in her Sunday best, stepped forward timidly.

"Hello, Susie! All of us want to thank you for coming to take a lesson from me today. You don't know me, and I don't think you know many of the teachers here either, so it might be a little scary. Your being here shows that you are a special, brave little girl. Let's all give Susie, her mom and her teacher a big round of applause to show our thanks!"

Susie smiled as she bowed. She had been playing the violin for only a few months and was going to play the 'Taka-taka' variation of 'Twinkle.' Susie seemed a bit frightened, but she carefully placed the violin in position, with a good bow hold and fine left-hand placement.

She began to play, with a nice tone, but consistently out of tune despite a set of bright yellow tapes on the fingerboard. Her hand was placed too high up on the fingerboard, so all of the fingers missed the tapes. Her attention was totally focussed on her bow and the bow's tape. She continued bowing straight with a clear tone and out of tune, never adjusting the fingers of the left hand. She didn't seem to hear that the pitches of the fingered notes had no relationship to the open strings!

At the end of her solo, we all clapped and I thanked her again for playing for us. I turned to the teachers and said, "Susie's now going to play 'Twinkle' again for us with excellent intonation!" I could feel the wave of disbelief from the teachers!

"Susie, you hold the violin and bow so well, I'd like to play a game with you. It's a silly game but it's easy. Will you play it with me?" She nodded warily.

"Good, Susie. Please hold your violin up in playing position. Thank you. In this game, I'm going to be your fingers and I'm going to talk to you like this." I then crouched down so that my face was even with the scroll, next to her left hand.

"Hi, Susie, we're your fingers. How are you?" I asked in a falsetto voice. No answer.

"Susie," I continued in my normal voice, moving back a little. "I told you this was going to be a crazy game, right? So please imagine your fingers are talking, okay?"

Back to the scroll and the falsetto voice. "Susie, I'm George, your second finger. The others are too scared to talk to you, so they asked me to talk for all of us. We've been talking together down here, and we wondered if you saw whether or not we came down on all the yellow tapes on your fingerboard. I don't think we did. Did we?"

Again, no answer. Susie just stared at me, obviously wondering what this crazy teacher was doing. "Susie, remember this is a crazy game. Why don't you answer George?"

Then Susie did answer, and a wonderful answer it was.

"I don't know," she said very softly.

George then said, "Susie, when you play 'Twinkle' again, please watch us to see if all of us go down on the yellow tapes. You don't need to pay any attention to the bow hand—he's doing a great job. If you watch us all the time, we PROMISE we'll all come down on the tapes. Will you please do that? Remember: I said we promise to do our best." Silence from the bewildered Susie.

"Susie, you agreed to play the game. Please answer George. You heard what he promised."

"All right. I'll watch," she said faintly.

I reminded her again of George's promise, and that he said he was speaking for all of the fingers.

Now came the moment of truth. I held my breath as Susie started to play and then relaxed through a fine performance in which all the notes were in tune. All of the fingers came down on the yellow tapes. The teachers clapped enthusiastically, surprising Susie so much that she stood there with her violin still up in playing position.

I could have responded to her performance in several ways. The temptation was to praise her. Instead, I crouched down and, in my 'George' falsetto, asked Susie, "How'd we do?" No answer.

"Susie, you said you'd play the game with me. Please answer George."

She glanced at her left hand. "Good," she said softly.

"What?!" George cried out. "We promised to play every note in tune if you kept your eyes on us. You did, and we thought we played great!"

"Well, Susie, do you have anything else you'd like to say to George?"

Her reply was slightly louder: "Great!"

"See what a wonderful job those fingers do if you just watch them, expecting them to go down in the right place? So, when you practice, watch them on the fingering and watch the bow on the open string notes. Then all of them will do a great job.

"Susie, thank you for playing that game so well. Now you can name your other fingers and tell them, as if they were little children, what you want them to do. You'll both be happy!"

Little Tommy, and Lully's G♯

Tommy was playing the Lully "Gavotte" for me. Each time he came to the G♯, high 3rd finger on the D string, his third finger slid up from G.

"Tommy, did you ever throw darts at a dart board?" I asked. "You have? Good. Did you ever, after you threw a dart way over to the side, run up to the board and shove that dart over into the bull's eye? Of course you didn't! That was a crazy question, wasn't it?

"But what about that third finger of yours? Didn't you shove it up into the bull's eye after you heard it was flat?

"Tommy, I'm going to play a little game with you. If you play it with me, you'll never again have any trouble playing that high 3rd G♯.

"I'd better tell you it seems like a silly game. I'm going to pretend I'm your third finger, and I'm going to talk to you. His name is Fred."

"Hi, Tommy. I'm Fred. You know why I've had so much trouble playing that G♯? I've never played high 3rd on the D string before! That's a real stretch for me! If you help me stretch out ahead of time, when you're playing that open D before the G♯, I'll try my best to reach far enough. I'm sure I can do it. Please remember to remind me ahead of time. If you don't, I might forget and play G. Then I'll have to slide up again to G♯."

I asked Tommy to play the piece, and when he got to the open D, stop, yell out, "Get up there, Fred!" and then put Fred down in the bull's eye. He did it!

"That was great, Tommy! Did you see Fred stretch? Try it once more, only this time don't say anything to him. Let's see if he remembers."

But Fred protested: "That's too soon, Tommy! I will probably fall into my old habit of playing G and sliding. Let me do it two more times while you give me directions ahead on the open D. Then I think I'll be ready to do it without any help from you."

After two more successful playings, Tommy tried it without saying anything to Fred. Success! Tommy thought that was cool!

If our fingers and bow arm and hand could talk like this, remember what they would most likely say: "1) practice slowly, 2) practice in small chunks and 3) please give us good directions ahead of time!"

The Finger Control Room in the Wrist

Debbie had wandering eyes. I decided she would benefit from an imaging game. "Debbie, imagine your left hand down at the neck of the violin. Inside your wrist is a little room. This room has several tiny men and women operating levers that control your fingers and bow arm. There's a TV with a big speaker set in the wall. The tiny people watch you and listen to your instructions. They've been working hard to follow your directions so that the fingers fall in the right place.

"Suddenly your instructions stop, Debbie! The tiny people look up and see you're not paying any attention to the fingers or the bow. Your eyes are wandering around the room. One of the tiny women says, 'Look, Debbie's not paying attention. Just leave everything on automatic. Time for a break. Let's go for some coffee.'

"They pour the coffee and, after drinking some, notice from the TV screen that you're still not paying attention. This is a group lesson and they see you gazing out the window. So, they bring out some cards and start playing a game.

'Debbie,' the teacher calls out in a loud voice, 'those are supposed to be C naturals, not C sharps! Are you paying attention?' You glare down at your fingers. The tiny people throw the cards down and rush back to work. Please don't be angry with them! Do you think you treated them fairly? They're like little children who wander off if nobody's watching them. These tiny men and women need your directions. They also want you to notice how well they're doing!"

Training the Cerebellum

"We're not training the fingers, we're training the brain," a teenager reprimanded me once after observing my imaging game. "Of course!" I readily agreed. "You're training your cerebellum to play the violin automatically like it does so many things for you. But John, small children can look down at their fingers and visualize them as little people whom they're teaching much easier than they can visualize a part of the brain as a person. Even you, if you try it, will agree that it's easier to visualize teaching your fingers rather than your brain.

"Try talking to your cerebellum, imagining questions and answers coming from it. You could ask, 'Okay, Do you understand that motion?' The reply: 'Which version do you want me to plot? You've done it three different ways.' Or you might say, 'That was just right! That's the way I want it!' And the cerebellum's answer: 'You need to repeat it many more times. I've got a lot of neurons to line up for this one. In fact, I'll need many repetitions before I can do this automatically! I've never had an assignment this complicated before!'

"If you decide to deal with the cerebellum, you must remember that it doesn't know right from wrong. You can repeat incorrect motions and it will assume you want it that way. It needs many good repetitions before it can put everything on automatic pilot. You must give very specific instructions if you want good results."

Practicing With A Timer

Suzuki often said, "Parents complain that their children cannot concentrate for more than a minute or so. At the beginning, if they can play through all of the "Twinkle Variations" without stopping, they are concentrating for four minutes at a basic level. It may be asking too much to insist that the bow is straight all the time when they are focusing on the next note to be played. I tell the mothers that the children's powers of concentration will grow in time and in strength, but the mother should ask her child to focus on *only one point* at a time. If the mother studies violin for a while, she will understand how well her child is doing when he's able to play through all the 'Twinkle Variations'!"

I do think we expect too much of small children. Asking them to practice new passages in small chunks, to practice in small chunks of time and then to change to another passage before they are tired of the first one helps them have greater success.

Monitoring a student's ability to focus can also be made into a game. Teachers and parents who have done this find the children not only receptive but also fascinated. I recommend that parents and teachers buy a timer that counts down and up in seconds, minutes, and hours.

I measured my own focusing time when I was practicing a brief (small chunks, remember?) but very difficult passage from one of the late variations in my book, *77 Variations on Suzuki Melodies*. In this passage there are two large shifts to be played at high speed. Practicing slowly and carefully, I found I soon became tired of the passage. I

looked at my timer, which was operating like a stop watch. Only two minutes had passed! I was shocked! Since I wanted to keep fresh, I went on to other passages. Later I went back to this one, set the timer for two minutes and quit when the bell went off. I determined focus times for all the passages and how much repetition they needed. I went from one to another and back to the first again, always keeping mentally alert. My practice efficiency was very high.

Later I gave a talk on practicing effectively to all the music majors in the College of Music at the University of Colorado. I explained how I used the timer and gave illustrations of its effectiveness with my own college and precollege students and with children of all ages in workshops throughout the world.

Marie's Vibrato Lesson

One of these illustrations concerned Marie, an impatient 15-year-old who had an irregularity in her vibrato. Her previous teacher assured her she could work it out easily, but she had become frustrated because it was taking so long to change that habit. Her present teacher brought her to a workshop where I was teaching master classes for teachers to observe. She asked me to work with Marie's vibrato.

Observing Marie play, I noted that she could play with a regular vibrato only for short periods and only on certain notes. We did some preliminary exercises and talked about the three aspects of the sound of vibrato: width, speed and regularity. She commented that regularity was her big problem.

"It's very good that you know your problem, Marie. Let's work on that. Please play, with vibrato, one note on the E string, using your best finger. Change bows when you need to. I want you to focus on one thing only: the beautiful regularity of your vibrato. This timer will act as a stop watch. Please stop playing as soon as you lose your focus. We'll see how many seconds you can focus easily. Don't force your concentration. Remember: You can't make a mistake except by continuing to play when you've lost your focus."

Marie started out with a very regular vibrato. She was doing so well I was surprised when she stopped and said, "That's it! I know that wasn't very long, but you told me to stop when I lost my focus."

"That was great, Marie! You did both things I asked for. You focused so well that a beautiful regular vibrato was the result. And you quit before we noticed any change in your vibrato. Thirteen seconds. Wonderful! You may think that was short, but I thought it was excellent! You'd have to search through a lot of music to find one note that is thirteen seconds long, if you could find one!" I shook Marie's hand, congratulating her for her cooperation.

"I wonder, Marie, if you would please try something else for me and all the teachers in this room. I'd like you to repeat what you just did. I'll set the timer, and when it rings, you stop. You should feel very comfortable about this because I'm setting it to go off in only eleven seconds. That should be very easy for you since you just played longer than that a moment ago."

The eleven-second demonstration came off easily. Marie looked surprised when the timer went off. "I don't know why," she said, "but I felt I could have gone on a lot longer, even longer than the first time!"

I suggested that she buy a timer and start timing periods of focus for different problems. After she found the times, she could experiment by setting the timer for a shorter period. She would feel so good, I assured her, when she reached her goal that it would spur her on, and every extra second would be a bonus, more than she aimed for. "Later when you time yourself again, you'll find the time span has increased. After that, set the timer just under the new record so you know it can be reached easily. As I said before, you'll feel so good reaching these goals, you'll want to go on! Remember that this is effective only if you are very sensitive to your mental state. You don't want your mind to slip away without your realizing it."

Focusing Time of the
University Music Majors

"All right, students, I want your best attention. When I say 'ready,' close your eyes and focus on mentally practicing a small part of a piece you're just learning. Choose a difficult part, focus on practicing it and then hold up your hand when you've lost your focus. Keep your eyes closed until you hear this timer go off. When you hear it, keep your hand up, open your eyes and look around the room. I'll tell you how much time has elapsed then."

After two minutes, the alarm went off. The students were surprised to see that almost everyone's hand was up. I

asked them how much time had elapsed. A few guessed two minutes; most thought it had been three or four. Some of the hands had gone up after only one minute had passed. I assured them that they were probably not used to mental practice and would do much better with live practice. "Please invest in one of these timers. Find your maximum focus time with different passages. Then set the timer at a period of time a little less than that maximum, and repeat the passage. Change the passages to be practiced frequently to keep your ability to focus at a high level. When you cannot focus anymore, take a rest. Just sit quietly and meditate for a few minutes. It may seem strange to you, but while you're resting your neurons will continue to work on the passage just completed, even if you are not consciously thinking about it.

"A question: In an hour of practice, how much of that hour do you estimate your practice is at a high level?" The answers varied, but most fell within a range of 50–60%. I told them this was probably a little too generous since it is possible and probable that during repetitions, the mind often slips away unnoticed. Some worried that if they didn't persist a longer time on a specific difficulty, they would not recall what they had learned.

"Ah, but that's not a valid concern. Consciously you may be concerned that you will forget what you had practiced, but the brain won't forget those repetitions. When you are assigned a new piece that may contain many new difficulties, go through it as you start your practice and estimate times for all the passages. Draw out a detailed practice time schedule. You may alter this if you find your estimated times are too short or too long."

The Takacs Quartet Rehearsal Schedule

I then told them a fascinating story about estimated time schedules drawn up by the world-famous Takacs String Quartet in residence at the University of Colorado. The quartet consisted of four young Hungarian string players who were catapulted into prominence in the musical world when their quartet won several prestigious international competitions.

Since their concert schedule was not as full as it would later become, they spent many hours rehearsing in the university music building. It was exciting for the string students to eavesdrop in the hall as the Takacs Quartet rehearsed new quartets to add to their repertoire. No one could understand what they were saying since they conversed in Hungarian. Philip, one of my students, became friendly with Karoly Schrantz, the second violinist of the quartet. Philip became curious about a sheet of paper pasted on the wall, filled with numbers and words in Hungarian. He noticed that they were constantly consulting this sheet as they rehearsed.

Mr. Schrantz told Philip that the sheet was their rehearsal schedule. It listed all the passages they'd chosen for rehearsing, identified by the name and movement of the quartet, with an estimated time for rehearsal of each passage.

"We don't want to neglect any passages that need special attention, nor do we want to give too much time to one, slighting others of equal difficulty. So if we work on a passage and the time is up, we go on to the next." "What if you felt that time period was inadequate?" Philip asked. "Oh, we re-adjust these schedules daily so as to learn all of the music equally. We may find that seven minutes was too little for Passage No. 4 and four minutes more than necessary for Passage No. 6. So the next day this may be changed to nine minutes for Passage No. 4 and two minutes for Passage No. 6. At the beginning, we know our estimates may be off, but as time goes on we become much more accurate in determining the best use of our time. When we finish a quartet that is new to us, there are no under-rehearsed passages. Of course, some of the very difficult excerpts may be practiced twenty times longer than other passages."

"If such an elastic estimated practice schedule is effective for a world-class string quartet," I observed, "all of us should pay attention to such a role model and imitate their method." I urged the students to get timers, and monitor both their ability to maintain a sustained focus, and their effectiveness in practicing.

I closed this talk with a quote from the book, *Inner Tennis*, by Timothy Gallwey: "The more attentive and relaxed the mind, the more able it is to pick up increasingly minute muscle and energy sensations in the body."

It is my hope that parents and teachers may want to read or tell these stories to their students of all ages. Better yet, I hope everyone will be stimulated to develop their own creative uses of imagination and humor in assisting their students and children to develop their innate abilities. I repeat Suzuki's plea to adults working with children: "We must continue to develop new ideas to help children learn to play more easily, and to help them enjoy their learning."

Suzuki never passed up an opportunity for colorful, vivid and humorous images when teaching children. Here are some examples: "You carry an elephant with your bow. Now carry a mouse!" "Pianists don't move the piano around the stage while playing!" "That was a homemade D!" "My English is made in Japan." "Not water-spider tone, tuna tone! Water spider moves on top of water, tuna swims down deep!"

Japanese American Differences

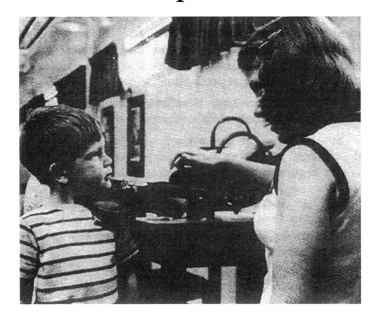

Susan Shields and student.

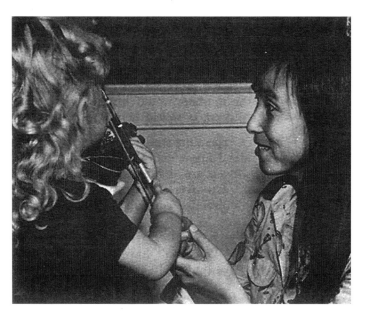

Hiroko Iritani and student.

(The following is an interview in which Susan Shields and Hiroko Iritani discuss with me the differences between teaching in Japan and in America. Both women have taught extensively in both countries and are graduates of Dr. Suzuki's institute in Matsumoto, Japan. The interview touches on 4 main topics—recruiting of students, practice, listening to the record, and lesson atmosphere.)

STARR—"How was recruiting done?"

SUSAN—"By word of mouth, mainly. That is, a student in the program would bring friends and neighbors to study. Also—in Japan national television specials are presented on the Suzuki method periodically, and Japanese teachers report an increase in students after such a special."

STARR—"How was the indoctrination done?"

HIROKO—"In Japan, prospective mothers were required to read Dr. Suzuki's book, *Nurtured by Love,* and to observe lessons. If they were still interested in taking lessons, they could start. After they were in the program, they attended mothers' meetings which were held once or twice a month."

STARR—"Were these meetings social?"

SUSAN—"Not really. The mothers were paying attention to the content of Dr. Suzuki's lectures which touched on such topics as the potential all children possess; how to motivate children and so on."

STARR—"Did the veteran mothers help in the indoctrination of new mothers?"

SUSAN—"Very much so. When I was teaching in Omachi, most of my students were young children whose mothers often became discouraged in the beginning stages. I was fortunate to have in the program Mrs. Totani, a woman whose daughter had studied about 10 years and who was very enthusiastic about Talent Education. She would always reinforce what I was doing and tell the young mothers how important it was to get a careful beginning.

Sometimes a young mother would take her child to the home of a veteran mother for some extra help in between private lessons."

STARR—"How much time do Japanese children spend practicing?"

SUSAN "There are numerous Japanese children, especially in Matsumoto, who practice several hours a day. The program has been going in Matsumoto more than 30 years under the direct supervision of Dr. Suzuki with spectacular results. Children in Matsumoto are constantly inspired by the presence of Dr. Suzuki, and also by the numerous visits of observing foreigners. When I was in Matsumoto, I knew of numerous 'instant concerts' in which the teachers in Matsumoto would phone their students and say, 'Be at the institute in one-half hour to present a concert for some American visitors who just arrived.' In addition, the students in Matsumoto are motivated by the chance that they might be able to go to America on one of the tours."

HIROKO—"In some of the more isolated cities in Japan the motivation is not as strong as in Matsumoto, and the children don't practice as much. Many Americans who go to Japan only observe the large branches of the Suzuki method (Matsumoto, Tokyo), and get a glossy picture of Talent Education. When I was studying with Dr. Suzuki, I went to Ina, a small town one hour from Matsumoto, about once a week to teach. I only had seven students, and I was the only teacher there, so I couldn't get together with other teachers for group lessons. Anyway my students in Ina didn't practice very much."

STARR—"Does it bother you very much that your American students don't practice as much as the students in Matsumoto?"

HIROKO—"Once in awhile I have a student who learns more than I expected, and I get so tickled. But it doesn't happen so often. I'm satisfied with the amount of time most of my students practice, but I wish some of them would practice more effectively. Along these lines, I think if the mothers would listen to the record as much as the children, it would help."

SUSAN—"I don't expect my students to practice several hours a day, because I know many of the mothers work, and American children are involved in more activities than the Japanese. However, I do get disappointed at children who don't practice consistently. Many of my students practice from ½ hour to 45 minutes a day and make excellent progress. I often remind my parents of Dr. Suzuki's slogan, 'You don't have to practice every day—only on the days that you eat.' "

STARR—"You've mentioned before that American children have a few more years than the Japanese—maybe through high school?"

SUSAN—"Yes, in Japan school pressure becomes intense around the junior high school level. Children have to take entrance examinations to get into junior high, so many children drop violin around age 13. This is one reason why they quit at this age. Another reason is that many Japanese Suzuki students begin violin at age 3 and then finish the 10 Suzuki books by age 13. In Japan there are no school orchestras or amateur orchestras, so the 13 year old student, having no outlets for his playing, drops violin.

In America, many elementary, junior, and senior high schools have orchestras for our students to participate in. Therefore, I feel very optimistic about the ability of our students to keep playing the violin."

STARR—"Generally speaking, do you think the American can learn as fast as the Japanese? Or is it just because they don't practice as much?"

SUSAN—"By comparing my 4½ years teaching in Japan with my 2½ years teaching in Knoxville, I feel that there are no physical differences between the Americans and Japanese. I haven't seen any coordination problems here which I didn't encounter in Japan. My American students who practice an hour a day have the same fluid bowing and good memory as my Japanese students who practiced an hour a day."

STARR—"What are some of the main problems you have getting children to practice?"

HIROKO—"Several times I asked my mothers to tape their practice sessions at home. When I did this, I discovered that some of the sessions were too long, and the children rebelled. I haven't asked any mothers to do this lately, because it's kind of artificial."

STARR—"Yes—the mothers can't can't swear or yell."

SUSAN—"I agree with Hiroko. Especially in the beginning stages I urge the parents to keep the sessions short. For instance a beginner's practice session might consist of playing one rhythm (ta-ka) 2 or 3 times; placing the left hand in position 2 or 3 times, which only takes 1 or 2 minutes. Then I ask the mother to repeat this practice several times a day."

STARR—"Do you have problems getting the mothers to compliment their child's success?"

SUSAN—"Most of the mothers pick up the cue from the teacher. We try to make each step seem important—in the beginning the child receives instant gratification from my saying, 'You have a beautiful bowhold', and usually the mother repeats this compliment. Mothers who can be firm enough to get their child to practice and yet praise the child at the same time can get the child to practice consistently."

HIROKO—"My mothers have said the mothers' meetings are always a shot in the arm. They practice better after these meetings."

SUSAN—"One of my calm, positive mothers came to me after a mothers' meeting and surprised me by saying, 'I can always be calm at the lessons, but at home I lose my temper. After Mr. Starr's speech at the last meeting, I decided to make a new resolution, and lately, our home practices have been much calmer.' "

STARR—"Do Japanese children listen to the records a great deal?"

HIROKO—"Many of the mothers in Matsumoto taped the records onto long-playing tapes so that the child could hear the same record over and over without turning the record over. Japanese houses are small, so when the mother plays a tape or record for the child, he can hear it no matter where he is in the house. One mother in Matsumoto came up with a unique idea. She had a little boy who was very active and was always riding his bike or running around in the yard playing, which made it difficult for him to listen to the record enough. Therefore she bought a tiny tape recorder (wallet-size) and strapped it onto his back. Then he could hear the tape no matter where he went."

SUSAN—"I've made tapes for all my students, and many of them listen each night at bedtime. A tape is a little more convenient than a record, because the mother can put the tape recorder in a child's room, whereas a stereo is not so portable.

One of my mothers told me a funny story in connection with this. Her 5-year old daughter was afraid to sleep alone, and the mother said this made it difficult to play the record for her at night. After I made the tape for her, the mother put it in the child's room, and it was the first time the child would sleep alone."

STARR—"How about deportment in the lessons? Did Japanese teachers have trouble with this?"

SUSAN—"No—there's a definite format to the lessons in Japan. A student bows before and after the lesson and then it's understood that he's not supposed to talk while the lesson is going on. I try to do the same thing here. Sometimes a child will try to say something during the lesson, and I tell him, 'Tell me after the lesson is over', or 'Don't talk during the lesson'. Eventually children learn not to talk during the lesson, and it helps them concentrate on violin."

STARR—"About concentration—in Japan you have a child who's not wild, who's not rebellious, but has trouble concentrating—how is that concentration built?"

SUSAN—"Largely by repetition on a single step until the child masters that step. One teacher I was observing in Japan told me that from the time a child starts violin until the time he finishes all the Twinkle variaitons, he has played the ta-ka rhythm 1,000 times."

STARR—"Could you compare the attention spans of American and Japanese children?"

HIROKO—"I think in both countries there are children who concentrate well and poorly. In the beginning stages, there's no difference. The difference is maybe American children show their lack of attention more openly. They look around the room and get wild. Japanese children, on the other hand, get a glazed expression, but keep doing what the teacher says. Japanese children are easier for the teacher to handle."

STARR—"Visitors who come here to observe are struck by the excellent attention spans of the Knoxville children. How do you get this?"

SUSAN—"I think it's partly getting the mothers not to talk to the child during the lesson and partly the way the teaching is programmed.

All of my mothers are cooperative about not talking during the lesson. When I was observing lessons in Japan I would often see a mother of a new beginner start to correct a child. The teacher would politely ask the mother, 'Let me do the teaching here—you can teach him at home.'

Also—the programming of the material is important. Hiroko and I both spend a year teaching Twinkle to a beginning student. The 1st lessons might consist of—:

1. Playing ta-ka on the E string 15 times (Teacher guides and student plays alternately).

2. Placing and dropping the left hand over and over.

It's easy for a child to concentrate if the lessons are short in the beginning."

HIROKO—"I think making the atmosphere is something the teacher can control. This also helps build a good attention span. The teacher should speak calmly and seriously without being angry. Some teachers are so anxious to make the child enthusiastic that they say very loudly, 'Let's do this.' It shouldn't sound like you're doing games, but that you're doing something serious."

STARR—"That's important. One time in an interview with Jascha Heifetz, he said people should be told that music is work. It can be enjoyable, but it is work."

SUSAN—"Also—what we, as adults, consider hard work, children enjoy very much. For instance when I'm teaching a beginner to play his 1st rhythm, he plays it perhaps 15 times at one lesson. I usually see an expression of real delight on the child's face. Unfortunately this enjoyment is often squelched by a parent who will demand, 'When is my child going to learn some pieces? It's boring to play rhythms over and over.'

Parents should keep such feelings to themselves and should praise the child at each step of development."

STARR—"You're always giving commands where to look, aren't you?"

HIROKO—"I don't know how many times I say, 'look at your bow'—maybe 30 times at a lesson."

STARR—"How do you get the child to keep his violin up during the lesson?"

HIROKO—"Maybe it's because they can hold it pretty strongly with the chin. If they feel uncomfortable, then they like to put the violin down."

SUSAN—"Holding its strongly involves taking enough time in the beginning stages. Some of the pupils I observed in Japan spent 6 months working on the right and left hands separately before putting them together and beginning work on Twinkle."

STARR—"Were students who were observing lessons in Japan sitting quietly?"

SUSAN—"Yes, most of the time."

STARR—"What was the behavior of new beginners who came in? Were they calm and collected?"

SUSAN—"Many of them had short attention spans in the beginning, but none of them were belligerent. One day when I was teaching in Omachi, a little girl came running into the lesson place. Her home was in the middle of the rice fields, and she was accustomed to playing outside all day. She ran around the room, and even tugged on my skirt, but when it was time for the lesson to start, her mother commanded, 'fuzakenai de' (don't goof off), and the little girl then tried to do whatever I asked her. Of course her attention span was very short, but she stood there until I told her the lesson was over.

In connection with this little girl, I should also mention that her mother used to give her a candy bar after the lesson if she had a good lesson."

STARR—"In other words, the mother had talked to the child before she went to any lessons."

SUSAN—"Yes—the mother supported the teacher at all times. Once I was observing a lesson of a 4-year old boy, and it was the only time I saw a child talk back to a teacher in the 6 years I was in Japan! The teacher had been asking the student to play something over and over. Eventually the little boy decided he had done it enough, and when the teacher asked him to do it again, the boy said, 'ya da' (I don't want to). Immediately the mother said, 'You shouldn't say "ya da" ', and the teacher said, 'You shouldn't say "ya-da" ', so the little boy did what the teacher requested."

STARR—"Is there a distance between Japanese teachers and students?"

SUSAN—"Yes, and the amount of respect a child has for the teacher is mainly determined by the mother. One of my students who cooperates very well has a mother who makes a point of putting me on a higher level than the child. She always tells the child, 'Try hard for Susan'.

Another student I have who frequently talks back to me has a mother who says at the lessons, in front of the child, 'I don't know why he won't do this for you; he always cooperates with the school teacher'. "

HIROKO—"I often saw examples of this in Japan. Once I was waiting in a studio to observe a new beginner, and the little boy ran into the room and hugged the teacher around the legs, saying 'oji-san' (Mr.) The mother told the boy, 'Don't call him "oji-san"; call him "sensei" (teacher)', and then the teacher gently brushed the little boy off."

STARR—"Would you describe how a Japanese mother observes lessons?"

HIROKO—"Many mothers in Japan tape the lessons. They sit at the lesson with the music in their hand, and whenever the teacher says something, the mother makes a note of it in the music. The mother keeps a calm expression on her face during the lesson no matter what happens. In this way the child is not distracted by her interruptions."

STARR—"Can you contrast this with American parents?"

SUSAN—"Most of my parents bring a notebook to the lessons and take copious notes. In the beginning, mothers would correct a child, but I asked them not to, and it rarely happens anymore. The hardest thing for American mothers, I think, is to write down what a teacher says without interjecting comments of their own.

For instance, I might correct a child's bowing distribution in one piece and then proceed to work on it over and over. A Japanese mother would mark it in the music, tape it on her tape recorder, and watch the teacher intently.

Most of my American mothers are just as serious as the Japanese, but some mothers will interject, 'Oh yes, I know he has trouble with that', and then neglect to write it down, unless I tell them to."

Group Lessons

Group lessons are an integral part of the Suzuki approach and can contribute greatly to the motivation of students. Suzuki recommends they be held bi-monthly or monthly at the very least. Their content may vary from instruction and group practice to mini-concerts with the children playing through their repertoire. Group lessons can be particularly a joy for the small child hearing the big sound of the collected violins, and playing with his peers, and more advanced students. He can also hear and see performances of the pieces he will later learn and play.

When our children were studying in Matsumoto, they participated bi-monthly in groups that were divided into several levels. At times these groups would meet together in the auditorium but this was not the regular procedure. Instructors teaching the advanced students always told the children the pieces that they should review for the next session. One day the teacher forgot this and announced, "Vivaldi G Minor Concerto, 3rd movement". A chorus of groans greeted this statement. "O.K. Next time we'll play Vivaldi G Minor, 3rd movement!"

Experienced teachers have found it inadvisable to have the more advanced students playing all of the beginning selections again and again. They should be taught a certain amount of *noblesse oblige,* in that they are helping the beginners as they themselves were helped, but this use of the older ones can be overdone. Teachers should be careful about this. Even in Japan one notices few of the older teenagers participating in the group lessons, especially older players who are not as advanced as some of the younger ones. In America we have more chamber and orchestral outlets for the older children. These opportunities are not as readily available for Talent Education students in Japan.

Suzuki is most ingenious at planning group lessons, entertaining and instructing at the same time. If the students were not well prepared in private lessons, however, these group lessons would be much less effective. Teachers should not use the same format each time for the group lessons, but should be constantly innovative as they teach.

It is very important that the best possible accompanist be found for the group instruction. This becomes more critical as the groups strive for fine musical expression. A poor accompanist can impair the growth seriously in these lessons. This is no place for a Suzuki organization to try to save money by using a pianist who is barely adequate, although Book I groups can get along without too much assistance from the accompanist.

Here are suggested activities for group lessons:

1) Performances of pieces with certain points being brought to the attention of all the students for each piece.

2) Preparation for concert performance with many musical demands being made of all. It is important that the children realize that the effectiveness of the musical expression of the group depends on each individual. This should prepare them for integrity in their orchestral work.

3) Demonstration of technical development, with each player playing some small fragment alone. This can be used for technical passages involving complex fingering or bowing problems, or for vibrato, trills, etc.

4) Tonalization. This may be done with the whole group, but it is very affective if the students play one by one, listening carefully to each other's tones.

5) Solos, duets and trios, etc. This is good preparation for solo recitals, and accustoms the children to playing for an audience.

6) Teaching of basic theory and notation.

7) Sight-reading.

8) Playing of games to entertain the children while developing their skills.

Listed below are many games for use in group lessons for beginning and advanced students. They are games that have been used successfully in Japan and in America. The teacher should use only those games with which he or she feels comfortable, and should be encouraged to be creative in the development of his or her own games.

1. Children stand in place. Clap rhythms with piano.

2. Children stand in place. Move right arms up and down with Twinkle rhythms played on the piano.

3. Standing in place, with arms at sides, children may practice rapid arm motions such as the one Suzuki uses: Upon signal, each child quickly raises his right hand to touch the top of his head, then lowers it quickly to his side.

4. Standing in place, children march in place to the rhythm of the piano, swinging arms freely.

5. Children stand in place. At teacher's request, they may 1) bow correctly 2) move their feet apart and turn the left foot slightly to the left 3) turn their heads to the left without moving their bodies in the same direction 4) raise their left arms into playing position, also moving left hands around to the left, simulating playing position.

6. Teacher turns back on students who have violins and bows in rest position. Upon request, children very quietly place violins and bows on floor in front of them. Teacher should not be able to hear any sound, or very little, depending upon age of the students.

7. Children practice hearing and remembering verbal orders. Teacher calls out numbers (Ex. 584 -

3528 - 47629 - 334265, etc.), with the children repeating each group after the teacher.

8. Children act out verbal orders. Best started without violins. "Raise your left foot", "Touch your nose with your right thumb", "Touch your right ear with your left hand", etc. This can be done with "Simon says . . ."

9. Children quietly place violins and bows on floor in front of them. When teacher claps, they quickly pick up the violins and place them in playing position. At the discretion of the teacher, the left hands may be 1) at their sides 2) under the right armpits 3) at the waist on the right side 4) at the neck of the violin in playing position.

10. Upon signal, children place violins in playing position, and hold them there without the support of the left hands. Teacher and parents count to see how how long this can be done. Children should be holding the violins without strain.

11. Violins and bows on floor in front of students. When teacher claps, they quickly pick up the bows, assume the correct bow holds, and hold the bows in front for the teacher to inspect. Both correctness and speed can be emphasized.

12. Children hold bows, in front of them, with the point upwards. As piano plays march or Suzuki Allegro, they move the bows up and down, using whole arms, like a drum major.

13. Children hold bows horizontally in front of them, and move bows up and down, tip moving with frog. Teacher can explain that their bow arms are like cantilever elevators (those with support on only one side).

14. Freeze game. This can be done on any level. Children play, then stop immediately when the teacher or one of the pupils calls out 'freeze!'. Posture, hand positions, and bow placement can then be checked.

15. Eye control game. Teacher moves bow through the air while children keep their eyes on the bow tip.

16. Children play through a piece, with teacher watching carefully to see how many can play through an entire selection without looking up or around the room.

17. Teacher picks two children who have trouble keeping their eyes on their playing. They are placed facing each other, scroll to scroll, with the other children gathered around. As they play a piece together, the rest of the children watch to see who looks up first.

18. Children play Twinkle, and imitate the teacher as he bends his knees, turns around, or walks around the room. Good posture should be maintained.

19. Children play Twinkle variations, answering questions directed by the teacher. They should continue playing without pause.

20. Children, upon command, raise violins from rest position to playing position with eyes closed.

21. Children do the same with the bow with the eyes closed.

22. Teacher starts piece without naming it. Children join in as soon as possible after recognizing selection.

23. Students take turns starting pieces, with the others joining in.

24. Teacher claps rhythm. Students, recognizing piece, begin to play it.

25. Teacher mimes bowing in air. Students guess piece and play it.

26. Teacher starts in middle of piece. Students join as quickly as possible.

27. Children are divided into groups. They play a selection with each group alternating as the teacher directs.

28. Children play with eyes closed to see if they can bow straight. As pieces are played, teacher may call, "Close your eyes", then, "Open your eyes. Are you bowing correctly?"

29. Parents come up to play, with each child preparing and checking his or her performance. This and the following game are good for parties.

30. Advanced student, wearing mask and clown suit, comes in to be given his 'first' lesson from the younger children. Naturally he does everything wrong.

31. Teacher walks behind each child. All are in playing position. Teacher plays Twinkle rhythm on any pitch and then asks child to imitate on same pitch.

32. Teacher asks individual children to play pitch sung or played on the piano.

33. Teacher plays new rhythmic variation of Twinkle. Children imitate. Students can take turns creating new variations of Twinkle for the rest to imitate.

34. Children face off in pairs. Play Twinkle, shaking hands at all the open string notes.

35. Students play Twinkle, holding the bow at the tip and trying to get the same volume as they do with the correct bow hold.

36. Children play, on open strings, successive full up-bows, accompanied by chords on the piano. As they reach the frog, they lift the bow and reach across the violin with the right hand, forcing the elbow to move upwards. Very slowly.

37. Children play short repeated down bows on open strings, accompanied by chords on the piano, trying to retake the bow strokes with a small round motion. Very slowly.

38. Children play 1st variation of Twinkle with stops, moving the bow as directed to a different place for each rhythm. They try to maintain the same volume.

39. Teacher plays short pattern of notes children have not heard. Students play immediately afterward. Teacher plays new patterns, adding a note each time.

40. Group lesson is turned into a marathon. The teacher starts with the easiest pieces, and progresses until only one child is left performing. Each child sits down as he can play no more.

41. Teacher plays piece with deliberate out-of-tune notes. Children call out every time they hear sour note.

42. Children play easy pieces, swaying back and forth with the beat.

43. Children play certain easy pieces, trying to breathe in and out with up and down bows.

44. Advanced children play Perpetual Motion with all down bows.

45. Children play Perpetual Motion, fingering and bowing separately. This is good for the acquisition of speed. Teacher calls out "Play". Children play the first note. Then teacher calls "One," and they put down first fingers quickly and with strength, but do not draw the bows. Next direction, "Play", etc.

46. Students group in pairs to play pieces, one bowing, the other fingering.

47. Teacher assigns a certain pitch to each child. They then play a piece, each playing only his note.

48. Advanced students play easy pieces, pizzicato, ponticello, sul tasto.

49. Advanced students play pieces in high positions, starting on different fingers.

50. Advanced students play scales, starting on different pitches all over the violin.

The following games are related to the development of reading skills.

1. After students have learned the names of the notes they have been playing, teacher calls out a pitch. Students play Twinkle rhythm on that pitch.

2. As the students perform from music, teacher calls out different students to play each measure.

3. As the students read, teacher conducts performance. Students should respond to attacks and cutoffs indicated by the conductor, but that are not indicated in the music. Conductor may change tempo as music progresses. This should be done with very easy music, preferably without piano accompaniment.

Teacher may conduct easy pieces at rapid tempo to speed up reading and to form the habit of reading notes in groups. For example, a 4/4 piece with only quarter and half notes might be conducted one to the bar.

5. One of the students may be guest conductor.

6. As the students read easy music, the teacher-conductor may ask them to look up from the music every measure. This helps them to look ahead and memorize patterns.

7. Without playing, students look at music, calling out names of pitches in slow steady tempo. Tempo can be increased as facility is gained.

8. Students call out fingerings in slow steady tempo.

9. Reading from blackboard or overhead projector. Teacher covers notes as they are reached by the students as they play. Forces them to look ahead.

10. Pianist plays unfamiliar piece. Students guess meter signature, and give appropriate tempo indication.

11. Teacher writes short melody on blackboard, then erases it. Students play melody from memory.

12. Teacher plays piece as students watch music. Purposeful errors are made. Students call out incorrect notes.

13. Students read music, playing all notes pizzicato. Good for rhythmic development.

14. Students read, performing in alternate groups as directed by the teacher.

Suzuki playing a game with the bow at a group lesson.

Concerts. Recitals. Suzuki's Summer School.

There are all levels of concerts in Talent Education in Japan from the home concert given by a youngster for his father to the mammoth annual concert in Tokyo that draws over two thousand children from all over the country. All of these concerts and recitals provide motivation for the child and parents.

The private recital given by students of a single teacher for their families is the beginner's introduction to public concert appearances. Here the little one may appear just to bow to the audience, or demonstrate his basic posture, or play the rhythm of the first Twinkle variation once on the open E string. The teacher does everything to keep the child relaxed. The teacher usually comes on stage with the beginner, helping the child fix his violin and bow hold properly, and often remaining by the child's side throughout the performance.

The behavior of the small children appearing on stage for the first time is often quite humorous and entertaining. All of this is enjoyed by the teacher and parents. The laughter doesn't seem to cause any discomfiture in the children.

The private concert usually features a number, if not all, of the children as soloists, and closes with group performances of several selections. When the music progresses in difficulty past the selections they know, the children run off stage and sit with their parents.

Again mention must be made of concert deportment which doesn't differ radically from the behavior at private and group lessons. The children are moderately quiet, although at concerts of very large groups of children, there is often considerable noise in the hall.

The concerts, city or regional in scope, given by large groups of children follow the pattern of the annual concert in Tokyo in that the music played progresses from difficult to easy with the number of performers on stage reaching its zenith at the end of the concert as the children play Suzuki's Twinkle Variations.

Most often the children are seated in the hall with their parents waiting for their turn to play. Suzuki feels it is better for them to hear the more advanced players rather than be crowded offstage in anterooms as they wait to play. "After all," says Suzuki, "these concerts are very special. They are primarily for children. They hear and notice more than we realize. This is all part of the favorable environment that helps them to want to play the instrument."

Between each number, new children come on stage and there is a reshuffling of position as the more advanced move to the rear of the stage. Occasionally a child will get on stage one selection early and then run off when he realizes that he can't play that piece. Tags with numbers indicating the first selection a child is to play are now used to help teachers know whether a child is coming on stage at the right time.

Private recital, Matsumoto. Teacher remains on stage.

Refreshments after recital in Matsumoto.

Summer School

In 1949 Suzuki conceived the idea of a summer school during which students of Talent Education from all parts of Japan could gather together to study and play together. At first the summer school sessions were small, family-size affairs.

Suzuki believes he remembers that twelve students attended the first summer school. "It was so small then we were able to rent one ryokan in the mountains for our study sessions and concerts. Gradually each year the enrollment grew to such a large number that we could not find a hotel in the mountains large enough to take care of all the students, teachers, and parents. We had to move out of the mountains into Matsumoto.

In recent years, we've had two sessions of five hundred children each. Some of these come from Matsumoto but we have enough visitors to crowd many of the inns in Matsumoto and its suburbs. The children and parents make many new friends during the summer schools and look forward to seeing their friends again each summer."

The summer school is usually held during the last days of July and the first days of August. Most of the Talent Education teachers are in attendance, even those who may have no students at the summer school. Attendance of the students is entirely voluntary. The parents pay their own expenses. Many families make the summer school a regular part of their vacation.

Each session lasts about five days, days that are filled with lessons, recitals and group performances. Since the new Talent Education Building was completed in 1967, this building has become the center of summer school activities. Group concerts are given in the municipal auditorium across the street from the Talent Education Building, with many lessons being given in a nearby high school.

The opening session is for teachers. During this period, held the evening before the students register, Suzuki gives a lesson to all the teachers who are to work with the students in the next few days. He sug-

gests points for study and procedures for teaching the children. The teachers have their violins with them and often throughout the evening the recital hall is filled with the sound as it were of one large violin as the teachers play passages from selections in the Suzuki books.

The next morning the students gather in the appropriate rooms for lessons. Selections from the inevitable Twinkle to one of the Mozart concertos have been chosen for study. Rooms are also reserved for cello and flute students.

In each room, for two hours a day, a team of three teachers instructs the students who are working on a particular piece. The youngsters do play together at times but there is a great deal of individual instruction as the teachers try to perfect each child's ability on that particular selection. There are approximately thirty students in each room. Mothers and fathers crowd in the back to watch. As the students come from different places and from different teachers, the parents as well as the children are able to compare their children's work with that of others.

Solo recitals and group performances are held in the early afternoons and on some evenings. The schedule is quite relaxed and allows ample time for the children to play and rest.

Annual concert. Tokyo, 1968.

Annual Concert 1968

March 24   **1:00 P.M.**

Nippon Budokan, Kudan, Tokyo

PROGRAM

Greeting --Chairman M. Honda

Address ---President S. Suzuki

Graduation Ceremony

Words of Congratulation ---Hon. President Y. Tokugawa

Performance by Graduates

Loure --Bach

Violin

    1. Sonata g min. 1st & 2nd mov. --Eccles
    2. Concerto a min. 1st mov. --Bach
    3. Allegro ---Fiocco

Cello

    a. Twinkle, Twinkle Little Star—Variations -----------------------------------arr. by S. Suzuki
    b. Long, Long Ago ---Bayly
    c. The Swan --Saint-Saens

String Ensemble

    Serenade ---Mozart

Violin

    4. Concerto d min. 1st mov. for Two Violins ---Bach
    5. Concerto a min. 1st mov. ---Vivaldi
    6. Humoresque --Dvorak
    7. The Two Grenadiers --Schumann
    8. Chorus from "Judas Macabeus" --Handel
    9. Menuetto No. 2 ---Bach
   10. Perpetuum Mobile --S. Suzuki
   11. Allegro --S. Suzuki
   12. Papillon ---Folk Song
   13. Twinkle, Twinkle Little Star—Variations ----------------------------------arr. by S. Suzuki
   14. Auld Lang Syne --Folk Song

Annual Concert 1969

March 30   **1:00 P.M.**

Nippon Budokan, Kudan, Tokyo

PROGRAM

Greeting --Chairman M. Honda

Address ---President S. Suzuki

Graduation Ceremony

Words of Congratulation ---Hon. President Y. Tokugawa

Performance by Graduates

Bouree --Bach

Violin

1. Concerto No. 4 1st mov. _____Mozart
2. Concerto a min. 1st mov. _____Bach
3. Sonata No. 4 1st mov. _____Handel
4. Allegro _____Fiocco
5. Concerto d min. 1st mov. for two violins _____Bach
6. Concerto a min. 1st mov. _____Vivaldi

Cello

a. Twinkle, Twinkle Little Star—Variations _____arr. by S. Suzuki
b. May Song _____German Folk Song
c. Perpetual Motion _____S. Suzuki
d. The Swan _____Saint-Saens

Concerto for two violins 1st mov. _____Vivaldi

William Starr, conductor

Violin

7. Menuetto _____Bach
8. Menuetto _____Boccherini
9. Bourree _____Handel
10. Menuetto No. 2 _____Bach
11. Perpetual Motion _____S. Suzuki
12. Allegro _____S. Suzuki
13. Song of the Wind _____German Folk Song
14. Lightly Row _____Folk Song
15. Twinkle, Twinkle Little Star Variations _____arr. by S. Suzuki

Auld Lang Syne _____Scottish Folk Song

Shinichi Suzuki's 1969 Talent Education Tour

PROGRAM

I.

1. Sonata in G minor _____H. Eccles
   1st Movement: Grave — Arr. by S. Suzuki
   2nd Movement: Courante — (played by 7 performers)
2. Allegro _____G. H. Fiocco
   (played by 9 performers)
3. Largo from Concerto in A minor _____A. Vivaldi
4. Concerto in A minor _____A. Vivaldi
   1st Movement: Allegro

II.

1. Rondo _____Mozart-Kreisler
   (Solo by Isako Fukasawa)
2. Fantasia in D minor, K. 397 _____W. A. Mozart
   (The first presentation of the Suzuki method in piano music) — (Piano solo by Mikie Naito)
3. Pièces en Concert (from Gouts Réunis) _____F. Couperin
   (Cello solo by Koji Yanagida)
4. Concerto in E minor, Op. 64 _____F. Mendelssohn
   1st Movement: Allegro molto appassionato — (Solo by Hitomi Kasuya)

INTERMISSION

45

III.

1. Concerto in D minor for Two Violins _____ J. S. Bach
   1st Movement: Vivace

2. Country Dance _____ C. M. von Weber

3. Bourrée _____ G. F. Handel

4. Menuetti No. 3 & No. 2 _____ J. S. Bach

5. Five pieces _____ S. Suzuki
   Rowing Lightly
   Song of the Wind
   Children's Song
   Allegro
   Perpetual Motion

PERFORMERS

Izumi Terada	5 years old	Mikie Naito	10 years old
Kumiko Kitazawa	6 years old	Hitomi Kasuya	10 years old
Shizuka Nakamura	6 years old	Yoko Aoki	11 years old
Junichi Higuchi	7 years old	Isako Fukasawa	11 years old
Nobuko Ohbayashi	7 years old	Koji Yanagida	14 years old

Summer School Schedule And Programs, 1973

July 27	3:30- 5:30	Teachers' meeting
July 28	9:30-11:20	Lessons in the classrooms
		(See list of selections below)
	11:20-12:00	Opening ceremony
	1:00- 2:30	Group lesson—city auditorium
	3:00- 4:00	Concert
July 29	9:30-11:30	Lessons in the classrooms
	1:00- 2:30	Group lesson—city auditorium
	3:00- 4:00	Concert
July 30	9:30-11:30	Lessons in the classrooms
	1:00- 2:30	Group lesson—city auditorium
	3:00- 4:00	Concert
July 31	9:30-10:50	Lessons in the classrooms
	11:00-12:00	Closing Ceremony and Concert

SELECTIONS FOR MORNING LESSONS

Twinkle Variations	Suzuki	Concerto No. 5	Seitz
Song of the Wind		Concerto in a minor 1st mov.	Vivaldi
Allegro	Suzuki	Concerto 3rd mov.	Vivaldi
Perpetual Motion	Suzuki	Concerto g min. 1st mov.	Vivaldi
Minuet No. 1	Bach	La Folia	Corelli
Minuet No. 3	Bach	Sonata No. 4	Handel
Gavotte	Gossec	Concerto in a minor	Bach
Bourree	Handel	Sonata	Eccles
Gavotte	Thomas	Concerto No. 5	Mozart
Minuet	Beethoven	Concerto No. 4	Mozart
Gavotte	Martini	(Flute)	
Humoresque	Dvorak	(Cello)	
Bourree	Bach		

OPENING CEREMONY

Group Concert Program . . . . July 28

Concerto in a minor 1st mov.	Bach
Concerto in a minor 1st mov.	Vivaldi
Bourree	Bach
Gavotte	Gossec
Minuet No. 2	Bach
Perpetual Motion	Suzuki
Allegro	Suzuki
Twinkle Variations	Suzuki

Group Lesson Program . . . . July 28-July 29

Concerto No. 5 1st mov.	Mozart
Concerto in a minor 1st mov.	Bach
Allegro	Fiocco
Concerto in g minor 1st mov.	Vivaldi
Bourree	Bach
Gavotte	Gossec
Minuet No. 2	Bach
Perpetual Motion	Suzuki
Allegro	Suzuki
Twinkle Variations	Suzuki

Concert . . . . July 28 - 3:00-4:00

Students 4 years and under
Allegro	Suzuki
Perpetual Motion	Suzuki
Minuet No. 2	Bach

Students 5 years and under
Bourree	Handel
Two Grenadiers	Schumann

Yumi Higuchi (7)   Nobuo Terada (7)   Matsumoto, Katsuno class
Concerto in a minor 1st mov.	Bach

Kyoko Takezawa (6)   Nagoya, Yamamura class
Concerto No. 5 1st mov.	Mozart

Reiko Hagiwara (5) Piano solo   Matsumoto, Kataoka class
Two Minuets and Gigue	Bach

Hisae Noguchi   Piano solo   Matsumoto, Kataoka class
Minuet	Paderewski

Shizuka Nakamura (11)   Fujisawa, Okamura class
Tambourin Chinois	Kreisler

Judith Starr (14)   Knoxville, Starr Class
Symphonie Espagnole 1st mov.	Lalo

Intermission

Cello Class
Minuet No. 2	Bach

Violin Class
Allegro	Fiocco
Concerto in g minor 1st mov.	Vivaldi
Concerto in a minor 1st mov.	Vivaldi

Concert . . . . July 29th - 3:00-4:00

Chorus from "Judas Maccabaeus" --Handel

Bourree ---Handel

Akiko Funatsu (4) Piano solo   Matsumoto, Kataoka class
   Sonatina 1st mov. Op. 36, No. 3 --Clementi

Akemi Kanda (5) Violin   Okaya, Yamashita class
   Concerto No. 5, 1st mov. --Seitz

Yoko Kashiwasako (10) Violin   Nakano, Kai class
   Concerto in a minor 1st mov. --Bach

Ryoko Nagamine (9)   Nakano, Matsui class
   Sonata in b minor 1st and 2nd mov. --Veracini

Kaoru Kuriiwa (12)   Matsumoto, Mori class
   Rondo --Mozart-Kreisler

Yukari Otani (9)   Matsumoto, Kataoka class
   Italian Concerto 3rd mov. --Bach

Intermission

Violin class
   Concerto in a minor 1st mov. --Bach
   Allegro ---Fiocco
   Bourree --Bach

String Orchestra   Conductor, C. Takasugi
   Minuet ---Mozart

Group Lesson Program . . . . July 30

Concerto No. 4 1st mov. ---Mozart
Sonata in g minor 1st, 2nd mov. --Eccles
Concerto for 2 violins 1st mov. ---Bach
Concerto in a minor 3rd mov. ---Vivaldi
Concerto in a minor 1st mov. ---Vivaldi
Minuet --Beethoven
Gavotte ---Gossec
Minuet No. 3 --Bach
Perpetual Motion --Suzuki
Allegro --Suzuki
Twinkle Variations ---Suzuki

Concert . . . . July 30 - 3:00-4:00

Students 4 years and under
   Twinkle Variations --Suzuki

Mio Murakata (7)   Piano solo   Matsumoto, Kataoka class
   Sonata in C major, 3rd mov. (No. 48) --Haydn

Sayo Kamata (4) Violin   Matsumoto, Mori class
   Humoresque --Dvorak

Mika Gojima (7)   Matsumoto, Toba class
   Sonata No. 4 2nd mov. --Handel

Yukie Ogura (10)   Nagoya, Asai class
   Rondo --Mozart-Kreisler

Fumiko Yamanaka (12)   Kichijoji, Matsui class
   Concerto No. 4 1st mov. _____Mozart

Seizo Azuma (10)   Matsumoto, Kataoka class
   Variations Brillante, Op. 12 _____Chopin

Intermission

Flute class
   Minuet from "L'Arlesienne Suite" _____Bizet
   Danse des Mirlitons from "Casse-Noisette" _____Tschaikowsky

Violin class
   Sonata in g minor, 1st and 2nd mov. _____Eccles
   Concerto in a minor, 1st mov. _____Vivaldi

String Orchestra   Conductor, C. Takasugi
   Minuet _____Mozart

Concert . . . . July 30 - 7:00

Matsumoto String Orchestra   Conductor C. Takasugi
   Serenade _____Elgar
   Minuet _____Boccherini
                                             Conductor Sister T. C. Murphy
   The Heavens Resounding _____Beethoven

Shakuhachi solos   Shizuo Aoki
   Shirabe and Sagariha _____Folk Tunes
   Byoh _____Ryohei Hirose

Koto solos   M. Wako
   Slumber Song Variations _____Y. Hirai

Duo for Koto and Shakuhachi   M. Wako, S. Aoki
   Haruno Umi _____M. Miyagi

Duo in B-flat Major for Violin and Viola _____Mozart
   Adagio-Allegro
   Andante Cantabile   Violin, Prof. W. Starr
   Andante con variazioni   Viola, Prof. W. Primrose

Teachers' String Orchestra   Conductor, W. Primrose
   Serenade _____Mozart
   Minuet _____Mozart
   Entr'acte from "Rosamunde" _____Schubert

CLOSING CEREMONY

Group Concert Program . . . . July 31

Concerto in a minor 1st mov. _____Bach
Concerto in g minor 1st mov. _____Vivaldi
Bourree _____Bach
Two Grenadiers _____Schumann
Gavotte _____Gossec
Minuet No. 1 _____Bach
Perpetual Motion _____Suzuki
Allegro _____Suzuki
Song of the Wind _____Folk Song
Twinkle Variations _____Suzuki

Shinichi Suzuki's 1975 Talent Education Tour

PROGRAM

I.

Allegro con fuoco from Concerto Sonata in E minor _____Veracini

Grave and Courante from Sonata in G minor _____Eccles-Suzuki

Gavotte _____**Martini**

Presto from Concerto in A minor _____Vivaldi

II.

Allegro from Concerto in A minor _____Bach
(Played by Mieko Kanno and Kiroaki Matsuno,
accompanied by a small string ensemble)

Rondo in G _____Mozart-Kreisler
(Played by Kyoko Takezawa, Yumi Higuchi
and Tomoko Kasai)

Fantasie Impromptu, Opus 66 _____Chopin
(Piano solo by Haruko Tanabe)

Concerto in E minor, Opus 64 _____Mendelssohn
3rd movement: Allegretto non troppo   (Violin solo by Tomoko Kasai)
Allegro molto vivace

INTERMISSION

Rhapsody in G minor, Opus 79 No. 2_____Brahms
(Piano solo by Kiroko Kasai)

Polonaise Brillante _____Chopin
(Cello solo by Tomoyuki Nomura)

III.

Allegro _____Fiocco
Country Dance _____Weber
Vivace from Concerto in D minor for Two Violins _____Bach
Allegro from Concerto in A minor _____Vivaldi
Allegro moderato from Concerto No. 5 _____Seitz
Bouree _____Handel
Gavotte _____Gossec
Perpetual Motion _____Suzuki

TOUR

Mieko Kanno	6 years old	Yumi Higuchi	9 years old
Maiko Kanno	7 years old	Hiroko Kasai	9 years old
Yumiko Takei	7 years old	Tomoko Kasai	10 years old
Nanako Imai	7 years old	Haruko Tanabe	10 years old
Hiroaki Matsuno	8 years old	Tomoyuki Nomura	14 years old
Kyoko Takezawa	8 years old		

Introduction to Tonalization

Mr. Suzuki has not only felt for years that a beautiful tone is a violinist's strongest asset, but that more students should acquire a fine sound earlier in their training, and that it is the teacher's responsibility to call attention to the quality of sound produced from the very beginning. Singers have always rated beauty of tone very highly and have been accustomed to begin voice lessons with vocalization. Suzuki says that many violin lessons, on the other hand, are given without any mention of tone. In order to remind his Talent Education teachers that attention to the acquisition of a beautiful tone should never be neglected, Suzuki preaches what he calls 'tonalization in all of his contacts with teachers, and has placed in the early books a series of tonalization exercises to be practiced daily by the students and heard at every lesson by the teacher.

In spite of limitations caused by the size and quality of the instrument and the student's lack of bow control, Suzuki believes that there is a good tone for each level of development, and that usually the quality of the child's tone is in direct relationship to the amount of attention brought to it by the teacher. Each teacher must determine the best tone for each level of the child's development. It is common to see Talent Education teachers in Japan borrow the small violins to see just what kind of tone can be coaxed from each particular instrument, and to give the child a tonal ideal for the piece he is studying.

In Suzuki's graded approach to tone production, the child is allowed, even encouraged, to play heavily at the beginning. What Suzuki calls "slip tone" is to be avoided at all costs. The plan is that the child is later taught to play "gradually lighter" as his control grows. Those who, disliking the heavy sound, teach lighter strokes too early may find that the children never acquire the ability to play what Westerners call "into the string". Even though Suzuki says again and again "Don't push" as he speaks of bow control, he is still more sympathetic to a heavy stroke with a beginner. This, however, is a matter of degree, and should not be interpreted as encouragement for a scratchy tone. Teachers of Talent Education note that application of arm and hand weight to the very small bows is very difficult to control, there not being much difference in degree between that which produces a "slip tone" and that which produces a crushed sound.

From the beginning Suzuki feels that the child should be taught to maintain the same volume during the bow strokes. The student must be made aware of the changes in volume that can occur involuntarily. Gradations in volume are introduced only after a solid "into the string" sound is established.

The children are first taught to produce changes in volume by bowing at different speeds. The first example is that of slowing the bow stroke to produce a diminuendo, a lessening of sound, at the ends of phrases. As the students progress, they are taught to bow with less weight. Advanced players are shown how to bow nearer the bridge for a loud tone, (Suzuki calls this the 'Kreisler highway'), and nearer the fingerboard for a softer tone. As the earlier pieces are reviewed, many refinements in tone production are taught. It is not unusual in a lesson to hear a small child play his current piece with short heavy staccato strokes, then return to an earlier piece and play legato with a big clear tone with longer bow strokes.

Suzuki intertwines the study of tone quality and intonation, stressing their relationship. He frequently refers to the "sound point" of notes, that is, the point at which the note is exactly on pitch. This is brought to the attention of the child at the beginning with notes which are octaves or unisons of the pitches of the open strings, that is, notes with the same names. The child is taught to listen to the open string vibrating freely as the fingered note is played on the same pitch, or to play first the open string and then the fingered note to compare their pitches.

Many pieces in the early books are given in the basic keys of A Major, D Major, and G Major in order to establish their tonalities in the student's ears. This is one aspect of his ear training. Suzuki feels that it takes a long time for the beginners to play well in tune, but believes that with the teacher's perseverance, much can be accomplished in this regard.

In this early portion of the manual, comments on tonalization have been limited to the presentation of the beginning tonalization exercises found in the Suzuki books. The main chapter on tonalization contains a thorough discussion of tonalization with many additional exercises used by Suzuki but not printed in the volumes of the Suzuki Violin School.

Holding the Violin and Bow in Rest Position. Bowing

When the student is given the violin for the first time, he is taught to hold the violin at rest under his right arm. This is called 'rest position'. At this time the student is taught the proper greeting and bow which always open the private lessons. Suzuki says that the bow signifies respect for the teacher and should not be quick or perfunctory. He also points out that the teacher's answering bow indicates the teacher's respect for the student, so that mutual respect is expressed by the bows. The formal Japanese bow is too low in Suzuki's opinion. He wants the students to have an 'international' bow. The child bows slightly and holds the bow until he counts to three, then he straightens up.

These routines taught by Suzuki are valuable in teaching the small child respect for the instrument. He learns to control himself as he handles the violin. Holding the violin properly 'at rest' and bowing correctly may be the first point the new student will proudly demonstrate to his father at his first home concert.

EXERCISE: *Teacher or parent places violin and bow in rest position. Bowing practice.*

1. Student faces teacher, standing straight with hands at sides and feet together.

2. Teacher raises child's right arm from side, placing violin under the upper arm so that the arm rests on the violin strings behind the bridge.

3. Teacher places bow in student's right hand. Student holds onto frog with right hand, with the bow pointing to the floor.

4. Student and teacher bow.

At group lessons, in order to ensure more deliberate bows, three chords may be played on the piano for the bows. The children bow on the first and straighten up on the third.

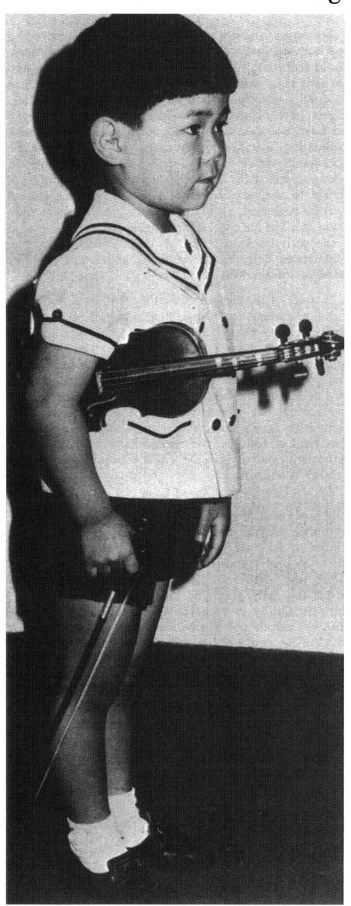

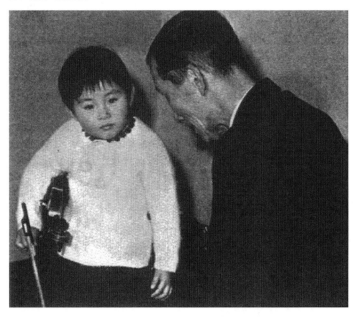

The bow shows mutual respect.

Rest position.

EXERCISE: *Student, taking violin and bow from teacher, places both in rest position.*

1. Student takes violin from teacher in left hand, holding violin securely by the neck.

2. Student places violin under right arm, strings facing out, with the arm resting on the strings behind the bridge. The right arm holds the violin, but should not press on it with undue force.

3. Student takes bow at frog in left hand.

4. Student puts bow in right hand, holding the bow at the frog, with the bow pointing to the floor.

5. Student and teacher bow.

EXERCISE: *Student takes violin and bow from case. Assumes rest position.*

1. Student takes bow from case, sliding bow carefully out of the holder.

2. Student holds bow at the frog in the right hand, with the bow pointing to the floor.

3. Student takes violin from case with left hand, holding the violin securely by the neck.

4. Student places violin under right arm, as above.

Holding Violin in Playing Position. The Proper Posture.

Suzuki is very particular about the stance of the children as they begin to play the violin. Musicians who have seen the groups of Japanese children touring America have been impressed by the excellent playing posture of the young performers. Those who have seen large groups performing in Japan have been even more impressed by the very large percentage of the young performers who have the same good natural playing posture.

After the child can hold the violin in rest position and bow properly, Suzuki's next move is to arrange the position of the student's feet in what he feels is the best natural position for playing the violin. A 'foot paper' guide for the placement of the beginner's feet has been recently adopted and advocated by Suzuki. The child's feet are placed in the correct position on a paper sheet or cardboard. An outline is then made with a pen or felt marker. Two copies of this guide are made, one for home use and the other for the lessons in the studio. Suzuki writes the child's name on the studio copy.

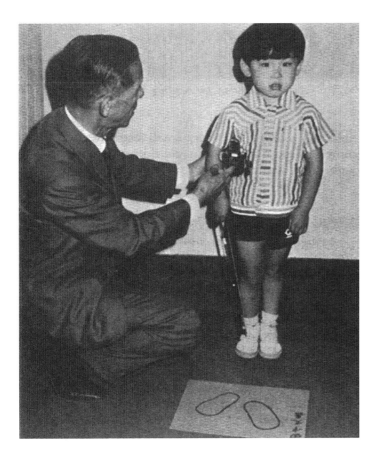

Suzuki's "foot paper."

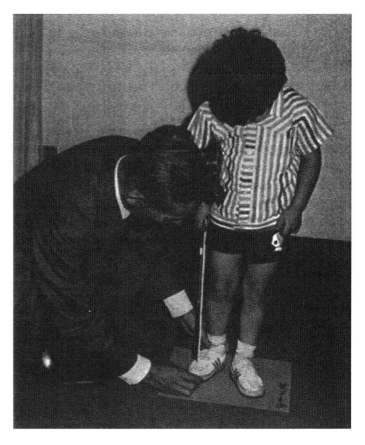

Placing the child's feet.

EXERCISE: *Teacher places the student's feet in the correct position.*

1. Student faces teacher, standing straight, with the feet together.

2. Teacher moves each foot approximately 45 degrees outward.

3. Teacher moves right foot slightly behind the left.

4. Student shifts weight to the left foot.

ALTERNATE EXERCISE: *Teacher places the student's feet in the correct position.*

1. Student faces teacher, standing straight, with feet together.

2. Student separates feet approximately six inches.

3. Teacher moves left foot approximately 45 degrees outward.

4. Teacher moves left foot forward slightly.

5. Student shifts weight to left foot.

Sometimes Suzuki asks the child to raise the right foot off the ground to impress upon him the fact that the weight should be on the left foot. "The left foot should be the center of the body vertically", says Suzuki.

After the student acquires the correct placement of the feet, he is asked to turn his head to the left, without turning the body, so that his nose is pointing in about the same direction as the left foot. The mother should sit so that the child's nose, turned at that angle, will be pointing toward her. The student should practice placing his feet and turning his head without holding the violin.

EXERCISE: *Student places feet properly, and moves head to the left.*

1. Student places feet himself according to the above procedures.

2. Student turns head to left in the direction of the left foot, without moving the body or the feet.

With the feet and head positioned properly, the student's arm is then brought into playing position as if to

Preparation for holding the violin.

hold the violin. The very small beginner may be required to go through this routine several times daily before the violin is placed in playing position.

EXERCISE: *Student's feet, head, and left arm are brought into proper position.*

1. Student's feet and head are positioned according to the above procedures.

2. Student's left hand is brought up into approximate playing position, with the palm facing the nose, level with it. The fingers are curved.

3. Student's left arm is turned further to the left until the four fingertips are in a line facing the nose.

4. Student moves left hand forward until the little finger touches the nose, and back again. The elbow should be in line with the nose.

54

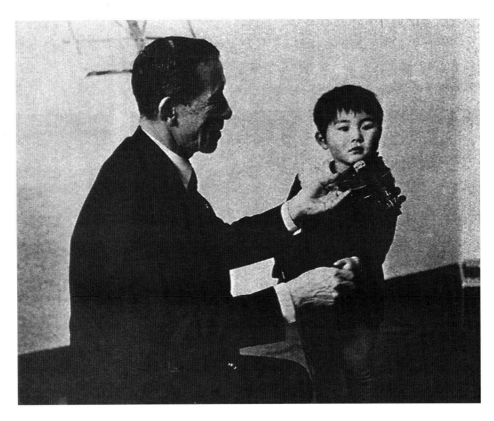

Suzuki places the violin in position.

Suzuki and his Talent Education teachers in Japan are very particular about placing the violin under the chin. They check carefully to see whether the child will need a shoulder pad to help him support the violin between chin and shoulder without the aid of his left hand. Many use a small Japanese shoulder pad of hard rubber which is connected to the violin under the brace holding the chin rest. A Kolitsch-type pad made in Japan is also used, along with homemade cushions fashioned by the mothers.

At the beginning, the violin is placed in position by the teacher, who should also show the parent just how this should be practiced at home. Since eventually the student will position the violin himself, it is important that he also be taught how to do it himself.

At the very beginning the student is asked to hold the violin between chin and shoulder without the support of the left hand so that he will not gain the habit of supporting the violin with his left hand. Some teachers have the student hold the violin between chin and shoulder with the left arm hanging down at the side, whereas others want the left hand placed in the right armpit, or on the right shoulder.

Mitsumasa Denda, a Talent Education teacher in Nagano, devised a 'pre-violin' for his very, very young beginners. This is a covered box with a ruler attached at one end for the fingerboard. Denda says that the box, being somewhat lighter than a violin, is easier to hold. He also finds that the very small beginner is motivated to work with the box so that he can 'graduate' to a real violin. The child looks forward with real eagerness to being given a real violin.

Some of the boxes used by Denda's students had four small circles drawn on the fingerboard so the child could practice putting the fingers down. Others had two lines drawn up the fingerboard so the child could shift his left hand up and down as he supported the violin between chin and shoulder. Denda has the children go through various postures and routines with the box held firmly between chin and shoulder. (See the game activities listed below.)

EXERCISE: *Teacher places the violin (or box) in playing position.*

1. Student assumes proper foot position.

2. Student turns head to the left. Keeps left hand at side.

3. Teacher, positioned on the child's left, inserts violin between chin and shoulder. The violin is tilted slightly, parallel to the floor. The student's nose should point to the strings. The nut of the violin should point to the center of the throat.

4. After making sure that the student has a secure hold on the violin, the teacher releases his hold.

5. Teacher counts to see how long student can hold the violin without allowing it to fall.

The above exercise may be done with the child's left hand placed in the right armpit or on the right shoulder.

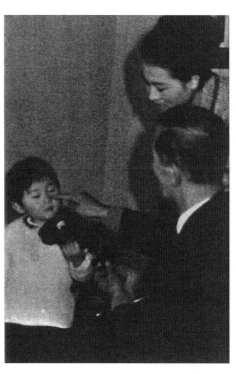

Please turn your head. *The nose should point this way.* *Please straighten your head.*

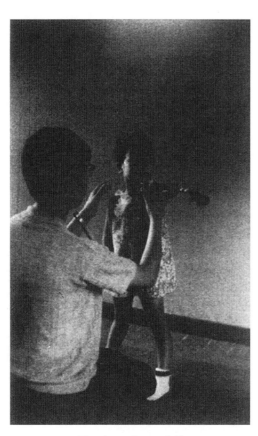

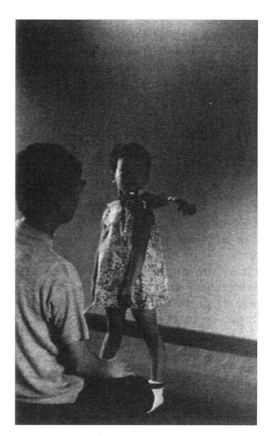

Teacher places violin. *Good position!*

It is common for teachers to make a game of seeing how long the student can hold the violin in the correct position, increasing the length of time at each succeeding lesson. At first, some children may complain that it hurts or that they tire very easily, but they gradually become adjusted to holding it without support. In fact, in order for the children to become free and comfortable with the violin held between chin and shoulder, the teachers and mothers play all sorts of games with them. During these games which entertain the children, their muscles will become stronger. The teacher and mother should constantly check to see if unneeded muscles are under tension. At this stage, the right shoulder often rises slightly as the violin is held.

GAMES TO BE PLAYED AS THE VIOLIN (OR BOX) IS HELD WITHOUT LEFT HAND SUPPORT

1. Teacher taps top of violin to see if it is held firmly.
2. Teacher tries to pull violin out from chin.
3. Student bends knees.
4. Student turns around in circles.
5. Student walks back and forth.
6. Student stands on left foot.
7. Student touches right ear with left hand.
8. Student shakes right or left hands with teacher or another student.
9. Student holds out both hands, waving them in the air.

EXERCISE: *Student places violin in playing position.*

1. Student holds violin in rest position.
2. Placing left hand on body of violin, student raises the violin to the chin, using the right hand also for support.
3. Student turns head to left as violin is brought up into position.
4. Student checks position. The violin should be slightly tilted, parallel to the floor. The nose should point down the strings. The instrument should be held without tension in the neck or back muscles.
5. Student lowers right and left arms to sides.

At the same time that the child is developing his ability to hold the instrument properly, he is also learning to hold the bow. These two holds are taught in the same lessons, but the children only perform one at a time.

Visitors often ask Suzuki or his teachers how long this or that procedure takes. Since Suzuki says, "Children like to do what they *can* do", he is careful not to push them too rapidly in order that they will not become confused and uncertain. Suzuki says that the rate of advancement varies according to the child's age, temperament, ability to concentrate, and his home environment.

Although Suzuki's program of instruction calls for the child to adjust to holding the violin and bow before starting to play the first variation of Twinkle, Twinkle

Child places violin in position.

Mother draws bow as child holds violin.

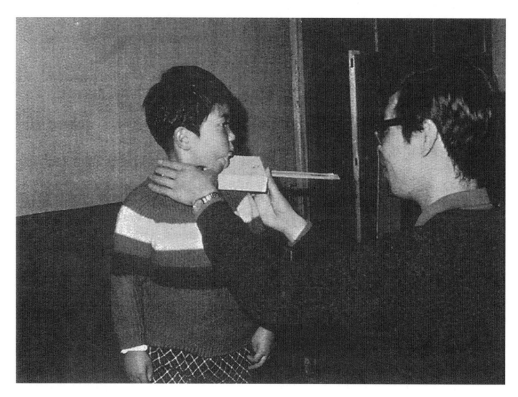

Denda puts box in position.

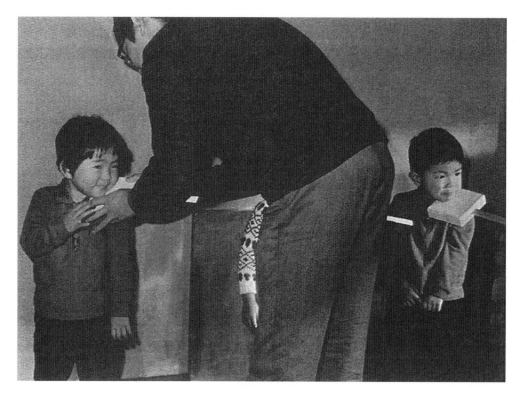

Group lesson with boxes.

Students place boxes in position.

Teacher pulls on box.

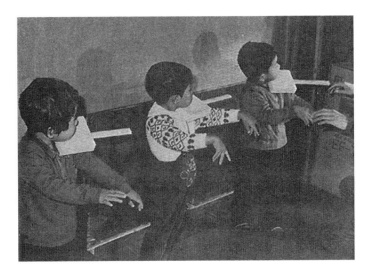

Students wave arms in air.

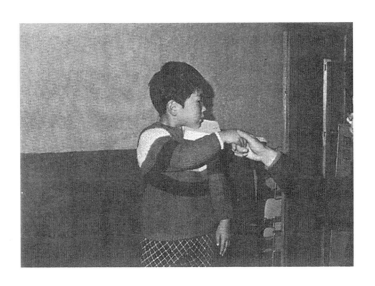

Student shakes hands.

Students put boxes on floor. Which way?

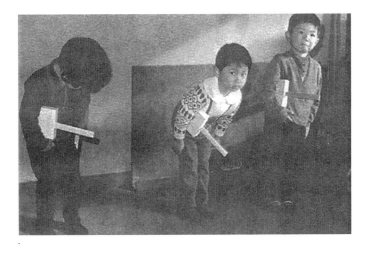

Bowing practice.

Little Star, the child is not restrained from starting to play Twinkle until he holds the violin and bow perfectly. Again and again the teacher aids the child in placing the violin properly until this becomes an easy and natural thing for the child to do by himself. It's not uncommon to see a Japanese teacher help the child place the violin in position before the beginner plays a short solo at a recital. Teachers are constantly adjusting the child's hold of the violin and bow even for children who are playing the early pieces of Book I.

Suzuki and his best teachers seem to know the propitious moment to move on with the child's development. The child and the mother both learn from experience that although the student is moving on to new techniques and new literature, he will still be required to improve his basic technique to a higher degree while he continues to play all of the previously learned repertoire.

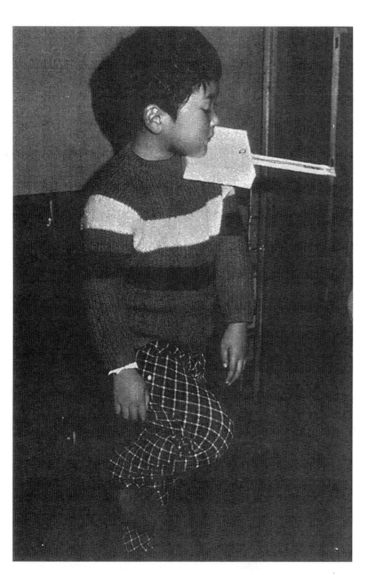

Student stands on left foot.

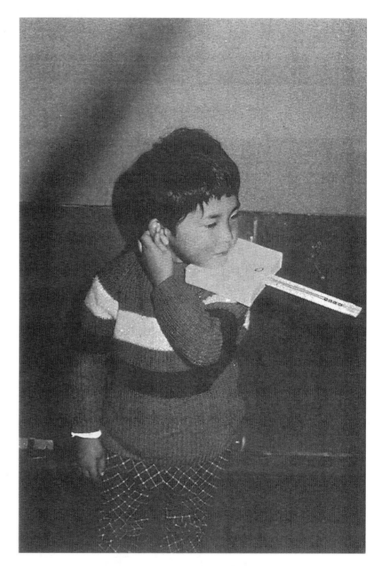

Student touches right ear.

Moving the Bow Arm Rhythmically

At the same time the student is learning to hold the violin and bow separately, rhythmic games may be taught the student to prepare him for the bow strokes used in the Twinkle variations. All of these rhythms should have been memorized by the student from listening to the recording. Many non-Japanese teachers make up word patterns that fit the rhythms, like "Mississippi River", or "Run, Susie, Run". Below is a list of the words used by teachers in Japan. Their translations show the use of praise and pleasant words for reinforcement.

Ta-ka-ta-ka taa - kaa
Yo-kat - ta (it was good)
Jo - zu-ni (play well)
Yo-i-o-to de-ma-shi-ta (a good tone was produced)

EXERCISES:

Student sings rhythms and claps rhythms.

Students clap rhythms together in group as teacher plays.

Teacher and student shake hands in rhythm.

1. Teacher and student clasp right hands.
2. Teacher raises right hands, says in tempo, "Ready, go", then lowers hands to start rhythm.
3. Teacher and student continue rhythm, saying the words aloud.
4. Teacher guides student to stop hand motion after the 8th notes. This is very difficult for many young children.

Teacher guides two students shaking hands in rhythms.

1. Students clasp right hands in handshake.
2. Teacher moves hands up and down as all say the words.

Two students shake hands in rhythms.

1. As above. Teacher watches for correct stops after 8th notes.

Teacher and student move hands in rhythms without touching hands.

1. Teacher and student put outstretched right hands parallel but not touching.
2. Student and teacher perform rhythms, moving hands down and up together.

Two students perform above exercise.

These exercises are fine for group activity. The most important point is that the children stop their motion at the proper places, that is, after the 8th notes. The third variation should be taught with a big motion for the first note, followed by a complete stop and then two very small connected motions for the next two notes. The next large motion, for the 8th note, follows the two small motions without a stop.

After the students are proficient, they should be asked to perform the rhythmic motions without saying the words to accompany them. This is sometimes difficult for those who need to be saying the rhythms at the same time.

Holding the Bow

Holding the bow properly has no counterpart in the child's activity. It is not easy. Suzuki realizes this and so he constantly urges his teachers to help the children form correct habits at the very beginning. As has been stated earlier, the bow hold is taught at the same time the child is learning to hold the violin, although these are done separately. The student's bow hold is corrected and refined again and again even as he progresses well into Book I.

There are a number of preliminary exercises used to show the beginner the proper way to approach the bow. From the beginning, Suzuki stresses curvature of the thumb and fingers, and the position of the thumb opposite the middle fingers.

EXERCISES: (preliminary to holding the bow)

Teacher teaches child to make circle with thumb and middle finger.

Teacher teaches child to pick up pencil with thumb and middle finger.

Student performs rhythmic exercises holding pencil as above.

When the child first holds the bow, Suzuki introduces a new position for the thumb. This is to facilitate the beginner's control of the bow. The thumb is not placed on the inside of the frog, but on the outside. It should approach the frog not at a 90-degree angle so often used, but at an angle of approximately 45-degrees, so that the thumb comes in contact with the frog on the thumb's right side near the nail. The thumb is also kept somewhat curved. The thumb and the curved little finger form an oval. Suzuki suggests putting bits of plastic tape on the child's hand to show the mother the places at which the bow contacts the hand.

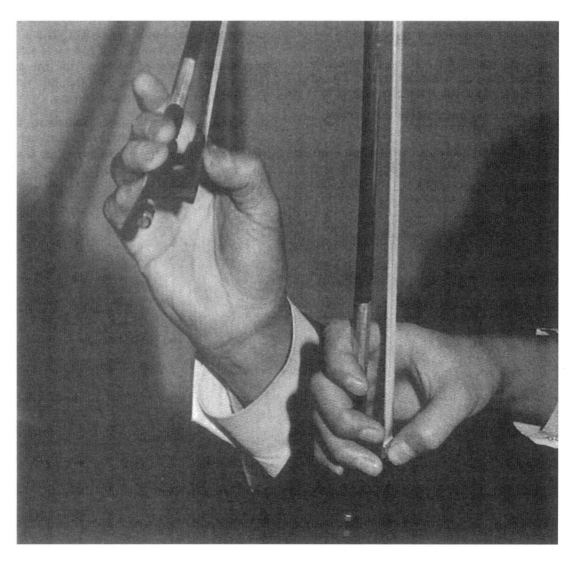

Suzuki's bow hold for the beginner.

62

EXERCISE: *Teacher sets student's bow hold.*

1. Student holds out right hand, palm up.

2. Teacher puts bow in upturned hand, placing the right corner of the student's thumb on the silver part of the frog, with the thumb curved slightly at a 45-degree angle.

3. Teacher wraps the two middle fingers around the frog, opposite the thumb and also at an angle. These fingers should touch the stick where the bow rests and also on the side of the frog. The fingers should be slightly separated.

4. Teacher separates the index finger from the adjacent finger. The bow rests in the second joint of the index finger.

5. Teacher places the tip of the little finger under the bow stick so that the tip will be on top of the bow when it is turned over into position.

6. Student turns the bow hand so that the stick points straight up.

EXERCISE: *Student sets own bow hold.*

1. Student holds out right hand, palm up.

2. Student takes bow in left hand at tip of frog, bow pointing to right.

3. Student puts bow in upturned hand, following the procedure in the preceding exercise.

ALTERNATE EXERCISE: *Student sets own bow hold.*

1. Student takes bow in left hand, holding bow stick near the middle. The bow hair is down, and the bow points to the left, over the left shoulder.

2. Student places right corner of thumb under frog on silver part, thumb slightly curved and at an angle.

3. Student puts fingers over frog, slightly separated. The index finger rests on top of the bow at the second joint; the middle two fingers touch the top of the bow stick at their middle joints and the side of the frog at their first joints; the tip of the little finger, which is curved, rests near the top of the bow, on the side nearest the hand.

Student sets bow hold vertically.

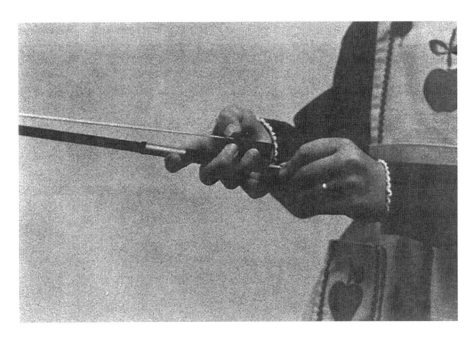

Student sets bow hold horizontally.

When the student holds the bow, Suzuki shows the mother how the hand should appear 'round' with both the thumb and the fingers somewhat curved. He also shows that the base knuckle of the first finger should be approximately level with the bow stick when the bow is turned over in playing position.

After the beginner learns how to place the bow in his hand and carry it properly, he is given important preliminary exercises for muscle development that are repeated for weeks, even long after the student is bowing on the strings. Advanced students are also frequently asked to review these exercises.

The bow hold should be 'round'.

EXERCISES TO STRENGTHEN MUSCLES USED IN THE BOW HOLD

1. Student sets bow in hand, then turns bow to ceiling. He raises his hand up, keeping the bow pointing straight upward. He then lowers the bow, watching to keep the bow pointing straight up.

2. Student sets bow in hand, turns bow point to ceiling, then performs rhythmic variations, moving bow straight up and down.

3. Student sets bow in hand, turns point up, then makes a small circle with bow hand, keeping the tip of the bow moving in the same circle.

4. Student sets bow in hand, turns point up. He then moves the bow hand back and forth, right and left, keeping the hand, elbow, and tip of the bow moving the same distance.

5. Student sets bow in hand, then holds the bow in front of him parallel to the floor. He then moves the bow hand up and down, keeping the hand, elbow, and bow tip moving the same distance.

At times Suzuki asks the student to hold the bow vertically. He then taps on the hair at the tip to see if the bow is held strongly enough for it to return quickly to its original position. "This shows thumb power", says Suzuki. "Thumb power is very important for tone production."

The thumb is not moved to its conventional resting place on the inside of the frog until the teacher is satisfied that the child is ready. This may not occur until the student is well into Book III.

The student should not exert undue energy in performing the above exercises. His little finger should gain in strength without pressing too hard on the stick. "Strong but relaxed," Suzuki advises.

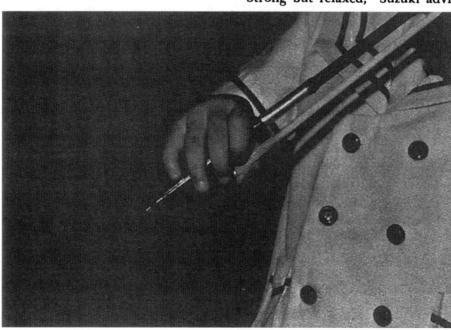

Four-year-old beginner.

Suzuki demonstrates . . . .   *bowing exercise No. 4, Page 52.*

Suzuki demonstrates . . . .   *bowing exercise No. 5, Page 52.*

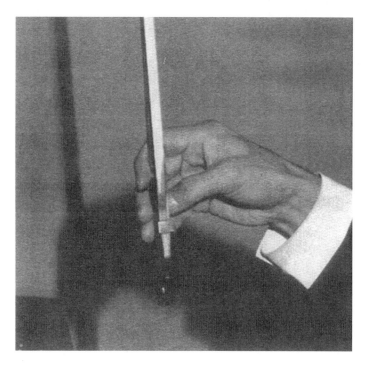

'Normal' bow hold as used by . . . .

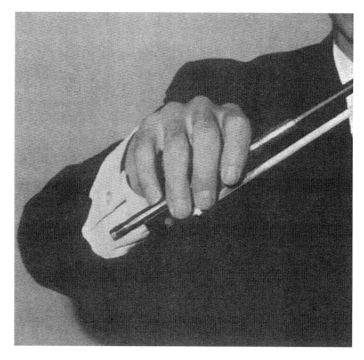

. . . advanced player.

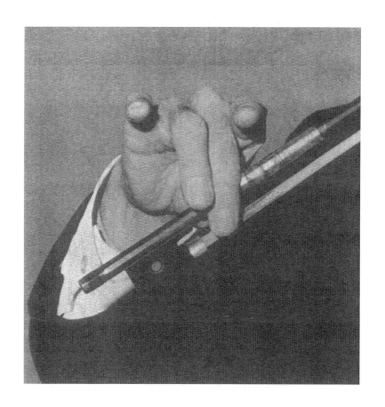

Center of bow hold: thumb and middle fingers.

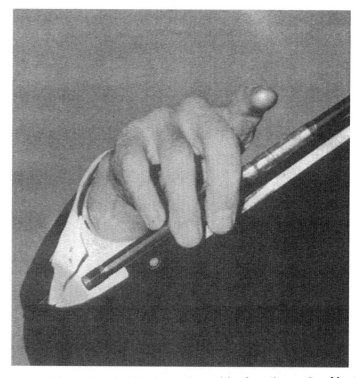

To avoid forming habit of pressing with first finger, Suzuki at times asks student to play with it off the bow.

Basic E String Posture

After the beginner has become fairly proficient at holding the violin and bow properly, Suzuki wants him to assume the "E string posture", a position Suzuki considers basic. When the student has developed the proper bow hold, and is holding the violin in playing position, Suzuki places the bow on the E string at the lower tape which has been put on the bow at the point where the forearm is parallel to the strings. He is careful to see that the elbow and entire right arm are close to the right side of the body.

Suzuki advocates the use of tapes on the bow to guide the student in placing the bow on the strings and in drawing short bow strokes at the beginning. He places two tapes on the bow for the Twinkle variations. The first, or lower tape, is placed at the point where the forearm is parallel to the strings, with the second tape being placed about 1½ to 2 inches above the first, depending on the child's arm length. All of the notes of the first Twinkle variation are played in this restricted area. No difference is made between the lengths of the bow strokes for the 8th and 16th notes. Suzuki just stops the bow after the 8th notes.

Suzuki observes correct E string posture.

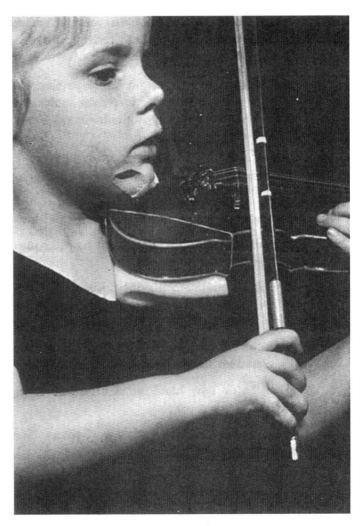

E string placement. Short forearm.

The student is now ready to play the rhythmic pattern that is used for the first variation of Twinkle. Previously he should have heard the rhythm many times, spoken the rhythm, and moved pencil or bow up and down to this pattern. This rhythmic figure has been identified as the rhythm of the opening of the first movement of the Bach Double Concerto. Actually, it contains within its brief statement two common bowing problems for the string player, the playing of connected notes in *legato* style (the first four notes) and the playing of separated notes, *staccato* (the next two notes). This rhythm, which has been called Suzuki's 'leitmotif', is a stroke of pedagogical genius in that it provides the beginner with an instructional unit that is a miniature piece in itself. Psychologically, the small child is less impelled to go on to try to play the whole Twinkle through before he should because he has in a sense played a complete entity, a musical idea, in these six notes. These notes are to be his first solo. In line with Suzuki's idea of early participation in concerts, many children may appear on their teacher's recital playing at first only this rhythm once on the E string.

When the student begins to play this rhythm, he does not at first play it himself, rather he holds the bow and violin while the teacher guides his hand, elbow and bow up and down.

EXERCISE: *Placing bow on E and playing rhythm of 1st variation.*

1. Student assumes rest position with violin and bow.

2. Student uses left hand to help right hand acquire proper bow hold.

3. Student raises violin to playing position with left hand, then lowers left arm, or supports violin by holding body of violin with left hand.

4. Teacher places bow on E string on lower tape, keeping student's right arm near side of body.

5. Teacher holds bow hand in right hand, elbow in left.

6. Teacher moves the bow and says rhythms. Student watches tapes.

7. Teacher repeats the rhythm several times, then disengages hands from student's bow arm.

8. Student then plays the rhythm, watching bow on the tapes.

9. Teacher comments on execution, commending and evaluating, ... "That's good. Please stay within the tapes. Can you play with a stronger tone?"

10. 7, 8, and 9 are repeated as often as necessary until the child tires.

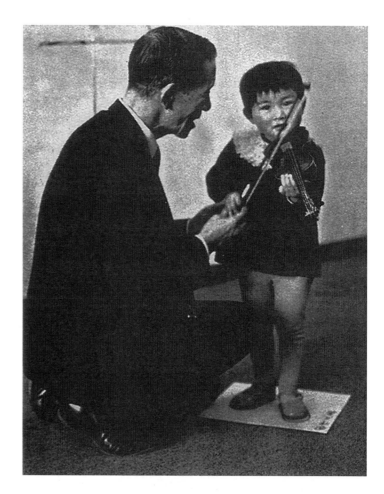

Suzuki places bow on E string for three-year-old.

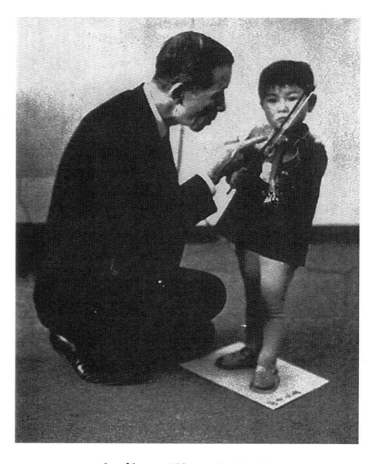

Suzuki says, "Please play here".

Suzuki . . . .   *assumes . . . . . .*   *E string posture.*

EXERCISE: *Placing the bow on the E string.*

1. As above, only student places bow on E.
2. Student plays rhythm.
3. Student lifts bow several inches in the air off E string.
4. Student places bow back on the E string, then plays rhythm.

During these first bowing exercises, the violin may be held with the left hand supporting it by holding onto the body of the violin on the right side. The left hand may also be kept at the left side of the body, or kept in playing position at the neck of the violin. All of these positions are used by Talent Education teachers. It is important that the student does not relinquish his firm hold of the violin between chin and shoulder while he is practicing his first bow strokes. If he holds his hand in playing position, it should not clutch the neck of the instrument.

Since the bow stroke is a short one near the middle of the bow, and the teacher guides the direction many times, there is a good chance that the beginner will not draw the bow crookedly. However, if the student persists in drawing the bow crookedly by pulling his elbow to the rear, the teacher may put his hand on the child's upper right arm to keep it from moving to the side. Some teachers provide a further guide to drawing the bow straight by placing a long white tape across the top of the violin below the strings midway between bridge and fingerboard and parallel to the bridge.

Suzuki comments that many children like to start with an up-bow stroke because from an early age they are accustomed to bring food up to their mouths. The teacher should strive to correct this immediately, by showing the child the difference between the feel of the up-bow and the down-bow.

From the beginning, Suzuki wants the child to produce a strong tone. Observers have noticed that Suzuki, in assisting a young beginner to play his first bow strokes, produces a much heavier sound than he does when he plays the same pattern himself. "Put the bow on the string. Don't push with the first finger. Let the weight of the arm rest on the strings. Draw a nice, full tone, then stop the bow without pushing into the strings.

Gradually you can play lighter". These are remarks of Suzuki's often heard during this period of instruction.

Teachers watching Suzuki play the first variation of Twinkle notice a flexibility in his fingers and wrist, and hear a well-controlled smooth tone, big but not forced. Teachers should not expect this of their beginners. Suzuki doesn't. He does not teach any finger or wrist action at this time. He has found that children need to develop control of the large muscular motions at the beginning. He also stresses heavy tone rather than light tone for the first bow strokes, and is averse to what he calls a 'slip' tone which usually results from the student drawing too long bows. Suzuki's beginning students almost always play much more heavily than he does. "Gradually lighter", he is heard to say. One never hears, "Gradually heavier."

In order that the beginning student not develop the habit of pushing or leaning heavily on the bow stick with the first finger, some teachers ask the student to touch the bow only lightly with the first finger. The finger may be straightened and protrude at this time. Later the finger is curved over the stick. This is a development of Suzuki's idea that the bow should be held chiefly between the thumb and the middle fingers, and that arm and hand weight should be applied at that point.

Suzuki doesn't use a slow tempo to introduce the first rhythm to children. "If the tempo is too slow, the child will draw too long bows. The small child can actually move more rapidly than the mother or teacher might expect. Of course, it takes time for the small child to do this well", he says. The metronome speed for this variation varies from 80-115 for the beginners.

If there were a subtitle to the first book of Suzuki's Violin School, Suzuki agrees that it should be 'preparation'. "Preparation", Suzuki says, "is the most important habit of practice. I tell the child that his father does not start the car moving until the doors are closed and all is ready. So the violin student must prepare every motion. After he plays the first rhythm once, he must then stop. His mother or teacher can then tell him, 'Very good. Please play it again', or, 'Very good. Please don't move your elbow', or some such advice, then when he is prepared he can play again. We say 'hai' (OK) when we want the child to proceed. If the student becomes accustomed from the very beginning to stopping and preparing when he practices, he will learn very rapidly".

E string posture.

Use Of Tapes On The Bow. Bow Distribution

As the student progresses in his ability to bow straight and maintain a firm tone throughout the duration of the bow stroke, a tape may be added below the first tape to increase the use of the bow below the middle. Some teachers, however, do not do this right away, but rather add a third tape above the higher tape, elongating the bow stroke in the upper part of the bow. The placement of this third tape depends upon the teacher's assessment of the child's needs and readiness. The third tape may be added when the Twinkle melody is studied, to differentiate between the quarter and half note strokes.

The two outer tapes may be moved outward by degrees as the child's bow control increases, until the frog and the tip of the bow are reached and the child can play full bow strokes. Teachers drop the use of tapes at different times with their students. Some use them only at the very beginning. Others use tapes for a long time, perhaps into Book II, as they give the student specific instructions regarding bow distribution for each piece. As one experienced Japanese teacher put it: "The children know what finger to use, what string to bow on, and the duration of each note and its pitch. I think it also helps them to know just how much bow to draw for each note".

Whether or not tapes are used for a long period, certain principles must be kept in mind regarding the tone produced by the bow. Experienced teachers have found that the child learns to bow straight and in the right path more quickly if he keeps his eyes on the bow stroke at the point of contact with the strings. With most pieces, as the child becomes freer and freer in his handling of the bow, the length of the bow strokes is increased. (Exceptions, such as Song of the Wind, are noted as the study of each selection is undertaken in this volume.) It is important to Suzuki that the student, as he elongates his bow strokes, maintains a firm tone, not losing control of the bow.

The illustrations given here show the first two tapes, and progressive uses of tapes. It is difficult to give instructions regarding exact placement of tapes and the bow distribution for all children for each selection with any one set of tapes. This is an individual matter for each student. In the text of this manual and in the exercises many bowing indications are given, some specific, as "Place the bow on the center tape", and some less so, "use longer bows on the quarter notes in the third measure". These instructions should be interpreted according to the needs of the student. It is Suzuki's intent that each student will become adept at using all parts of the bow with ease. On the one hand the child should not be required to use a long stroke that is too difficult for him to control, but on the other he should not be kept on small bow strokes without being given the opportunity of gaining facility gradually with longer strokes. Well-trained Suzuki students use the whole bow with ease, having been given a great deal of training and experience in the more difficult lower half of the bow.

One of the main applications of Suzuki's principle of reinforcement is that of requiring bow strokes of different lengths as the student reviews selections. For instance, the Twinkle melody might at first be played between the first two tapes, then later with three tapes as a third is added below the first tape, and then much later with whole and half bow strokes for all the notes.

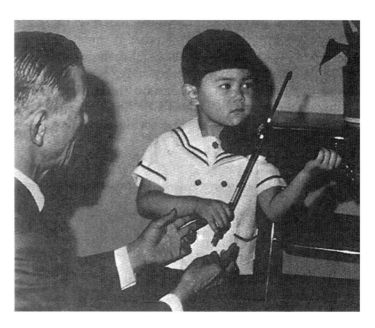

First set of tapes.

Tapes for more advanced player.

Changing String Levels

Throughout Book I, Suzuki constantly refers to the problem of changing from one string level to another with the bow. He urges teachers to teach the student to stop the bow motion before each change of string level, and to move the arm carefully to the next level so that the same kind of tone can be produced on the new string. "It would be easy to get a good tone on the violin if it had only one string", Suzuki jokes with students, reminding them to get the same quality and quantity of tone on both strings. "Don't play with a slip tone on the new string."

There are three basic kinds of string changes possible to the string player: 1) changing the level by using the whole right arm as a unit, that is, hand, forearm, elbow and upper arm together; 2) changing the level by using the hand and forearm only, with the elbow following if the player remains on the new string; 3) changing the level with a hand or finger motion only. Suzuki favors the second of these for the beginner, saying,

"The bow hand and forearm should move first to the new string level. The elbow should follow the hand".

In spite of Suzuki's insistence on the change mentioned above, many teachers in Japan use the first type of string change at the very beginning. One sees them move the child's whole arm to the new string level. It's not long after, however, that they ask for the second type of change, which involves less elbow motion.

EXERCISE: *Changing string levels.*

1. Play Twinkle rhythm on E. Stop.
2. Raise hand and forearm until bow rests on A string. Teacher checks level.
3. Play rhythm on A. Listen to tone. Same volume as that on E?
4. Lower hand and forearm until bow rests on E. Teacher checks level.
5. Play rhythm on E.
6. Repeat above again and again.

Suzuki demonstrates: "Elbow is too high".

Denda helps child place bow on A.

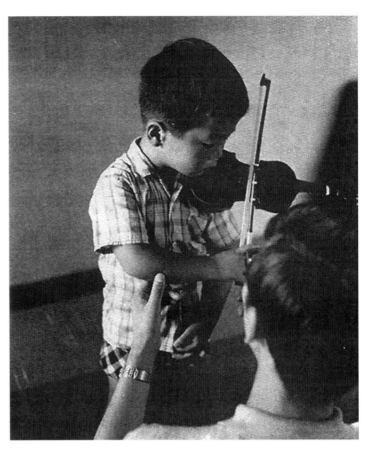

Denda guides bow on A. Note hand guiding elbow.

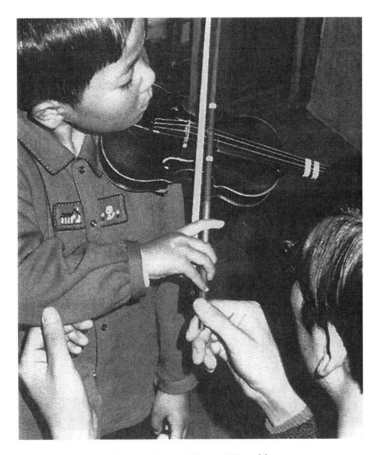

Bowing on the A string with guidance.

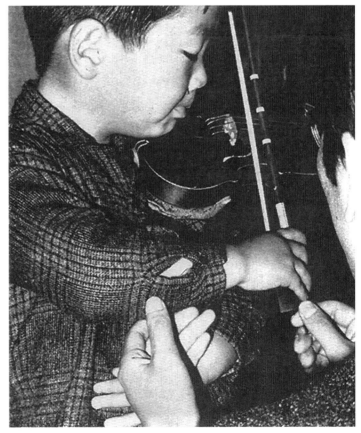

Bowing on the A string with guidance.

73

E string level.

A string level.

D string level.

G string level.

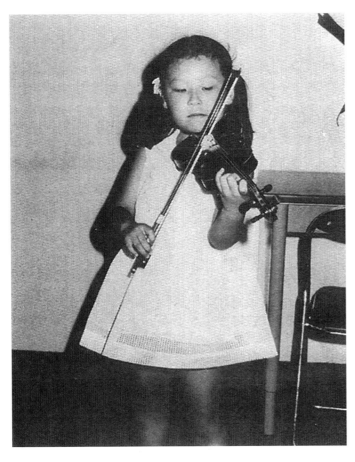

E string level.

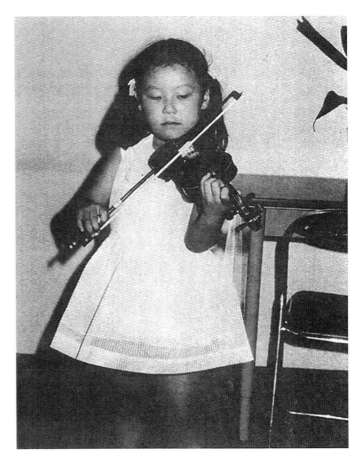

A string level.

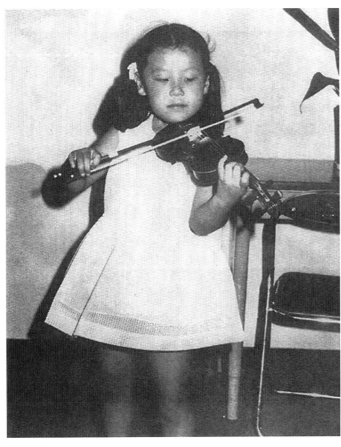

D string level.

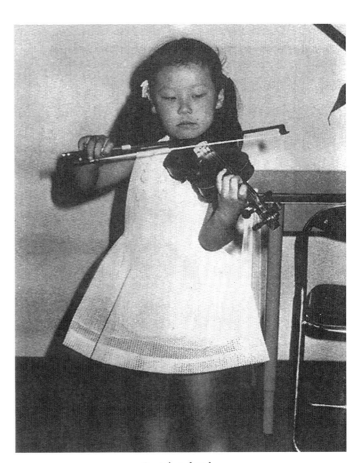

G string level.

Suzuki demonstrates:

the hand leads as the bow . . . .

crosses to lower strings.

A string level.

A string level.

Holding The Violin. Placing The Left Hand

At the same time the student is learning his first bow strokes, he learns to use the fingers of his left hand. Before the beginner places his fingers on the fingerboard, three white tapes are affixed to the fingerboard. The first tape, placed one whole-step above the open string, indicates the notes, from the G string up, A-E-B-F#. Another whole-step up the second tape is placed. This indicates the notes B-F#-C#-G#. The third tape, placed one half-step above the second, indicates the notes C-G-D-A.. This is the first finger pattern to be used. "These are guides for the student and mother", says Suzuki. "The tapes must be carefully placed taking into consideration the size of the tips of the child's fingers".

EXERCISE: *Student places left hand and fingers in playing position. Violin in rest position.*

1. Student holds violin in rest position, without the bow.

2. Student brings left hand up to neck of violin. The thumb touches the neck of the violin at the base of the first joint, behind the first tape. The first finger touches the opposite side of the neck of the violin at the base of its second joint.

3. Student curves the other fingers over the fingerboard.

4. Student brings down three fingers one by one on the A string tapes, keeping all of them down.

5. Student then raises violin to playing position with the right hand.

EXERCISE: *Student places left hand and fingers in playing position. Violin in playing position.*

1. Student places violin in playing position, holding the left hand down at the side.

2. Student brings left hand up to violin neck. The thumb touches the neck at the base of the first joint, behind the first tape. The first finger touches the opposite side of the neck at the base of its second joint.

3. Student curves the fingers over the fingerboard.

4. Student brings the fingers down one by one on the tapes, on the A string, keeping all of them down. The fourth finger is kept over the fingerboard.

5. Student lifts the fingers one by one, keeping them poised in the air over the tapes.

Although Suzuki does not ask the pupil to use the 4th finger at the beginning, he points out that it should be kept over the fingerboard insofar as is possible at this time. This keeps the left hand in better position and draws the elbow under the violin.

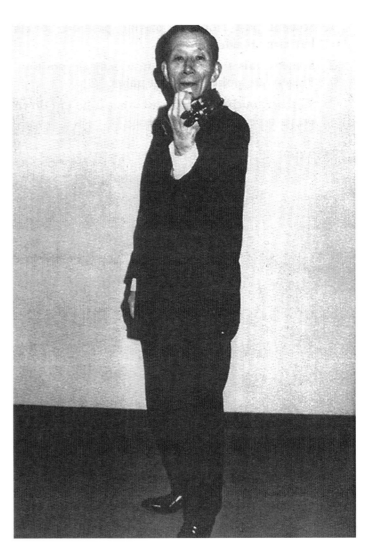

Nose, string, elbow, foot in line.

The teacher or mother should check the hand position after the fingers are put down. Suzuki advises the mothers to see that the thumb is not too high or curved toward the neck, that the hand is not slumped, that the base of the first finger touches the neck lightly, that the fingers are not flat, and that the elbow is under the violin.

Suzuki likes and uses simple formulae that he can repeat again and again to impress young students. He often uses these words to sum up the correct position for the violin and left hand, "Nose, string, elbow, foot . . . in a line together. Nose, string, elbow, foot."

Some teachers ask students to form a "house" with the curved fingers placed on the fingerboard. Collapsed fingers ruined the house, the students were told.

Suzuki tells students whose fingers are too high or not poised above the tapes that their fingers are asleep. The students are also reminded not to clutch the violin tightly, not to "hurt" the violin. Suzuki's teachers are aware that a firm grip of the violin at the chin may be accompanied by an equally firm grip by the left hand.

EXERCISE: *Placement of individual fingers.*

1. Student puts violin in playing position, lowers left arm to side.
2. Student raises left hand into playing position. Fingers are poised over the tapes.
3. Teacher touches a finger, asks that it be put down on its tape on a specific string.

4. Teacher asks that the finger be raised and kept in position over the tape.
5. Teacher continues with other fingers in same manner.
6. After child is ready, teacher continues to call out finger action, but does not touch fingers.

Although rapid and strong finger action is the goal from the beginning, it does take the small child a long time before this control comes. The building of finger strength and rapid finger action is a gradual thing. The hand is never allowed to slump to assist the child's fingers to be brought down with strength. In the early stages, the teachers are chiefly concerned with the correct hand position. Later the child will be asked to move the fingers more quickly and bring them down with more strength. When Suzuki demonstrates for children, his finger action is quick and percussive.

In discussing the beginner's use of his fingers, Suzuki mentions the importance of preparation. The student should keep his fingers prepared for use. To call attention to the period of preparation, Suzuki writes a rest between each fingering at the beginning of Book I.

Suzuki stresses that the fingering and bowing exercises should be done separately until the child feels at ease with them. "Children like what they can do", Suzuki reminds his mothers, pointing out that the child may be unhappy being asked to do too many things at once too early. He sets no time table for this. "The teacher must watch to see how free the child is", is a familiar expression of his regarding speed of technical advancement.

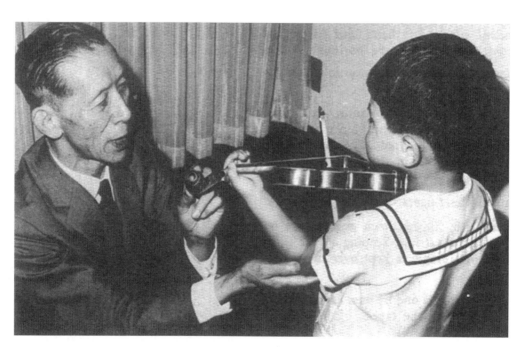

Suzuki moves elbow under violin.

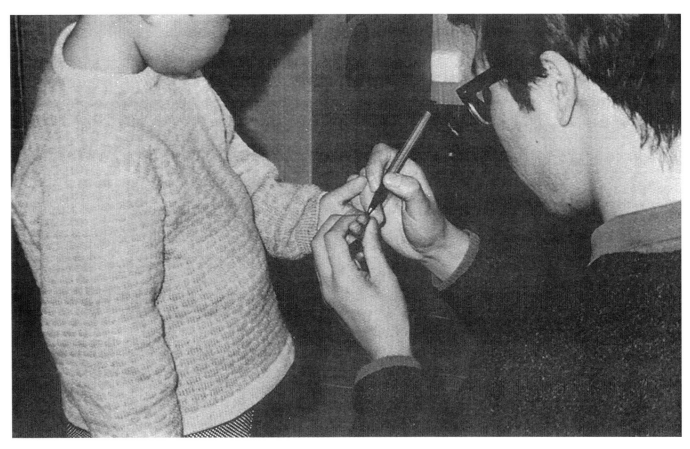

Denda marks point at which finger should touch neck of violin.

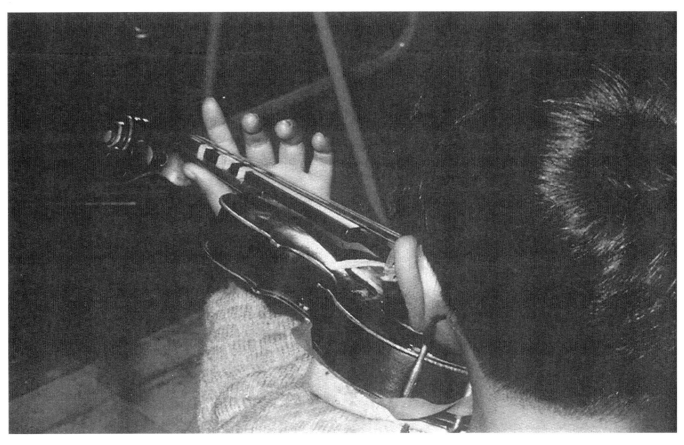

Beginner bringing fingers over fingerboard.

79

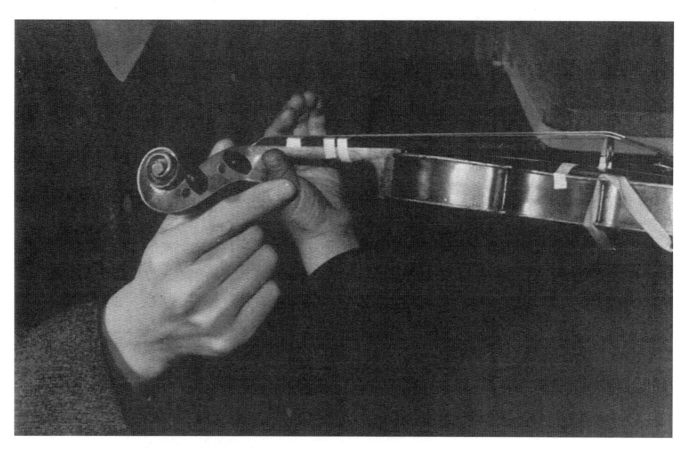

The thumb should touch the neck at the base of the first joint.

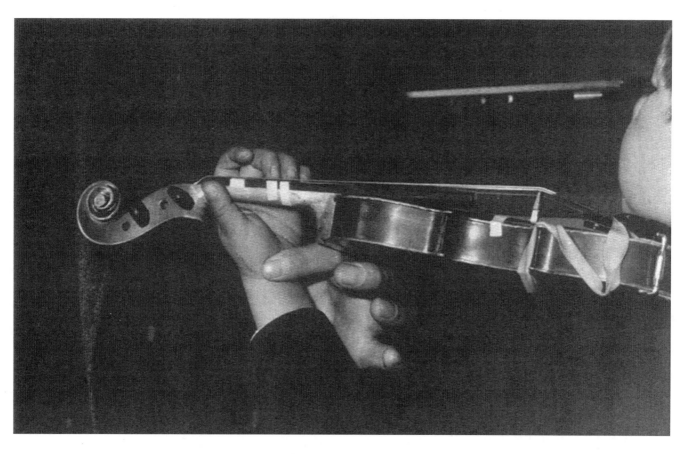

The wrist should not collapse inward.

Please keep 4th finger over the fingerboard.

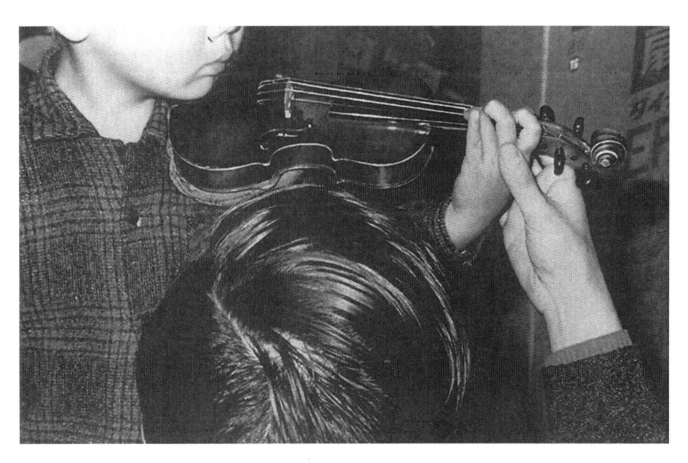

Fingers should be slightly separate.

81

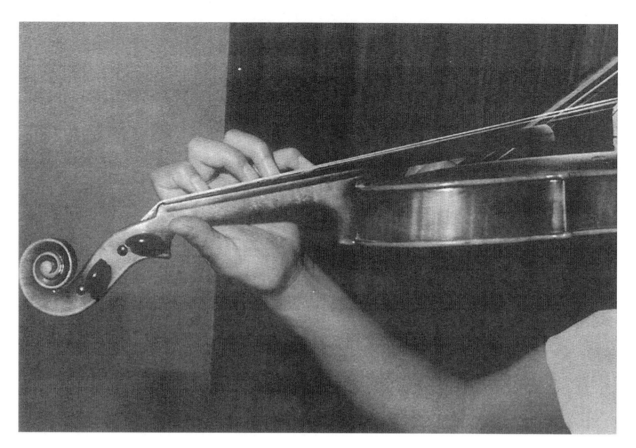

Left hand. Member of Japanese tour group.

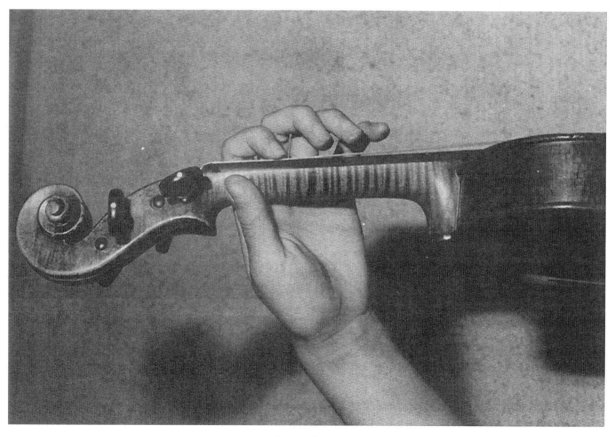

Left hand. Member of Japanese tour group.

Bowing and Fingering Together

The first exercise for bow and fingers together utilizes the rhythm of the first variation of Twinkle.

EXERCISE: *Bowing and fingering, first finger on E*

1. Assume E string posture, with bow on the string at lower tape. Left hand in playing position, fingers poised over tapes.

2. Play rhythm on open E. Stop.

3. Put first finger down on E string. Teacher checks hand position.

4. Play rhythm on 1st finger, sounding the note F#. Stop. Is tone clear? If not, finger may not be on string with enough weight.

5. Lift 1st finger. Play rhythm on open E.

6. Repeat 3, 4, 5 again and again. Much later the stops between may be omitted.

EXERCISE: *Bowing on A string, using three fingers*

1. Assume E string posture. Left hand in playing position.

2. Raise bow hand and forearm to A string level.

3. Play two short, separated bow strokes on open A. Stop.

4. Put first finger down firmly. Play two short, separated bow strokes with the first finger down. The note B sounds. Stop. Is the tone clear?

5. Keep 1st finger down, put 2nd finger down. Play as above. The note C# sounds.

6. Put 3rd finger down, keeping 1st and 2nd down.

7. Play two strokes as above. The note D sounds.

8. Lift 3rd finger. Play as above.

9. Lift 2nd finger. Play as above.

10. Lift 1st finger. Play as above. Were all the tones as clear as the open A?

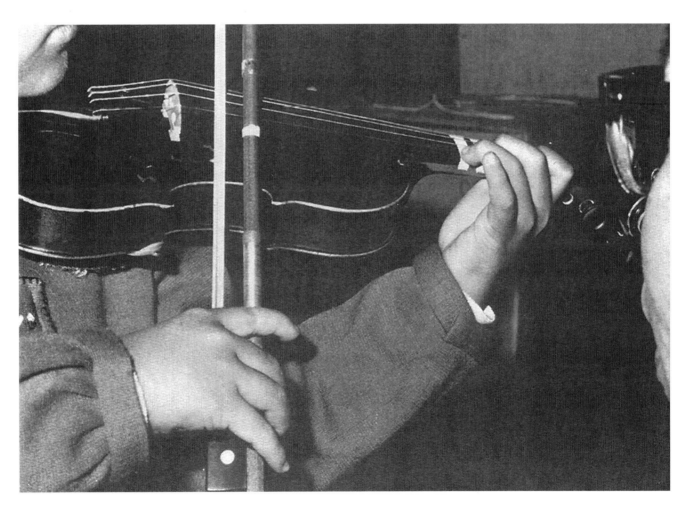

First use of both hands together.

EXERCISE: *Bowing and fingering the A Major Scale. A and E strings. Var. A rhythm.*

1. Assume E string posture, with the bow on the string at the lower tape. Move bow hand and forearm to A string level.

2. Play rhythm on open A. Stop. Fingers should be poised over fingerboard.

3. Bring all three fingers down one by one, playing the rhythm on each finger, and stopping between each rhythm for finger preparation.

4. Lift all three fingers together. Move bow to E level. Play rhythm on open E. Stop.

5. Bring all three fingers down one by one, playing the rhythm on each finger, and stopping between each rhythm for finger preparation.

6. Lift all three fingers one by one, playing the rhythm after each is lifted and stopping between each rhythm. Keep the lifted fingers poised over the fingerboard.

7. Move hand and forearm to A string level.

8. Put down 1st, 2nd, and 3rd fingers on A tapes. Play rhythm on 3rd. Stop.

9. Lift all three fingers one by one, playing the rhythm after each is lifted. Keep the lifted fingers over the fingerboard.

EXERCISE: *Preparatory fingering for Twinkle, on A string. Var. A rhythm.*

1. Assume E string posture. Move bow to A string level.

2. Put down all three fingers quickly, one by one.

3. Play rhythm. Stop.

4. Lift all fingers one by one, playing the rhythm after each is lifted.

5. Repeat steps 2, 3, 4 above.

Although the goal is to put the fingers down and lift them quickly, this is an ideal not easily achieved for some time. The teacher is often satisfied if the beginner does not raise the fingers too high and does keep them well over the fingerboard. The practice of stopping before putting a finger down or lifting one should be well ingrained into the student and continued as he progresses.

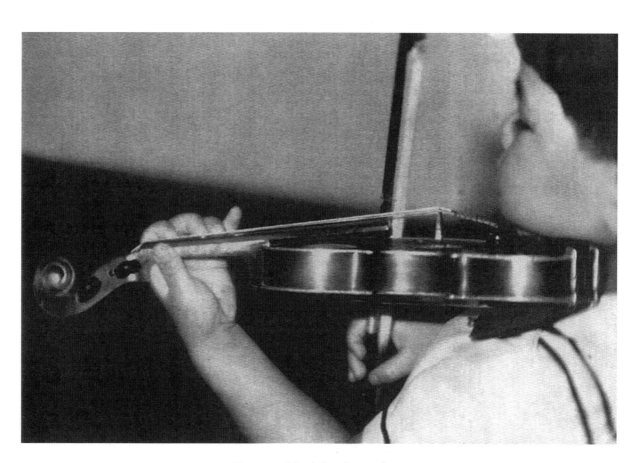

First use of both hands together.

Twinkle Variation A

Since so much time has been spent in preparation for this variation, the transition to practicing this variation is an easy one. There are many points for the teacher to check, however, because as the activity of playing becomes more complex the beginner is apt to forget many details he did well separately. The teacher must have a constant check-off list for his inspection: 1) bow hold 2) bow placement 3) direction of bow strokes 4) bow lengths 5) violin hold at chin 6) left hand position 7) tone volume and quality.

At the beginning the entire variation is played through with stops after every rhythm for the preparation of the fingers and the string level changes. Suzuki asks that the student be given plenty of time for finger and bow preparation at the points where the melody moves down to the note D, played by the 3rd finger on the A string. (The preceding exercise dealt with this fingering problem.) Suzuki wants the fingers to be brought down on the A string separately 1, 2, 3 again and again many times for three reasons: first, the student needs much practice bringing the fingers down correctly on the tapes; second, the first and second finger placement strengthens and guides the third finger which may be the weakest; third, using all the fingers induces a correct position in the left hand. Suzuki admits that the 1, 2, 3 action is not necessary after the child has acquired good control of this fingering pattern. More advanced students playing Twinkle put down only the 3rd finger for the note D, then the 2nd, and then 1st separately. If this independent fingering is done too early, the intonation and hand position may suffer. However, if enough independent finger action has been practiced without the bow previous to this point, the student may be playing that way very soon.

At no time does Suzuki recommend to beginners 'block' or group fingering where all three fingers are put down at the same time. This does become necessary with chords and double stops later on, but is not a goal at this point. Even when the student is putting all three fingers down in Twinkle, he is putting them down rapidly one after another, not simultaneously.

EXERCISE: *Playing Variation A with independent finger action on A string.*

1. Play first four notes of Twinkle with stops.

2. Put 3rd finger down on A, alone. Move bow to A. Play rhythm. Stop.

3. As 3rd finger is lifted, put down 2nd on A. Play rhythm. Stop.

4. As 2nd finger is lifted, put down 1st on A. Play rhythm.

5. Continue Twinkle, using above procedure for each passage where melody moves down from open E to the note D, played by the 3rd finger on the A string.

As the student progresses in his ability to bow and finger correctly, the stops used in this variation become shorter in duration and eventually disappear, although the pause before each appearance of D (3rd on A) remains long after the other pauses are no longer necessary.

Suzuki guides bowing of Variation A.

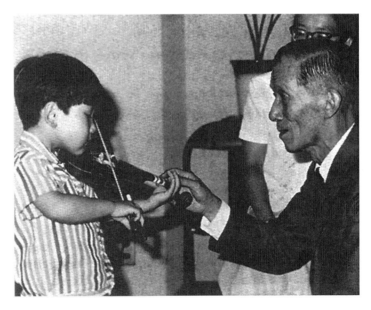

Suzuki assists with proper fingering.

Variation B

As the student is learning Variation A, he begins his study of Variation B. The teacher does not wait until the child can play Variation A without error before this variation is introduced.

Long before the student begins to play this variation, he has already practiced its rhythm, with the handshake exercise, and by moving the bow through the air to this rhythm. Suzuki also asks the students to clap the rhythm before they start to play it. He states that all of the rhythms found in the Twinkle Variations should be practiced at first on the open A and E strings only. His demonstrations show that the teacher should guide the bow to introduce the rhythms to the student, as was done with the very first bow strokes on the open E string. The mother can also follow this procedure. The teacher, or parent, and the student can alternate playing the rhythms.

Stops for preparation of all finger actions and string crossings cause this variation to have a peculiar syncopated rhythm as the beginner starts work on it. This variation in its entirety is not attempted until the student becomes fairly proficient at playing the rhythm on the open strings.

EXERCISE: *Playing Variation B with stops for finger placement and string crossings. (At the outset, teacher may guide bow)*

1. Put bow on open E at lower tape.
2. Move bow hand and forearm to A level. Play two short, separated bow strokes, open A. Stop for the rest written in the music.
3. Play single short bow stroke on open A. Stop.
4. Change bow to E string level.
5. Play two short separated bow strokes on E. Stop for the rest.
6. Play single short bow stroke on open E. Stop.
7. Put 1st finger down on E.
8. Play two short separated bow strokes on 1st finger, F#. Stop for the rest.
9. Continue in the same manner.

Variation C

The rhythm of this variation can be found in many study books. It bears many repetitions, not only at the beginning, but also as a review exercise, because it is invaluable in developing the student's ability to mix bow strokes of different lengths and speed with freedom. It has been found very helpful if the student has already practiced this rhythm, with the handshake exercise, and by moving the bow through the air to the rhythm.

Suzuki points out that the most frequently encountered mistake made by children first playing this rhythm

is that of using too much bow on the 16th notes. The student often continues to use the same breadth of bow stroke for the faster 16ths as he employed on the 8th notes, causing him to bow awkwardly and fall behind in the tempo.

In order to keep the student from squandering bow on the 16th notes, some teachers apply a third tape midway between the existing tapes, resulting in very small bow strokes for the 16th notes.

EXERCISE: *Teacher guides rhythm on open strings* (three tapes on bow)

1. Place bow on A string at lowest tape. Hold on to the child's elbow with the left hand, and the bow hand with the right.
2. Move bow to upper tape, drawing the bow hand and elbow down together. Stop bow.
3. Draw two short connected strokes (the 16th notes) between upper and middle tapes, keeping the elbow in place, moving only the bow hand. Stop.
4. Move bow to the lower tape, moving both bow hand and elbow up together. Stop.
5. Draw two short connected strokes between lower and middle tapes, moving the bow hand only. Stop bow.
6. Move bow to E string level. Continue as above.

The student and the teacher can now alternate producing this rhythm in this manner. If the strokes are quite small, it may be difficult for the student to acquire the proper elbow motion at this time. This may be more effectively taught later as the bow strokes for the 8th notes are lengthened.

After a certain proficiency has been attained by the student playing alone, the preceding exercise may be repeated with the following exception: the stop after the pair of 16th notes should be eliminated. This results in three notes, the two 16ths and the following 8th, being played without pause. The 8th notes are always played staccato at this stage.

When the student begins to play the variation through, he should continue to make a noticeable pause to prepare each finger placement, and each change of string level.

Suzuki says that this is the most difficult of all the variations and should be practiced with care. Some teachers teach this variation after Variation D. When the more advanced student reviews this variation, he is asked to elongate the bow strokes for the 8th notes. Much later the variation may be played in a legato fashion, with flexibility in the wrist and in the fingers. Suzuki demonstrates for the beginners with this flexibility, but never requests it of them. Many of the advanced students develop a rather flexible finger and wrist action naturally through many careful repetitions of these variations.

Variation D

It is important that this variation be played with short bow strokes from the beginning.

Suzuki, noting that it is quite difficult for the child to count "one-two-three-four-five-six-seven-eight" rapidly as he bows eight notes on each pitch, asks the student to think of these notes as two groups of four each. "One-ta-ta-ta, Two-ta-ta-ta", Suzuki says to the beginner, allowing the child to stop between each group of four notes until he feels them as a unit.

Again, as in the other variations with 16th notes, no wrist or finger action is taught at this time, although Suzuki and the teachers demonstrating are quite flexible in the fingers and wrist. Many of the more advanced students, playing these rapid bow strokes, do naturally adopt a flexible wrist and finger action. It should never be exaggerated, however, to the extent that the child's bow hold becomes loose with corresponding loss of control.

Suzuki is often heard to ask advanced students, playing this variation, to play with "small bows, strong tone, but relaxed". These three directives are difficult to do simultaneously, but they provide a fine guide for the acquisition of a flexible wrist and finger action. Suzuki feels that all of the variations can be repeated profitably many, many times by more advanced students for the development of their bow arms.

Twinkle Melody

At the outset, the bow strokes for the Twinkle melody are short, remaining within the original two tapes put on for the first variation. The same length of bow is used for both the quarter and half notes, the bow merely being stopped for the second beat of the half note. Suzuki advises, however, that longer bow strokes be introduced gradually as the child's ability grows. As slightly longer bow strokes are introduced, another tape is frequently put on the bow, about two inches above the upper tape. Solid bands of tapes are used by some teachers, with different colors for the two halves of the bow stroke. Teachers using these bands of tape for beginners state that the bands are somewhat easier for the child's eyes to follow than thin strips placed at intervals.

The melody is played, as were the variations, with Suzuki's special stroke, "legato with stops". By this phrase Suzuki means that the tone of each stroke should be free, the ending of the stroke not crushed. The separation between notes is for preparation. "It is much better", says Suzuki, "to play a short controlled bow stroke and stop to put a finger down or change the bow level with care, than to draw a long slow bow and proceed to the next note without any preparation." Suzuki has found that children can control short bow strokes at the beginning better than they can long ones. "Even so", Suzuki reminds his teachers, "the teacher should be ready to introduce longer strokes as the child becomes freer with his bow strokes".

If a third tape has been added to elongate the bow strokes, it is best if the teacher guides the bow strokes at the beginning, moving both the student's bow hand and elbow the same distance. The tempo should not be too rapid at first as the student acquires the feel of the longer bow stroke.

As the student progresses further, a tape may be placed about two inches below the lower tape in order to introduce the lower part of the bow. Again the teacher should guide the student's bow hand and elbow, moving them up and down together. Suzuki keeps the elbow slightly lower than the hand. He does not advocate a high elbow even though he does want the elbow raised on up-bow strokes in the lower half of the bow. Later, on the down-bow strokes from the frog, Suzuki moves the elbow down with the hand at the outset of the stroke. Many times he says, "The whole arm plays the violin".

Students who are well into Book I, still using short bow strokes as they learn new selections, are frequently asked to review the Twinkle melody, using as much as half of the bow for the quarter notes, with a whole bow for the half notes. The first quarter notes are played in the lower half of the bow, with the elbow moving down and up with the right hand. With the first half note, the bow is carried to the point and the next quarter notes are played in the upper half with most of the motion in the lower arm.

The following open string exercise is given for use at the time deemed appropriate by the teacher. (It has been introduced successfully as early as the child can play the Twinkle melody with short bow strokes. It should be practiced for a long time slowly and deliberately before being applied first to the Twinkle melody and succeeding pieces that lend themselves to the half and whole bow stroke. There are three points to be carefully observed by the teacher: 1) the maintenance of a straight bow stroke, parallel to the bridge, 2) the sustenance of a solid tone with unvarying dynamics, well "into the string", and 3) the proper use of the whole arm, that is, the raising and lowering of the elbow with the elbow kept slightly lower than the hand.

EXERCISE: *Preparation for long bow strokes.*

1. Student puts bow on E on middle tape.
2. Teacher, holding bow hand and elbow, raises both as bow is moved to frog with up-bow stroke.
3. Teacher, still holding bow hand and elbow, draws a down-bow stroke, moving elbow and hand down to the original position.
4. Student draws up-bow to the frog, moving hand and elbow together as the teacher did.
5. Teacher straightens bow if necessary, and raises or lowers elbow if necessary.
6. Student returns bow to middle, lowering elbow as hand moves down.
7. Continue as above on the A string.

The above procedure may be used for the upper portion of the bow, with much less involvement of the elbow. In working with the upper part of the bow, the teacher should be careful to indicate just how near the point the student should draw the bow at this time. If the student's arm is not long enough and he is trying to draw the bow all the way to the point, the bow will tend to slip off toward the fingerboard and the bow hand may slip out of position.

Suzuki observes correct placement of bow at the tip.

Suzuki raises elbow with hand as bow moves.

Hirose aids bow movement to frog.

Suzuki continues hand and elbow motion to the frog.

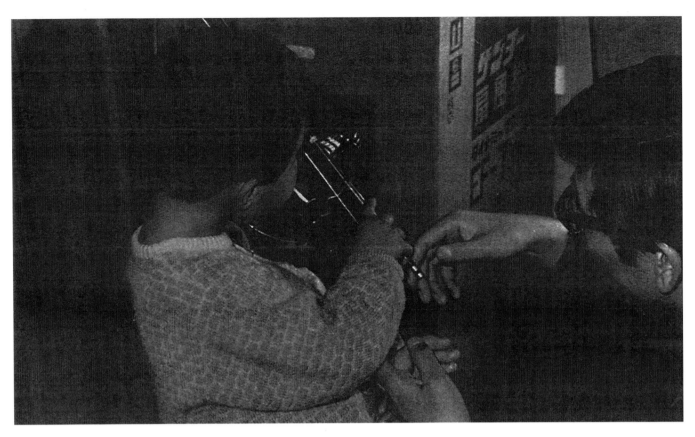

Denda moves elbow and hand up to frog.

Denda aids bow motion to frog.

Student places bow in middle.

Student moves to frog.

90

Member of Japanese tour group. Middle to frog bow motion.

Bow at frog. Note hand, wrist and elbow relationships.

Japanese tour group. Full bow strokes. At tip . . . . . .

. . . . . at frog.

Tour performer. Bow at frog. A string.

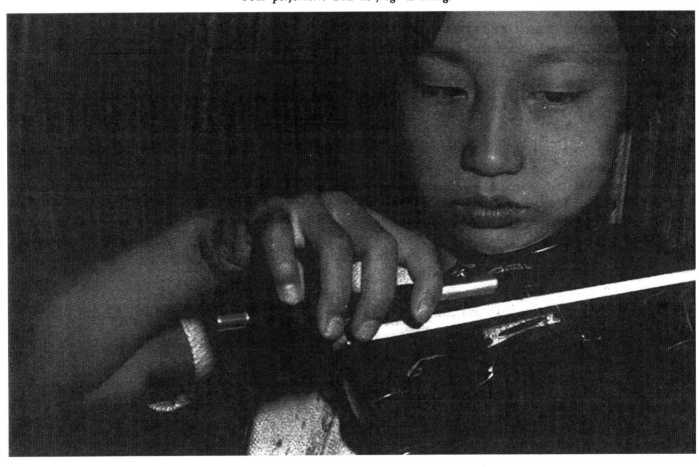

Tour performer. Bow at frog. D string.

93

Lightly Row

For this piece, the student is asked to use the same length and same character of bow strokes as used for the Twinkle melody. Stops are made for fingering and changes of string. If he has listened to the recording many times before attempting to play this piece, the student will most likely be delighted to see how quickly he can learn to play it.

Lightly Row is introduced as the child is still trying to improve his playing of the Twinkle melody and variations. In fact, Suzuki most often continues the study of the Twinkle variations up through Perpetual Motion. At lessons, sometimes only the first variation of Twinkle is heard by the teacher to see how the student has progressed in regard to good tone, correct posture, and correct bow movement.

Suzuki likes to use the rhythm of the first variation of Twinkle as the child is introduced to new finger patterns.

EXERCISE: *Finger practice* (1st and 2nd measures)

1. Play 1st variation rhythm on open E.
2. Put 1st and 2nd fingers down on A. Move bow to A. Play rhythm.
3. Put 3rd finger down. Play rhythm.
4. Lift 3rd and 2nd fingers. Play rhythm.

EXERCISE: *Finger practice, more advanced*
(1st and 2nd measures)

1. Play 1st variation rhythm on open E.
2. Put 2nd finger on A. Move bow to A. Play rhythm.
3. Put 3rd on A. Lift 2nd. Play rhythm.
4. Lift 3rd. Put 1st on A. Play rhythm.

EXERCISE: *Change of string levels* (1st measure)

1. Put bow on E at middle tape. Play short stroke on open E.
2. Raise bow hand to A string level. Play open A, short up-bow stroke.
3. Draw short down-bow, open A. A string tones should have same volume as that of E string.

EXERCISE: *Finger practice* (7th and 8th measures)

1. Play rhythm on open A.
2. Put 2nd finger down on A. Play rhythm.
3. Lift finger. Move bow to E. Play rhythm.
4. Put 2nd on A. Move bow to A. Play rhythm.

When this piece is first played, it is played staccato for preparation of fingering and string crossings. Later, it can be performed legato with small bows and, much later, legato with half and full bows for the quarter and half notes respectively. Advanced students may be requested to play with diminuendos on the half notes at the ends of each of the four-measure phrases. Suzuki likes to see the diminuendos effected by the slowing of the bow on the half notes.

More advanced students at the proper age level can be given instruction in musical structure as they review the pieces of Book I. The phrase should be pointed out as a unit of music that is most often four or eight measures in length and is terminated frequently by less motion in the music, an effect that is called a cadence. Lightly Row consists of four phrases, each four measures in length. They can be diagrammed A A' B A'. Recognition of musical structure often helps students in memorization, and is helpful to them should they want to compose their own pieces.

Song of the Wind

This piece is played by the beginner with the same length and character of bow stroke as that used for the 8th notes in the Twinkle Variations.

The first difficult problem involves the use of the third finger on the A and E strings consecutively in the third measure. The child is not asked to cover the two strings with the same finger. This is the only new finger pattern. All others have already been encountered in the two previous selections.

EXERCISE: *Finger practice* (3rd measure)

1. Put 1st finger on E. Play rhythm.
2. Keep 1st down. Put 3rd on A. Move bow to A. Play rhythm.
3. Lift 3rd, put 3rd on E string. Move bow to E. Play rhythm.
4. Lift 3rd. Play rhythm.

The next problem Suzuki focuses on is that of the repeated down bows in the fourth and fifth measures. He tells the mother that the hand, bow, and elbow should all move in a small round motion as the bow is lifted a few inches off the string and then placed back on the string at the lower tape. Suzuki states that this bowing problem is main problem of this piece. At first the beginner is given plenty of time to replace the bow correctly, then he is asked to do it more quickly, but always with a round motion as the bow is lifted off the string. The student should retain a good grasp of the bow. The bow is not to be moved horizontally up the string, but should be always moved with a round motion and replaced carefully on the string.

EXERCISE: *Repeated down-bow strokes* (4th and 5th, 6th and 7th, 10th and 11th measures)

1. Put bow on E at lower tape.
2. Draw bow to upper tape. Stop.
3. Lift bow in round motion to reset carefully on string at lower tape
4. Repeat.

Song of the Wind is always played staccato with short bows. As the student progresses in his ability, he may play this piece at a more lively tempo, which does make the repeated down bows much more difficult.

Go Tell Aunt Rhody

Suzuki chose this piece to contrast with the preceding one. Song of the Wind calls for a more sprightly tempo. This piece, played a little slower, can be played with longer bow strokes. Suzuki demonstrates with a bow stroke for the quarter notes almost twice as long as the stroke used in Song of the Wind. Eventually this piece is to be played legato but at the beginning Suzuki wants a slight space between the notes for preparation. He asks for a slow bow on the half notes closing the phrases.

The bow strokes for the 8th notes are not big or rapid, but well-controlled. The small strokes should have the same firm tone of the longer strokes.

None of the finger patterns in this piece are new. They are all found in the earlier pieces.

Some teachers introduce this piece with the same bow strokes as those used by the student for the Twinkle melody. After the student can play through the piece well, he can repeat it with the 8th notes legato, and all the quarter notes staccato. From this, he can then graduate to all legato articulations. Much later, the piece can be used for training in drawing full and half bow strokes.

The musical form is rather simple, three phrases of four measures each, diagrammed A B A.

Advanced students enjoy playing these pieces with dynamic contrasts. This selection could be played in this manner: first phase forte (loud) with a diminuendo on the last note, second phrase piano (soft), and third phrase forte with a diminuendo and ritardando (gradually slowing) at the end.

O Come Little Children

For the first study of this piece, Suzuki demonstrates small bows comparable to those used for the Twinkle melody, and detaches each note slightly. All of the phrases are started up bow. Very small bows are used for the last note of each phrase so that each phrase is played in the same part of the bow. The beginners start the bow strokes with the bow placed on the middle tape. Stops of sufficient duration should be made for preparation of finger placement and change of string level.

EXERCISE: *Fingering* (3rd line, four measures)

1. Put 1st finger down on A, Play rhythm.
2. Put 3rd on A, lifting 1st. Play rhythm.
3. Lift 3rd, putting 2nd down on A. Play rhythm.
4. Put 1st on E. Lift 2nd. Move bow to E. Play rhythm.

EXERCISE: *Fingering* (4th line, 1st and 2nd measures)

1. Place bow on E. Play rhythm.

2. Put 3rd down on E. Play rhythm.
3. Lift 3rd. Play rhythm.

Students who have achieved sufficient freedom of the bow arm gradually use more bow as they play this piece. Eventually the piece is played with full and half bows, legato. Suzuki chose pieces starting with up bows to emphasize the elbow motion. Students playing this piece with full bows start the first note at the middle, going all the way to the frog with the right hand and elbow moving upward together. All of the phrases end near the middle of the bow with a slow stroke on the last quarter note of each phrase.

(If the edition has first and second endings of the first phrase, and a repeat sign, these should be explained to the advanced students.) The selection consists of four four-measure phrases and can be diagrammed as A A B C.

A musical interpretation by advanced students might include diminuendos at the ends of the first and last phrases with a crescendo in the B phrase leading to a climax on the high A in the C phrase. A ritardando may close the piece.

Tonalization

Although this is the first tonalization exercise in Book I, Suzuki in his teaching will have mentioned one in each lesson up to this point.

In this first exercise devoted exclusively to tone, the child is asked to listen to the tone produced by a string as it is plucked. The attention is brought not to the rather sharp sound of the actual pizzicato but to the tone of the freely vibrating string after it is plucked. "This is the true sound of the string," Suzuki says to his students. He then bows on the open A and E strings, using short detached strokes, calling his student's attention to the sound of the string vibrating. He says that the player should hear the same quality of sound as that heard when the string is vibrating freely after the pizzicato. There should be the same resonance as the bow moves, and the player should hear a continuing "echo" after he stops the bow as it rests lightly on the string.

The next exercise involves the use of the same kind of bow stroke with fingering on the A and E strings. The student should listen for the resonance of each tone. "Don't push with the first finger of the right hand," warns Suzuki. "The middle fingers and the thumb are the center of the bow hold. Just put the bow on the string and balance it properly. Arm weight should be used to produce a deep tone that is not forced."

A very young beginner may find this a considerable challenge. Some teachers defer this kind of study until later, since the beginner may be still playing with a rather heavy bow stroke, and still playing staccato, probably with a very definite ending to each note.

May Song

As the student begins to study this piece, he should be introduced to the D string level, which will be used in Long, Long Ago which follows May Song. Suzuki thinks this is best done by asking the student to play Twinkle Variation A on the D and A strings.

In May Song there is the first example of what is called dotted rhythm. In this case, the first quarter note is followed by a dot, which increases the duration of a note by half its value, thus the first note is one and a half beats long. It is followed by an 8th note, which is only a half-beat in duration. It will not be difficult for the student to feel the correct rhythm since by this time he should have heard the song many times on the recording.

Suzuki often caricatures the fault common to many beginners as they begin this piece. He draws a long bow for the first note, followed by an ungainly quick up bow on the short note following. "Not too much bow on the first note," he advises. "Just draw a short bow. Stop the bow before the next note." Suzuki also stops the bow on the half notes ending every second measure. This keeps the bow in approximately the same place for the whole piece.

Even if the beginner has begun to elongate his bow strokes by the time he studies this piece, it is still best for him, as he learns each new piece, to use only short bow strokes similar to those he used in the first variation of Twinkle. He will learn the new piece more quickly and with less effort if his concentration is focused only on new patterns of fingering and string crossing. Longer bow strokes are best introduced with music he can already play.

EXERCISE: *Bowing the first four notes on the open strings.* (Teacher may guide bow first)

1. Place bow on A string on lower of tapes used for the 1st variation of Twinkle.
2. Draw down-bow to next tape. As bow stroke begins, count first beat.
3. Stop the bow on the count of the 2nd beat.
4. On the second half of the 2nd beat, move the bow quickly back to the first tape. Move bow to E string level.
5. On the count of the third beat, draw down-bow again to upper tape. Stop.
6. On the count of the fourth beat, move bow up to lower tape.

EXERCISE: *Fingering* (1st and 2nd measures)

1. Place bow on open A on first tape. Play rhythm.
2. Put 2nd finger down on A. Play rhythm.
3. Lift 2nd. Move bow to E string. Play rhythm.
4. Put 3rd finger down on E. Play rhythm.
5. Lift 3rd. Put 1st finger down on E. Play rhythm.
6. Keep 1st down. Put down 3rd on E. Play rhythm.
7. Lift 3rd. Play rhythm.

EXERCISE: *Fingering* (3rd measure)

1. Place 3rd finger on A. Play rhythm.
2. Lift 3rd finger. Move bow to E string. Play rhythm.
3. Place 2nd on A. Move bow to A. Play rhythm.

Later, when the student reviews this piece, he may be asked to play it legato. However, the bow is always stopped or slowed to a stop on the dot of the quarter note with the weight released at this point. It is common to see May Song played by more advanced students with rather short bow strokes for the 1st and 3rd measures, and contrasting long lighter strokes for the middle phrase.

May Song is in three four-measure phrases, A B A. Youngsters enjoy playing this along with Twinkle as a duet.

Long, Long Ago

The beginner should practice this piece with short bow strokes, separated as in the earlier selections. Gradually, after the piece has been learned, the bow strokes are lengthened and the separation between strokes grows smaller and eventually disappears as the student plays the piece legato. At the beginning, Suzuki asks that not too much bow be used on the 8th notes.

Long, Long Ago, Go Tell Aunt Rhody, and the Twinkle melody are later used to develop the child's facility with longer bow strokes.

This is the first time the D string is needed and careful preparation is given to the change of string level and the placement of the first finger on the D string.

EXERCISE: *Fingering and bowing on A and D* (9th and 10th measures)

1. Put 1st finger on A. Play rhythm.
2. Lift 1st, and replace 1st on D string.
3. Move bow to D string. Play rhythm.
4. Leave 1st on D. Put 3rd on A, then lift 1st.
5. Move bow to A string. Play rhythm.

Again and again Suzuki reminds his teachers to check to see that the volume is the same as the student moves the bow from one string level to another.

The form of Long, Long Ago is A A[1] B A[1], four phrases of four measures each.

For an expressive performance, advanced students can play legato with long bow strokes on the quarter notes, slowing the bow speed on the half notes to create a good diminuendo. The B phrase, which starts on the third line, may be played forte for the first two-measure motive, then piano with an echo effect on the next two measures. A ritardando in the next to last measure adds to the musical effect.

Allegro

"Many years ago when I started teaching small children," said Suzuki, "I used a short Japanese children's song that was a very good exercise for quick movement with the bow arm. I wanted a longer, faster stroke than the beginners were accustomed to play. The song was only seven notes long, with only two different pitches on the E string: A A E E AE E. After six months of study with this same children's song, the small children I was working with protested, 'Isn't that enough, sensei?', so I then wrote this piece to provide them with variety. I had them working on it for so long because I wanted them to be able to move the elbow up and down with the bow hand, to play with 'whole arm' motion."

The beginner usually starts his study of Allegro with small strokes with stops after all of the notes. Later the 8th notes are played legato. If the student has been practicing the exercise given under the Twinkle melody and entitled, *Preparation for long bow strokes,* he should be able to start work on a quick motion with the bow hand and elbow moving together. The bow should be placed on the E string below the middle for the first stroke. It is important that the elbow and hand go down together at the very beginning of this stroke. Suzuki asks more advanced students to use more and more bow, with a quick motion. The stroke he demonstrates for them is lighter than previous slower bow strokes.

As Suzuki begins to place more stress on the elbow motion, he mentions an exercise with the rhythm of the first variation of Twinkle. It is played in the middle on the E string, but, on the last note of the rhythmic figure the child is to raise the bow hand quickly up over the violin on the G string side. "The elbow must move because you cannot reach that far without the whole arm moving," exclaims Suzuki. This elbow activity seems to be very difficult for many students to learn, particularly at the early stages. It is a very common occurrence to see Suzuki working diligently on this problem with advanced students.

The advanced students are also asked to play the middle section almost legato with sweeping bow strokes.

Many small children have difficulty lifting quickly two fingers at once. There are two melodic figures in Allegro that present this problem. It has been found effective to teach them to lift one finger as the other is put down. "When I press the button (put a finger down), the other finger pops up!" exclaimed one five-year-old who was being taught in this manner. The following exercises are based on this principle.

EXERCISE: *Fingering* (2nd measure)

1. Put 1st finger on E. Play rhythm.
2. Put 2nd on E. Keep 1st down. Play rhythm.
3. Put 3rd on E. Lift 2nd at same time. Play rhythm.
4. Lift 3rd. Play rhythm.

EXERCISE: *Fingering* (4th measure)

1. Put 1st finger on A. Play rhythm.
2. Put 2nd down on A, lifting 1st at same time. Play rhythm.
3. Lift 2nd. Play rhythm.

This piece consists of four phrases of four measures each. The form is A A B A. The word "dolce" at the beginning of the third line means "sweetly." "Rit." at the end of the third line is an abbreviation for ritardando. At the end of that measure is a "hold" or "fermata," indicating a pause in the rhythmic flow.

Perpetual Motion

This piece, along with the Twinkle variations, is played many, many times by the students of Talent Education. Much technical ability is developed through countless repetitions of Perpetual Motion. If this piece is practiced correctly, observes Suzuki, it will do much toward developing the student's ability to play rapidly.

The student starting to work on this piece is told to practice only one phrase at a time. When he practices slowly, he should use very short strokes, played quickly with a stop between each stroke. Suzuki asks the student to put the finger down between each bow stroke, pointing out that the finger action should

anticipate the bow stroke. Also, fingers that are lifted off of the string should be raised quickly before the next bow stroke.

EXERCISE: *Fingering* (4th line, last 4 notes of 1st measure, 1st note of next measure)

1. Put 1st finger on E. Play rhythm.
2. Put 2nd on E, lifting 1st at same time. Play rhythm.
3. Put 3rd on E, lifting 2nd at same time. Play rhythm.
4. Put 2nd on A, then lift 3rd on E. Move bow to A. Play rhythm.

It should be noted here that by no means all of the child's growth in ability is the result of conscious effort. Suzuki recognizes this in his insistence upon repetition in group lessons. He feels that the children advance a great deal as a result of participation in group lessons. Many learn to play this piece rapidly by trying to play it in group lessons with more advanced players.

The kind of quick and strong finger action Suzuki requests is not easily forthcoming from the beginner. Perpetual Motion is often used as a review piece for advanced students who need to accelerate their finger action. Suzuki suggests ample time for mental preparation for each finger action, followed by a strong rapid motion. The child should not press the finger into the string, but only strike the string with moderate force. Some strike too forcefully, slowing the action. The fingers should be kept well over the fingerboard at all times. The lifting action should be done as quickly as the striking action. Suzuki finds this kind of practice invaluable in developing the finger action. "Ten minutes a day for two months," he was heard advising one student who was having trouble "keeping up" with her group in the Allegro of Fiocco.

The single-note version of Perpetual Motion is always played staccato. Beginners will frequently be found using rather heavy bow strokes, with a definite beginning and ending. Much, much later the stroke, still staccato, may go into the string for each note, and come to rest lightly on the string at the end of each note as the weight is released.

The double-note version of Perpetual Motion is not attempted until the student knows the fingering. In order to demonstrate the proper bowing, Suzuki often shakes his right hand and arm in the air as though he were bouncing a ball on the ground. He moves the elbow slightly with the forearm, with the hand traveling somewhat farther back and forth. "If you can move this way and relax at the wrist, you can play this piece with double notes," Suzuki encourages the child. He feels that the student should feel the two repeated notes as one motion, a rapid "down-up," and suggests that the piece be practiced with stops after each pair of repeated notes. He also wants the fingers to move during the pause between bow strokes.

Even though Suzuki asks for a relaxed wrist, most beginners play with the entire forearm with no sign of finger or wrist flexibility. Suzuki is not alarmed by this. He knows from experience that, after hundreds of repetitions of the double-note Perpetual Motion and Variation D of Twinkle, most of the students will acquire a natural flexibility as they become freer in their bowing. This rapid double-note version of Perpetual Motion is not played with long bow strokes by the advanced students. Rather, Suzuki is often heard to ask them to play it (as he does with Variation D of Twinkle) with short bows, strong tone, but relaxed. These three directives are difficult to do simultaneously, but they provide a fine guide for the development of the bow arm for rapid short strokes.

Advanced students will profit by playing the double-note version of Perpetual Motion and Variation D of Twinkle rapidly at the tip of the bow for practice in keeping the bow straight and the tone strong. This is a very common orchestral bowing.

Perpetual Motion is in four phrases of four measures each, A B C A. An interesting aspect of its form is that each four-measure phrase, except that of C, consists of two two-measure units alike except for their endings. Dynamic contrasts, forte and piano, between these two-measure units make for an effective musical performance.

Exercises for the 4th Finger

Up to this point, the only direction given concerning the 4th finger has been for the child to keep the 4th finger over the fingerboard as much as possible as he plays with the other three fingers. Suzuki has one preparatory exercise to be practiced before the child begins to play with the 4th finger. He says that this exaggerated stretching will make the normal stretch of the 4th finger playing one whole-step above the 3rd not so difficult.

EXERCISE: *Stretching the 4th finger*
1. Put the first finger down on the A string. Do not use the bow.
2. Keep the 1st finger down. Stretch to see how far the 4th finger, flattened, can reach on the A string. Move the elbow to the right as the finger is stretched.
3. Lift 4th finger.
4. Stretch the 4th again. Repeat several times. Do not continue if pain is felt is felt in the hand.

Although Suzuki's first exercise with the 4th finger involves the student's comparison of the pitch of the open E with the pitch of the E produced by his 4th finger, teachers may put a new tape on the fingerboard as a visual guide for the placement of the 4th finger. These exercises on the A and E strings should be played with a slight pause between each bow stroke, so that the student can prepare for the next note and can listen for the resonance of the vibrating string.

Tonalization on the D and A Strings

The tonalization exercises here consist of two common arpeggios (horizontalized chords) from the key of D Major. The student is to use the longest bow strokes he has been drawing, and eventually to use the whole bow, tip to frog. He should strive for the best tone he can get, full but not forced. Each bow stroke should have a uniform dynamic level. Suzuki considers intonation of paramount importance here. "Be sure to find the 'sound-point' of each pitch," he urges. He has found that even small children can become very sensitive to the sympathetic vibrations of the open strings as they finger and bow the notes that are an octave higher. "Not more than two seconds for each full bow," Suzuki says. "Please don't push on the bow stick with the first finger. Always put the bow carefully on the string before starting the first bow stroke."

The tonalization exercises are followed by the D Major scale which is to be played in the same manner. These short exercises make excellent review material for the more advanced student who is capable of producing a better tone and can give more attention to correct intonation.

Often in America the request "play into the string" is heard as teachers ask for a good clear tone. Suzuki's way of putting it is similar. He asks the students to "put the bow on the string" or "touch the string." He wants contact to be maintained with the string as the bow is drawn. If it slides along the surface of the string, he calls the undesirable result a "slip tone." He also avoids the opposite extreme, saying "don't crush the tone, don't push with the first finger." He wants the bow to be kept on the string by application of weight of the hand, arm, and elbow.

Perpetual Motion on the D String

As the student moves to the D string level for the next few pieces, Suzuki is concerned that the student does not raise his elbow too high as he starts on the D string. He asks the student to assume the A string posture, then raise his bow hand until the bow rests on the D string. Particular attention must be paid to the intonation the child plays on the D.

At the same time this piece is played on the D string, the student should be introduced to the G string level, which will be used in Allegretto which follows. The student should play Variation A of Twinkle on the G and D strings. Care must be taken that the elbow does not move too high.

Allegretto

Allegretto has the same rhythm and is played with the same kinds of bow strokes as Twinkle Variation C. Suzuki asks the student to review Variation C before starting work on this piece so that he will know what kind of bow strokes should be used. At the very beginning, as the fingering and string crossings are learned, all of the notes should be played staccato.

Later all of the eighth notes are played legato. Allegretto is always performed with small bows, although some teachers have used it, played in a much slower tempo, as an exercise for full and half bows.

There are dots below all of the eighth notes in the music, in addition to accents and dots below almost all of the quarter notes. Suzuki, in his performances of Allegretto, does not separate the eighth notes, makes only a very slight accent on the quarter notes, but separates them from the next pair of eighths. He asks for a small round motion with the right hand and elbow as the repeated down bows occur. A strong, heavy tone is avoided throughout.

If the student can reach the correct pitch with the 4th finger on the D string where that finger is indicated in brackets, he will find the string crossings much easier than if he uses the open A string. The exercises below cover both fingerings.

EXERCISE: *Fingering and bowing*, with open A string (1st measure)

1. Set bow on middle tape, A string.
2. Raise forearm until bow rests on D string.
3. Put 2nd finger on D Play short down-bow stroke. Stop.
4. Keep 2nd down. Play short up-bow. Lift 2nd.
5. Lower bow hand to A level. Play short down-bow on open A.
6. Put 3rd on D. Raise bow hand to D level. Play short up-bow.
7. Keep 3rd down. Play short down-bow.
8. Put 1st on A. Lift 3rd. Lower bow to A level. Play short up-bow.

EXERCISE: *Fingering*, with 4th finger on D (1st measure)

1. Put 2nd finger on D. Play rhythm.
2. Keep 2nd down, put 4th down on D. Play rhythm.
3. Lift 4th, put 3rd down. Play rhythm.

EXERCISE: *Fingering* (8th and 9th measures)

1. Set bow on D, middle tape. Play rhythm.
2. Put 2nd down. Play rhythm.
3. Lift 2nd, put 1st down. Play rhythm.
4. Lift 1st, move 1st to G string, put down.
5. Move bow to G string. Play rhythm.
6. Lift 1st, move 1st to D string, put down.
7. Move bow to D string. Play rhythm.

This piece is another example of four four-measure phrases, A A¹ B A¹. It starts on the 4th beat, so the last measure has only three beats. This is the second use of a fermata, indicating a pause in the rhythmic flow.

In line with the principle of giving the student a preview of new problems, it is a good idea for the teacher to introduce to the student, as he starts Allegretto, the low 2nd finger pattern found in the G Major scale. When he has completed Allegretto and Andantino, he should be able to progress fairly quickly to Etude.

Andantino

Both this and the preceding piece by Suzuki are great favorites of the Japanese children, perhaps because of the humorous rhythmic pauses which they must remember in performance. Suzuki laughs when the little children forget the fermatas and keep on playing.

This piece opens with the same kind of bow strokes as those used in Allegretto. Suzuki warns the students not to use long bows on the half notes at the ends of the phrases. "Short, slow bow. Stay in the same part of the bow for the next phrase," he advises. At the beginning all of the notes should be played staccato. Later all of the eighth notes are legato. Depending on the freedom acquired by the child at this point, Suzuki asks for quick, longer bow strokes in the middle section. Here the elbow is moved noticeably with each stroke.

Andantino consists of four four-measure phrases, A A¹ B A¹. Advanced students always perform the A phrases with small bows, with very long bows used for the B phrase.

EXERCISE: *Fingering* (7th and 8th measures)

1. Put 1st finger on A. Play rhythm.
2. Put 2nd on A. Play rhythm.
3. Put 3rd on A, lifting 1st and 2nd. Play rhythm.
4. Lift 3rd, move over to D string, put down on D.
5. Move bow to D string. Play rhythm.
6. Lift 3rd, put down 2nd at same time. Play rhythm.
7. Lift 2nd, put down 1st at same time. Play rhythm.

Tonalization, G Major Scale

Heretofore, the pieces and exercises in Book I have been in the keys of A and D Major and could be played with the same finger patterns. The 2nd and 3rd fingers were always played close together, one half-step apart. Suzuki felt that this pattern should be mastered before another was attempted by the student.

In the key of G Major, the 2nd finger must be moved back and placed close to the 1st, one half-step above it, to produce the new notes, C and G. (The "high" second fingers used in the preceding pieces produced C♯ and G♯ on the A and E strings.) This is the first time "low" 2nd finger is necessary. The G Major scale should be studied before the Tonalization exercise in G Major, since it introduces the "low" 2nd finger in a simpler manner. Practice of this scale is often started while the student is still learning the previous two pieces. Each note of the scale is played with the rhythm of Twinkle Variation A, with stops for finger preparation.

The teacher should watch carefully the placement of both the 2nd and 3rd fingers. Often the student puts the 2nd finger down too close to the 1st, causing a flat pitch. A tape applied in the correct place on the fingerboard under only the A and E strings may be helpful as a visual aid. The 3rd finger has a tendency to be pulled back by the low 2nd finger. It should be kept in the original position.

Suzuki considers G Major the basic key of the violin. It was not introduced at the beginning because of the difficulty of bowing on the lower strings, and the difficulty of playing two different finger patterns at the same time. Once introduced, it is reinforced in selection after selection. Suzuki considers the presentation of many different keys at this level detrimental to the child's developing sense of intonation and his increasing sensitivity to the resonance of tones. He feels that a child later studying a piece in E flat Major will be more likely to play it well in tune if he has been thoroughly grounded in G Major rather than having played material of comparable difficulty in a number of different keys.

"I tell my teachers that it takes a long time for the child to be able to play well in tune, even in this key," Suzuki says. "Sometimes it takes a very small child two years before he can play G Major well in tune."

EXERCISE: *Fingering fragment of G Major scale*

1. Put 1st on E. Play rhythm.
2. Put low 2nd on E. Play rhythm.
3. Lift low 2nd. Play rhythm.
4. Lift 1st. Play rhythm.
5. Put down 1st and then 3rd on A string.
6. Move bow to A. Play rhythm.
7. Lift 3rd, put down low 2nd on A. Play rhythm.
8. Lift low 2nd. Play rhythm.

Practicing the new low second finger pattern.

EXERCISE: *Fingering tonalization*

1. Put 1st on A. Keep down. Put 3rd on D.
2. Put bow on D. Play rhythm.
3. Move bow to A. Lift 3rd. Play rhythm.
4. Keep 1st down. Put 3rd on A. Play rhythm.
5. Lift 3rd. Keep 1st down. Put low 2nd on E.
6. Move bow to E. Play rhythm.
7. Keep 2nd down. Put down 3rd on E. Play rhythm.
8. Lift 3rd. Play rhythm.
9. Put 3rd on A. Keep 1st and 2nd down.
10. Move bow to A. Play rhythm.
11. Lift 3rd and 2nd. Play rhythm.

Although Suzuki does want full bows used eventually for the tonalization exercise, he allows the beginner to use a shorter stroke, and asks him to lengthen the strokes as he becomes freer with his bow arm. "Careful attention should be given to the intonation," he says. "These are very resonant tones if played in tune."

Etude

Etude is played with the same kind of bow stroke as that used for Perpetual Motion. The bow is stopped after each note. The double-note variation is played as was the variation of Perpetual Motion, with very short strokes.

This is the first piece in G Major. Careful attention must be given to the fingering, the second finger being low on the A and E strings, and high on the D and G strings. Although fingering problems are important, Suzuki points out the many changes of string level for careful practice.

The student should begin with the arm on the A string level. The hand and forearm should be raised for the notes on the D string. The elbow should be kept in the same place as the student plays on the A and D strings and moves down as the bow is brought to the E string. Suzuki mentions that the same volume must be maintained as the string crossings are made. "It would be so easy to get a good clear tone," remarks Suzuki jokingly, "if the violin had only one string. So many students change the tone when they cross from one string to another."

EXERCISE: *String crossing* (2nd measure)

1. Put bow on A, in the middle of the bow.
2. Draw short down-bow on A. Stop.
3. Raise bow hand to D level. Keep elbow on same level.
4. Draw short up-bow on D. Stop.
5. Move bow hand back to A level.
6. Draw short down-bow on A.

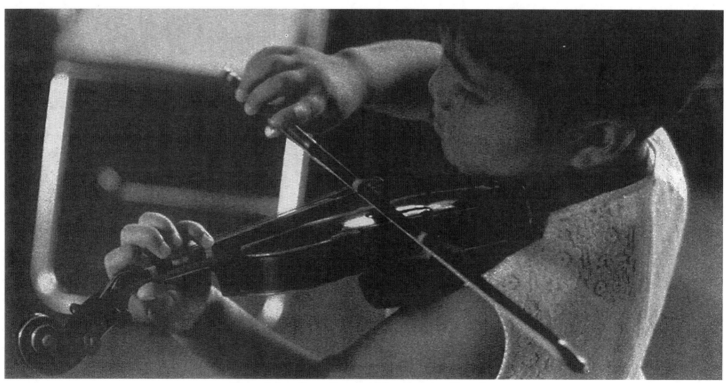

Practicing fingering and bowing on G string.

EXERCISE: *Fingering and bowing* (8th measure)

1. Put 1st on A. Play rhythm.
2. Keep 1st down. Put 3rd on D. Move bow to D. Play rhythm.
3. Move bow back to A. Lift 3rd. Play rhythm.
4. Put 3rd down on A. Keep 1st down. Play rhythm.
5. Lift 3rd. Keep 1st down.
6. Place 2nd on E next to 1st on A, then lift 1st.
7. Move bow to E. Play rhythm.
8. Lift 2nd, put 1st on E. Play rhythm.

EXERCISE: *Fingering* (10th measure) (to be played with rhythm, then single notes)

1. Put 2nd on D. Play.
2. Lift 2nd. Play open D.
3. Put 2nd on D. Play.
4. Lift 2nd. Move bow to A. Play.
5. Put 1st on E, then 3rd. Move bow to E. Play.
6. Lift 3rd, put down low 2nd on E. Play.
7. Lift 2nd. Play.

The fingering in the preceding exercise may be modified later. When the student becomes more accustomed to placing the low 2nd finger, he may place 3rd finger on the E (step 5 above) without the 1st to guide the 2nd.

Many students have a difficult time memorizing this piece because of its irregularity. There are four phrases: the first two, four measures each, the last two, three measures each. It can be diagrammed A A[1] B A[2]. The confusing measure is the fourth where four notes of the beginning are used to lead into a repetition of A. It is helpful if this is pointed out to students who forget at this point.

Minuet 1

"The child's musical education begins with this minuet, with Bach as his teacher," exclaims Suzuki. He adds that everything heretofore has been preparatory, in order that the child be ready for this musical education. "Of course the mother has been playing the recording every day so that the child already knows the melody," Suzuki affirms.

This minuet is to be practiced with small bows, staccato. After the fingerings and string crossings are learned, the bow strokes should be legato except where dots on the notes indi-cate staccato. Small bows should be retained. Students with good elbow action can use longer bows on the quarter notes.

As in the Etude, Suzuki asks that the string crossings from the A string to the D string to be done with only the lower arm changing level. The elbow is kept in pretty much the same place.

Suzuki begins to mention musical phrasing more and more often as the child begins his study of the Bach minuets, asking him to play the endings of the phrases softly.

The first measure offers a new bowing problem: two staccato notes bowed in the same direction. Suzuki advises, "Use a small elbow motion for the 2nd up-bow stroke. Don't push the bow with the first finger."

EXERCISE: *Staccato bowing* (1st measure)

1. Put 3rd on A. Place bow in middle. Play short down-bow. Stop.
2. Play short up-bow. Stop.
3. Play another short up-bow stroke, lifting elbow slightly.

The same bowing is found in the next exercise. Different fingers are used for the up-bow staccato notes.

EXERCISE: *Staccato bowing* (3rd measure)

1. Put bow on A string in middle. Play short down bow. Stop.
2. Put 3rd on A. Play short up-bow. Stop.
3. Lift 3rd, put down low 2nd on A.
4. Play another short up-bow. Stop.

Up to this point, the use of the 4th finger has been optional, except for the exercises introducing its first use. In this minuet the student must use the 4th finger to play the note B on the E string. The 3rd finger must remain down on the A string until the 4th is placed on the E.

EXERCISE: *Fingering* (3rd line, last two measures)

1. Put 3rd on A. Play rhythm. Keep 3rd down.
2. Put 4th on E. Lift 3rd. Move bow to E. Play rhythm.
3. Lift 4th. Put low 2nd on E. Play rhythm.

This same finger pattern is found in the second line, 1st and 2nd measures, only on the D and A strings. If the student can play 4th finger on the A without strain, he should employ this fingering. Otherwise, he must make a string crossing from the D to the E string.

EXERCISE: *Fingering* (2nd line, first two measures)

1. Put 3rd on D. Play rhythm. Keep 3rd down.
2. Put 4th on A. Lift 3rd. Move bow to A. Play rhythm.
3. Lift 4th. Put low 2nd on A. Play rhythm.

EXERCISE: *Fingering* (4th line, first three measures)

1. Put bow on open A. Play rhythm.
2. Put 2nd on A. Play rhythm.
3. Put 3rd on A. Lift 2nd. Play rhythm.
4. Lift 3rd. Put down low 2nd on A. Play rhythm.

EXERCISE: *Fingering* (4th line, last two measures)

1. Put 1st on A. Play rhythm. Keep 1st down.
2. Put 3rd on D. Move bow to D. Play rhythm.
3. Lift 3rd. Put low 2nd next to 1st on A. Move bow to A. Play rhythm.

This minuet is in two sections, both of which are repeated. This is known as binary form. The first section, A, consists of one eight-measure phrase. The second section, B, consists of two eight-measure phrases.

This piece may be performed with a crescendo in the fifth measure of every phrase, leading to a climax in the sixth measure, followed by a diminuendo in the seventh and eighth measures.

Minuet No. 2 - Bach

This minuet is one of Suzuki's favorites, and seems to be a great favorite with the children.

Suzuki is quite concerned that three bowing problems in this piece be taught and practiced carefully: the complicated string crossings in the first two measures, the slurred triplets, and the slurs with string crossings. He feels that problems like these should be practiced first, before the youngster goes through the piece, practicing it from beginning to end.

The elbow remains near the A string level for the following three exercises.

EXERCISE: *String crossings and fingering* (1st measure)

1. Put 1st on A. Put bow on A,
2. Keep 1st down. Put 3rd on D. Move bow hand to D level. Play rhythm on D3.
3. Lift 3rd. Return bow hand to A level. Play rhythm on A¹.
4. Keep 1st down. Put 3rd on A. Play rhythm.
5. Lift 3rd. Keep 1st down. Put low 2nd on E. Move bow to E. Play rhythm.
6. Lift 1st and 2nd. Move bow to A. Play rhythm on open A.
7. Put 1st on E. Move bow to E. Play rhythm.
8. Put low 2nd on E. Play rhythm.

After the student can play the above exercise with some facility, he may then play it with a short single staccato bow stroke for each note, rather than the rhythm.

EXERCISE: *String crossing, E to D* (2nd measure)

1. Put bow on open E. Play rhythm.
2. Move bow to D level. Hand and forearm first, elbow following slightly.
3. Play rhythm on open D. Same volume as preceding note.

EXERCISE: *String crossing as above, with fingering* (2nd measure)

1. Put 1st and low 2nd on E.
2. Put bow on E at middle. Play short down-bow stroke.
3. Lift 1st and 2nd. Put 3rd on D. Bow must be stopped during this finger action.
4. Move bow to D. Play short up-bow on D3.
5. Play another short up-bow on D3.

If the children have not learned independent finger action by this time, their fingering in the first two measures of this minuet will be very awkward. It was pointed out in the discussion of the fingering of Twinkle that Suzuki never advocated "block" fingering, that is, putting down two or three fingers simultaneously, yet many children try to play this piece with "block" fingering.

In the 5th and 6th measures it is advisable to keep low 2nd finger on the E down, since it will be used again after A3.

This next exercise deals with the first legato slur (two or more notes on one bow, without separation) in Book 1. Suzuki says that children encountering slurs for the first time usually play rhythmically erratically, and draw too fast long bows. To counteract this tendency, he asks that all slurs be first practiced slurred staccato with slow bow strokes. The direction of the bow is not changed, but there is a stop between each note. It is helpful if the teacher guides the bow at the beginning of this practice.

EXERCISE: *Slurred triplet* (4th line, 3rd measure)

1. Teacher puts bow on open A in middle.
2. Teacher draws short down-bow. Stop.
3. Student puts down 1st finger. Teacher draws another short down-bow.
4. Student puts down low 2nd. Teacher draws third short down-bow.

This exercise is then repeated with the student drawing the bow. The same exercise is then practiced on the E string (line 6, 3rd measure). Later the student plays the passage without stopping the bow between each note. "Small bows. Keep same volume," Suzuki requests.

EXERCISE: *Slurred string crossings* (8th line, 1st measure)

1. Put bow on open A in middle. Draw short down-bow. Stop.
2. Lift bow hand to D level. Draw another short down-bow on D. Stop.
3. Play short up-bow on D.

Now the student is ready to practice the minuet from the beginning. He will be happy to see that he already knows the difficult spots.

The beginner first practices with short separated bow strokes. Later all of the notes, except those with dots, will be played legato. As the student becomes freer, Suzuki asks for the second line to be played with contrasting long bows. The dotted half note A, at the end of the line, is played with a shorter bow stroke so that the bow will not move past the middle. The two Gs on the D string, in the second measure, are played softly with short bows.

Advanced students enjoy playing this piece with marked dynamic contrasts. Diminuendos are effective at the ends of the phrases at the ends of the 2nd, 4th, and 8th and 10th lines. The mf (medium loud) measures in the 5th line should be in marked contrast to the two "piano" measures preceding. Advanced students can practice reducing bow breadth by making a gradual diminuendo throughout the entire 7th line.

Very advanced students might imitate a brush stroke Suzuki often uses with the six eighth-note figure as it appears in the first measure. The bow scarcely leaves the string. The strokes are played below the middle with ample elbow motion.

The form A B A was used many times by Haydn and Mozart and other composers of their time. B begins at the double bar.

Minuet No. 3 - Bach

This minuet is approached much as the preceding ones. Difficult bowing and fingering problems are practiced first, before the piece is assigned to be practiced phrase by phrase. Suzuki feels that eight measures may be enough for one lesson's assignment, since the child will need time to reinforce earlier pieces, particularly the very latest acquired.

Short, separated bow strokes for all notes, including the slurs, are advocated for the beginner. Later, all of the notes, except those with dots, will be played legato. Somewhat longer bow strokes are used after the child knows the piece well. Long bows are particularly effective for the 4th and 5th lines, to be played forte. Ends of phrases are to be played with slower bow strokes, effecting a diminuendo.

EXERCISE: *Slurred string crossing* (1st measure)

1. Place bow on upper tape on D with 3rd on D.
2. Play short up-bow. Stop.
3. Move bow to A. Lift 3rd. Play another short up-bow. The volume should be the same for both notes.

EXERCISE: *Fingering and string crossing* (2nd measure)

1. Put 3rd on A. Put bow on lower tape on A.
2. Play short down-bow. Stop.
3. Lift 3rd. Move to D string.
4. Move bow hand to D string. Play 2 short up-bows.

EXERCISE: *Fourth finger placement* (3rd line, last measure: 4th line, 1st measure)

1. Put 3rd on D. Play down-bow. Stop. Lift bow.
2. Place 1st, low 2nd, then 4th on E.
3. Lower elbow. Place bow on E string at lower tape. Play short down-bow.
4. Lift 4th. Play short up-bow on low 2nd. Stop.
5. Put 3rd down. Play another short up-bow.
6. Put 4th down. Lift 3rd. Play short down-bow.
7. Lift 4th. Play short up-bow on low 2nd.

EXERCISE: *String crossings and fingering* (4th line, 2nd and 3rd measures)

1. Place 3rd on E, bow at lower tape. Draw short down-bow.
2. Move 3rd to A, then bow. Play short up-bow. Stop.
3. Move bow to E. Lift 3rd. Play another short up-bow. Stop.
4. Put 1st on E. Play short down-bow.
5. Keep 1st down. Put 3rd on A. Move bow to A. Play short up-bow.

6. Lift 3rd. Put low 2nd on E. Move bow to E. Play short down-bow.
7. Lift 1st and 2nd. Play short up-bow, open E. Stop.
8. Put 1st down. Play another short up-bow.
9. Put low 2nd down. Play short down-bow.
10. Put 3rd down. Lift 1st and 2nd . Move bow to A. Play up-bow.
11. Put 2nd on A. Lift 3rd. Play down-bow.

Each 2nd finger placement, high and low, should be made carefully. These are difficult, but should be initiated with care. The problems of careless fingering habits will multiply later and will severely limit the acquisition of speed and good intonation.

After these exercises are covered and the student begins to go through this piece, it might be a good time to give a preview of the difficult 8 16th notes in the Gossec Gavotte, line 5, 4th measure. The steps of the exercise are given in that section.

The form is A B, with both sections repeated.

Happy Farmer - Schumann

The main difficulty in this piece occurs in the first measure — the slurred staccato, with dotted rhythm and string crossings. Suzuki advises the teacher to present the rhythm on the open strings, then as a variation for Twinkle. The teacher should guide the bow at first.

Suzuki asks the beginner to draw only a short stroke for the dotted quarter note. It actually sounds like a quarter note followed by an 8th rest. Much later, this note will be played with a longer stroke that slows to a stop before the next note is played.

The beginner should have no trouble feeling the dotted rhythm. He should have heard the recording many times, and he has played the rhythm in May Song.

The piece is first practiced with small separated bow strokes on all notes. Later, all of the quarter and eighth notes, except those with dots, are played legato. Suzuki demonstrates, for very advanced students, (Book IX?) a brush stroke for the 8ths, played slightly below the middle of the bow. The bow remains near the middle in all of these versions.

EXERCISE: *Slurred staccato and fingering* (1st measure)

1. Put 1st on A and 3rd on D. Put bow on D at lower tape.
2. Draw short down-bow. Stop.
3. Lift 3rd, move bow quickly to A level.
4. Draw another short down-bow on A.
5. Keep 1st down. Put down 3rd on A. Draw short up-bow.

6. Lift 3rd and move it quickly to D string.
   Move bow quickly to D level.
7. Draw another short up bow on D3.

The child may forget this piece because of the similarities in phrases. It is helpful for him to know the phrase endings. The form is aaba'ba'.

Gavotte - Gossec

This is Suzuki's first graduation piece. It should be explained that the graduation tape submitted to Suzuki is usually not made until the child is well past this piece, not just as the child has first learned it. This is a good approach for solos in recitals, also.

Suzuki's suggested practice procedure deserves mention again. He believes that difficult "points for study" be taught before the child proceeds through the piece. It has already been suggested that the 16th note passage in the 5th line be introduced two selections earlier.

The following exercise should be played at first with short separated bows, then slurred staccato (4 notes on each bow stroke, but with stops between each note), and then finally slurred as written, with short bows and the same volume throughout.

EXERCISE: *Fingering* (5th line, 4th measure)

1. Put 1st on A. Draw short down-bow.
2. Keep 1st down. Put 3rd on A. Draw short up-bow.
3. Put 2nd behind 3rd. Lift 3rd. Play.
4. Put 3rd down again, lifting 2nd at same time. Play.
5. Keep 3rd down. Put 4th down. Play.
6. Lift 4th. Play.
7. Put low 2nd down. Lift 3rd. Play.
8. Lift low 2nd. Play.

The remaining 16th note passages of four notes should be practiced with the bowings as described for the exercise above. The grace-notes (as in the second and fourth measures) should be practiced as indicated by Suzuki.

The double string crossings, (D to E string, E to B, G to A) as found in the 7th and 8th lines, should be practiced with care. The elbow should be lowered immediately as the bow moves to the higher pitched string, but the hand should lead the change on the moves from the higher to the lower strings.

The beginner first practices this piece with short separated bow strokes. Later the first section (the first four lines) is performed detaché, non-slurred notes played with no appreciable space between them. Very advanced students may be asked to play this section with a brush stroke played slightly below the middle of the bow with elbow motion with each stroke. The bow scarcely leaves the string as this stroke is executed.

The first part of the next section (the first two lines) is played eventually with much longer bow strokes, except for the 16th note passages. The last two lines are played with smaller, slightly separated bow strokes.

If the last two bowed notes are played up-bow, the hand is brought into position for the pizzicato (plucked) notes. These are played with the first finger. The bow hold remains the same, only the first finger is disengaged from the stick to pluck the strings well over the fingerboard.

D.C. al Fine, an abbreviation for Da Capo al Fine, indicates that the first section is to be repeated to the word Fine (end). The Gavotte is in a large A B A form.

Always keep good posture, especially in group lessons.

Book II

By the time the student approaches the study of Book II, he should have had ample experience (in his review of earlier pieces) with the use of longer bow strokes, even full and half bows. Pieces from Book I frequently used by experienced teachers for the development of control of long bow strokes are: Twinkle, Lightly Row, Go Tell Aunt Rhody, Long, Long Ago, and O Come Little Children.

Suzuki mentions these objectives as paramount as the child progresses through Book II: development of musical sensitivity, with more attention to softer phrase endings; refinement of tone and intonation; and the use of more bow with freer movement.

The first tonalization exercise develops the perception of the resonance of the correct octaves above the open strings. Occasionally the teacher may pluck the open strings as these notes are played.

The second tonalization exercise is the one most frequently used by Suzuki. It consists of pitches that are very closely related to the open strings, pitches of maximum resonance. All kinds of variations of the exercise are introduced by Suzuki in his work on tonalization with advanced students.

The indication that Suzuki wants the G minor tonalization exercise taught at the same time as Handel's Bourrée is another example of Suzuki's interest in introducing new problems ahead of time, before they are encountered in the pieces.

Chorus from "Judas Maccabeus" - Handel

This piece, slow and sustained and with few fingering or bowing problems, is welcomed by the children. Psychologically, it is well placed. They are now in Book II and it is not so difficult. The students begin to feel that they have learned something basic that applies to new pieces!

It is instructive for the teacher to point out passages that are related to ones previously studied. In the 4th measure of the 3rd line, there occurs a passage with a D# to be played with high 3rd finger on the A. This use of the D# resembles that in Minuet No. 2, line 6, 3rd measure. Also, the very first measure contains the dotted rhythmic figure of May Song.

EXERCISE: *Fingering* (3rd line, 3rd and 4th measures)

1. Place 2nd on D. Play rhythm.
2. Place 4th on A, holding 2nd down until 4th is placed, then lifting 2nd. Play rhythm on A4. (Match 4th finger pitch with that of open E.)
3. Place high 3rd close behind 4th, then lift 4th. Play rhythm.
4. Move bow to E. Lift 3rd. Play rhythm.

The beginner uses short separated bow strokes as he learns this piece. All of the slurred passages are played slurred staccato. After the notes are learned, the bow strokes are elongated until the full bow is used. Suzuki says, "Middle finger and elbow move together, particularly in the lower half of the bow." Students at this level often have considerable difficulty maintaining a constant volume throughout long bow strokes. This is stressed by many teachers until well mastered. Later, the ends of the phrases are played with a diminuendo produced by slower bow strokes.

In the third measure, the notes with lines over them are at first played quite separately, but later with only a very slight separation.

Suzuki asks that this and the next selection be taught at the same time to highlight the contrasting bow strokes.

It would be helpful to the student if the teacher would also assign at this time the first exercise of the Hunter's Chorus as a preview of a difficult problem.

Musette - Bach

The Musette of Bach was placed here by Suzuki for contrast to the Chorus. This is played with short bow strokes above the middle of the bow. Suzuki regards the slurs and string crossings as the principal problems. All of the slurs are to be played at first as slurred staccato, then played as written with careful attention to uniform volume on the slurred notes, unless otherwise indicated. The diminuendos indicated are produced by smaller and slower bow strokes.

At first the beginner maintains the same bowing procedure previously mentioned many times — as the notes are learned, short separated bow strokes are used. Later, all of the notes are played legato. Gradually, "as the child becomes freer," says Suzuki, "he uses slower bows at the ends of phrases, and faster bows for more volume where it is indicated."

EXERCISE: *Fingering* (3rd line, 1st and 2nd measures)

1. Put 1st on E. Play rhythm.
2. Keep 1st down. Put 3rd on A. Move bow to A.
   Play rhythm.
3. Move bow to E. Lift 3rd. Put down low 2nd on E.
   Play rhythm.
4. Lift 2nd. Play rhythm.
5. Keep 1st down. Put 3rd on A. Move bow to A.
   Play rhythm.
6. Keep 1st and 3rd down. Put 4th on E. Lift 3rd.
   Move bow to E. Play rhythm.
7. Put down low 2nd on E. Lift 4th. Keep 1st down.
   Play rhythm.
8. Put 3rd on E. Lift 2nd. Play rhythm.
9. Lift 3rd, play rhythm on 1st.

Hunter's Chorus - Weber

Another lively piece, like the Gossec Gavotte, this contains slurred fast passages of four 16ths that should be practiced slurred staccato, with particular attention given to the volume in the passages where string crossings are present. Suzuki urges that all of the slurred 16th note passages be played with short bow strokes and a clear even tone. He says it is natural for the child to move the bow rapidly with quick finger action. This usually produces an uneven "slip" tone.

All of the 16th note passages should be practiced first. The exercise below deals with the one most difficult because of the rapid string crossing.

EXERCISE: *String crossing and fingering* (5th line, 3rd measure)

1. Put 1st on A. Play rhythm.
2. Lift 1st. Play rhythm.
3. Put 3rd on D. Move bow quickly to D. Play rhythm.
4. Move bow to A quickly. Lift 3rd. Play rhythm.

1) Play the above pattern with single separate bows for each pitch, 2) play all of the notes on one bow, slurred staccato, 3) play as written with short bow strokes.

Beginners perform this piece with staccato articulations in the middle of the bow, except for the slurred passages. More advanced players continue to make a slight space between the

quarter notes throughout and the notes following, so they are staccato along with the notes with dots on them.

Suzuki demonstrates an advanced bowing to older students. He performs this piece below the middle of the bow, raising and lowering the elbow slightly with each stroke. "Elbow and middle finger together," he says again and again.

EXERCISE: *Fingering, slurs* (7th line, 1st measure)

1. Put 3rd on A. Put bow on A at middle. Play rhythm.
2. Put low 2nd on A as 3rd is lifted. Play rhythm.
3. Lift 2nd. Play rhythm.

Play the preceding exercise 1) with single notes, separate bows, 2) with slurred staccato for the first two 16ths, and 3) as written. Do not put the first finger down. Listen carefully to the intonation, making sure that the fingers don't fall in different places as the pattern is repeated.

The quick string changes in the 3rd and 4th measures of the 8th line are really difficult for many children. These should be done with a very small forearm motion and with very short bow strokes. Usually children confronted with rapid motions such as these make gross motions and stiffen perceptibly. These changes of string level should be practiced slowly, and then gradually faster.

Long, Long Ago

The Variation of Long, Long Ago provides the student ample practice of up-bow slurred staccato. Suzuki does not present the staccato as a bite into the string made by pressure of the first finger on the stick, but a result of thumb articulation. Actually, the beginner plays the slurred staccatos in this piece much as he played them in the beginning of Minuet No. 1. Short bow strokes are used at the beginning, with the same volume for both notes. More advanced players use more bow on each note. Some Japanese teachers teach staccato as a lateral motion of the forearm with stops between the notes. Suzuki moves the elbow up a little as the bow nears the middle on the second up-bow note.

Suzuki asks the beginner to play this bowing at first on only the open D string.

Waltz - Brahms

The chief problem in this piece is the uneven bowing rhythm. Throughout the piece is found a down-bow of two beats duration followed by an up-bow lasting one beat, only half the duration of the down-bow.

Suzuki teaches beginners to practice the entire piece with stops between all the slurred notes. "Play the first tone of each slur with a deep tone, then stop the bow. The next note should be clear, with the same volume."

The melody at the beginning should be played with short bows, the bow having been placed on the string slightly below the middle. "Don't make the initial down-bow too long," says Suzuki.

To make the crescendo in the 4th and 5th lines, Suzuki asks the student to lengthen the bow strokes gradually, raising the elbow as the bow moves to the frog on the up-bows. "If the elbow does not move up, then practice my exercise, that of reaching across the violin with the bow hand."

If the down-bows in the forte measures are played with a strong tone throughout, and the faster up-bows are played more lightly, the up-bows should not sound louder.

Well-controlled dynamic differences are an exciting challenge to advanced students reviewing this piece.

In group performances one often hears children forgetting this piece at several crucial points. It is helpful to point out to them the following: in the 2nd and 3rd measures of the 2nd line, and in the passage at the end of the 3rd line and beginning of the 4th, the melody moves B D F♯, played A1, A3, E1. However, the next two similar passages are not identical. The melody moves B D G, played A1, A3, and E low 2. (These "almost alike" passages are found in the last two measures of the 6th line, and in the last line, the 3rd and 4th measures.)

G Minor Tonalization

The teacher should remember to teach this exercise given at the beginning of Book II as the child begins Bourrée. Suzuki's written suggestions should be observed.

It might be well for the teacher to put a new tape across the A and E strings to guide the placement of the low 1st finger. The student should move the finger back for the low 1st position without lowering it. The 1st finger should contact the neck lightly at the same point (the base of the 3rd joint) for regular 1st and low 1st position.

Bourrée - Handel

This is one of Suzuki's favorite pieces for review work. He uses it again and again for development of bow control, asking more advanced players to vary bow speed and to play in the lower half of the bow.

The beginner at first practices with separated bow strokes in the upper third of the bow, stopping the bow on the long down strokes to prevent the bow from going all the way to the point. After he learns the notes well, the beginner should move to the

middle third of the bow, using more bow on each note of the passages marked with a crescendo.

EXERCISE: *Bowing* (1st 8 measures)

The following are instructions concerning bow distribution given to advanced students by Suzuki:

1. Start in middle of bow. Move to frog on first up-bow stroke. Use elbow.
2. Draw next bow to middle. Elbow moves down with middle finger.
3. Play next four 8th notes with short bows in middle of bow.
4. Draw down-bow on open E to point.
5. Use full bow on half note G. Increase the speed to help with crescendo. Don't push on bow with first finger.
6. Play the next 8th notes with short bows. Lower part of bow.
7. Play end of phrase in 4th measure with slowing bow stroke. Half-note G should end with bow near the middle.
8. Play crescendo passage below the middle, using the elbow motion on each stroke. Bow strokes become longer and nearer the frog. When the top A is reached, the bow should be at the frog.
9. Play A full down-bow. Also next A and C♯ full up-bow.
10. The dotted half D is the end of the phrase. Make a diminuendo by slowing the bow on D. Stop near the middle to begin next phrase up-bow.
11. Continue as above.

Memory slips are common in similar passages. The student losing his place should be shown that the measure at the end of the first line occurs again (open A after the G.) The exact repetition is in the 3rd measure of the 3rd line. The next two occurrences differ slightly. F♯, not A, follows the G in the 4th measure of the 6th line and in the last measure of the 9th line.

Two Grenadiers - Schumann

This piece is another favorite of Suzuki's for development of free motion of the right arm. Advanced students practice with quick long bow strokes as they study this piece with Suzuki.

The first point for study is the dotted rhythm (the dotted eighth note followed by a sixteenth note) found in the first full measure. It occurs eight times in the piece, with and without a change of string. It should be practiced first without the string change.

EXERCISE: *Bowing* (2nd line, 1st measure)

1. Put bow on A midway between middle and point.
2. Play short up-bow. Stop.
3. Play another *very short* quick up-bow stroke, followed without stop by a down-bow stroke. The two bow strokes should be felt almost as one motion — up-down.

Play the preceding exercise with 1st finger down on A for 1st note. At step 3, lift 1st finger after quick up-bow so that open A sounds on the down-bow.

EXERCISE: *Bowing and fingering* (1st measure)

1. Put 3rd on A. Put bow on A midway between middle and point.
2. Play short up-bow. Stop.
3. Move bow quickly to E. Lift 3rd.
4. Play another very short quick up-bow stroke. Stop.
5. Place low 1st on E. Play down-bow.

After the student has gained facility with the placement of the low first finger, he may modify step 4 as follows:

4. Play another very short quick up-bow stroke, on open E, followed without stop by a down-bow stroke. Quickly place low 1st on the E for the down-bow stroke.

Suzuki reminds the students of the repeated down-bows in Song of the Wind as he points out the repeated down-bows in the piece. Ex. (3rd line, 2nd measure) "Small round motion with bow hand and elbow."

At first the beginner practices with short separated bows in the upper part of the bow. Later he uses the lower half freely. Advanced students slow the bow at the ends of all phrases and play the D major section (the French National Anthem, the Marseillaise) with long sweeping bow strokes separated slightly for rhythmic effect.

If this melody is preceded by: a soft passage (3rd line, 3rd measure), and crescendo (4th line), a píu mosso (more motion, a little faster, 5th line), and slight ritardando (6th line), the climax will be very stirring.

A very effective ending can be made at the last note if the bow is taken off the string abruptly as the piano plays the last chord on the 3rd beat.

Witches' Dance - Paganini

This piece has many repetitions of the dotted rhythm introduced in Two Grenadiers. In performance the short 16th note is not separated from the following note, but from the preceding note. In practice, however, there should be a stop after the 16th for preparation for change of string and/or fingering. Even though one stops for preparation, the string change and fingering should be done as quickly as possible. The quick change of bow direction is difficult and causes many children to make a big awkward motion, therefore the sixteenth notes should be played with very short bows.

At first Witches' Dance is played in the upper third of the bow, with very short bow strokes used for the triplet passages.

Much later Suzuki advocates quick, long bow strokes for the dotted eighth notes. The triplet passages are still played with short bow strokes.

EXERCISE: *Fingering and bowing* (1st line, 3rd measure) (an alternate fingering is suggested here)

1. Put 1st and low 2nd on E. Put bow at middle.
2. Play short down bow. Stop.
3. Lift 2nd. Play another very short quick down bow, on 1st, followed without stop by an up-bow stroke on the open E. Stop.
4. Place high 3rd on A. Move bow to A.
5. Play another very short quick up-bow, then put 4th down next to 3rd, playing a quick down-bow on A4.

The triplet passages should be played with only a single finger used for each note. The finger patterns for the following passages should be prepared in the preceding rests.

1) The 5th line ends with a quarter note D, A3. During the rest the student should lift the 3rd, and place 2nd and 4th on the E.

EXERCISE: *Fingering* (end of 6th line)

2) The 6th line ends with a quarter note A, E3. During the rest that follows the student should lift the 3rd and place low 1st, low 2nd and 3rd on the E.

The closing triplet passage, starting at the very end of the 9th line, should be practiced with short separated bow strokes. As the student practices to learn the notes, he should bring the fingers down and lift them quickly between bow strokes. This will help him acquire speed.

Gavotte "Mignon" - Thomas

This piece may seem long to a youngster beginning to learn it. The teacher who teaches by phrases can point out that it's actually not that long since there are so many repetitions.

After the notes are learned by the students (practicing staccato), this Gavotte is first performed above the middle of the bow with staccato 8th notes, but not staccato 16ths. The 16ths are played detaché, legato. All quarter note down-bows are played with a stopped bow. The bow is lifted for placement at the middle for the next 8th. Suzuki asks that the 32nd notes (as in the 1st measure of the 2nd line) be played with very short bow strokes and strong finger action.

Later the student plays the 8th notes slightly below the middle, with elbow action used for each note. The 16th notes are still played detaché until much later (Book IX) when the student may use a short brush stroke that barely leaves the string. By this time, there is flexibility in the fingers and hand. This stroke is also below the middle.

Some teachers use the B flat major scale as a preliminary intonation exercise for the middle section this piece (from the last measure of the 9th line to the return of the principal melody on the end line of the next page). The finger pattern is the same for both A and E strings. This is the first time for the low 4th, E♭, on the A string.

Play Twinkle variation rhythm on the following notes of the B flat major scale:

B♭ (low 1st, A string), C (low 2nd on A), D (3rd on A) E♭ (low 4th on A)

F (low 1st on E), G (low 2nd on E), A (3rd on E) B♭ (low 4th on E)

As in the Gossec Gavotte, the pizzicato notes at the end are plucked with the 1st finger of the right hand, the bow hold being maintained. The pizzicato chords are difficult. The strings should be brushed lightly with the first finger. The child should not try to pluck each string individually.

The teacher should always teach the child how to practice each piece, and should keep in mind the following principles.

1. Fingers should not be put down in "blocks."
2. Fingers that are to be used again should not be lifted.
3. Fingers that are to be moved to a new position, high or low or across the string, should be lifted before the change.
4. Each fingering and string crossing should be prepared. Separated bow strokes are still useful as these are learned.
5. The same volume should be maintained on down and up bows and on string crossings.
6. Memory aids should be given the student: "This melody is the same, except for the ending." "This pattern (last 4 notes of line 6) is repeated three times."
7. The length, position, and character of the bow strokes vary as the child advances.

Ear Training

The study in octaves that follows is rather difficult for a small child whose tone may be still quite heavy. Many children press very hard on the bow to sound two strings at once. Playing two open strings together may be a good preliminary exercise for this one.

Many teachers use this ear training exercise again and again with more advanced students.

Gavotte - Lully

This Gavotte, used many times by Suzuki for development of the bow arm, is at first played in the middle of the bow with short separated bow strokes for the quarter notes, the 8th notes being played with detaché strokes.

Suzuki marked "grazioso" (gracefully) at the beginning indicating that he felt this piece should be performed with a lighter bow stroke. Even though he says again and again, "Don't push with the first finger," he realizes that children should start with a heavier sound. "Gradually lighter," he says as the student progresses. Many Japanese teachers are still more concerned with "slip tone" at the time the student learns this piece. More advanced players are asked to play Gavotte slightly below the middle of the bow, with continual elbow action.

EXERCISE: *Fingering* (end of 2nd line)

Several specific points need mentioning:

1. Last 2 notes of 2nd line: D G♮, then A. Placement of G♮ can be helped by playing the notes in this order: A (D4), G♮ (D high 3), then A. G♮ is usually low here. As A (D4) is played, its pitch can be checked with that of open A.

EXERCISE: *Bowing* (3rd line)

2. 3rd line, last 3 measures. The slurs in these measures should at first be practiced slurred staccato, with not much bow. Very short bows should be used for the two 16ths at the very end of the 3rd line.

EXERCISE: *Trill and Bowing*

3. Line 6, 1st and 2nd measures. After the long trill, short bows should be employed for the two As to produce the diminuendo that is indicated.
4. Suzuki's exercises for practice at the end of the piece should be played first with his Twinkle rhythm, then staccato, then as written. He says, "The hand should not clutch the violin neck or the student will not be able to reach up for the extended 4th on C." The 1st and 2nd fingers should not be down here.

The second measure of Suzuki's exercises involves a big stretch between high 2nd finger (G♯) and low 1st finger (F). These fingers should be placed with care.

Below will be found fingerings given by teachers as substitutes for stretching the 4th finger (line 6, 3rd measure). Both of these involve shifting the hand. The whole left hand should move as a unit, thumb and first finger together. The wrist should maintain the same curvature.

1. First four notes, as written. Student shifts hand up, as open E is played, to place 1st finger on 3rd finger tape, or where 3rd normally falls. The next notes, CBA, are fingered 3, 2, 1. The hand is shifted back into its first position for the G♯ in the next measure. This fingering involves moving the hand into what is called 3rd position, that is 1st finger is placed where 3rd normally falls.

This next fingering involves a shift of the hand into 2nd position, that is, the 2nd finger moves up one note. (This is probably the easiest fingering if teachers forget that 2nd position has been considered difficult because of previous training.)

2. First four notes, as written. Student shifts hand up, as open E is played, to place 2nd finger on the 3rd finger tape or where the 3rd finger normally falls. The next notes, CBA, are fingered 4, 3, 2. After the A is played with the 2nd finger, the student moves the 2nd finger back to G♯ and continues as written.

Minuet in G - Beethoven

Bow distribution is particularly important in this piece. Beginners may find themselves running out of bow at the point if the bow lengths are not calculated.

Suzuki has one preliminary exercise for the staccato bowing of the Trio, (5th line, last measure). He suggests that this be played on one open string, D or A, in the upper part of the bow. The down-bow, lasting one beat, should be faster and lighter than the 4 staccato up-bows, so that the bow remains in the same place as the measure is repeated. There should be no accent on the down-bows.

At first the beginner just stops the bow between each 8th note. (About one inch of bow for each 8th.) He does not press on the bow stick with the 1st finger. Later the bow will go into the string as a result of thumb pressure for each staccato note. The thumb relaxes between notes. More advanced students use more bow for the staccato notes, "which should always have a nice sound," says Suzuki. "Melodic staccato," he calls it.

Very advanced students (past Book X) may play this quite rapidly with a bouncing bow, using flexible finger action.

Suggestions for study:

EXERCISE: *Beginning*

p con grazia

1. Beginning. Start in middle of bow, going to the frog to prepare for full down-bow.
2. 1st full measure. At first played with full, even volume. Later, in line with the accents marked, Suzuki asks the student to "sink into" the string on each D, letting up lightly on the 16th notes.

EXERCISE: 2nd and 3rd measures

3. 2nd full measure. Slow the bow on the half note, D, both to phrase and to save bow for the next beat.
4. 3rd measure. Slow bow on C. Next up-bow moves to frog.

EXERCISE: 2nd line, beginning

5. 2nd line, end of 1st measure. Start this phrase near middle. Go to the frog.
6. 2nd line, 2nd measure. Stop bow after 1st note, move 1st finger back quickly for A♮. Don't bend the hand. Don't clutch the violin neck with 1st finger. It is very difficult for small children to move the finger without a noticeable slide. This can be corrected later when the hand is stronger and larger.

EXERCISE: 3rd line

7. 2nd ending (3rd line, 2nd measure). Last two notes. Start up-bow at middle. Move to the frog.
8. 3rd line, 3rd measure. Last note, G. Big up-bow to frog, with elbow rising.

Five-year-old playing.

114

EXERCISE: 6th line, 3rd measure

9. 6th line, 3rd measure. Lift 2nd when 3rd is put down, to prepare low 2nd.

EXERCISE: 6th line, 4th measure

10. 6th line, 4th measure. Move 1st back and forth quickly without a slide if this is possible. Play the B and A♯ slurred staccato.

Minuet - Boccherini

In the beginning this is played in the upper third of the bow. The bow strokes grow longer as the child becomes freer with the use of his right arm, particularly in the lower half of the bow. Suzuki urges teachers to ask more advanced students for more varied bow lengths for dynamic contact. He is particularly interested in the development of freedom in the lower part of the bow, with corresponding elbow action. As these pieces are reviewed, Suzuki hopes for lighter, more graceful bowing.

Suggestions for study:

1. 1st five notes. 2nd and 3rd fingers should be down before starting. This figure should be practiced at first with the Twinkle rhythm, then separate bows, then slurred staccato, then as written. The bow should be put on the string before being moved, and the stroke should be short.

2. The quarter notes on the 2nd beats of the 2nd and 4th full measures should be played more softly with a slower bow stroke. This improves the phrasing.

3. The trills should be played with short bow strokes. The beginner may play only 7 notes for the whole trill figure. (2nd line, 3rd measure. 1-2-1-2-1-0-1- F♯ G♯ F♯ G♯ F♯ E-F♯)

4. 2nd line, 1st ending. Stop the bow between the two down bow Es.

Book III

As the teacher leads the student through this book, he should continue to look ahead to new problems that the student will confront. This may lead to introduction of problems from the early pieces of Book IV at the same time the student is completing the last pieces of this book.

Tonalization

At this point in the student's growth these tonalization exercises should be performed with full bow strokes. The changes of bow direction should become smoother, even without the use of finger flexibility.

Careful attention should be given not only to the production of a fine tone but also to the maintenance of uniform volume. The student should become aware of accidental changes in volume. Heightened perception of volume levels leads to expressive playing as the student uses volume changes for phrasing.

Exercises for Changing Strings

These exercises are to be practiced with hand and forearm making the string changes. The motions should become more and more refined as the student increases speed. The exercises should at first be practiced staccato.

EXERCISE: 3rd and 4th measures

The student will begin to be sensitive to the fact that there are several different arm levels possible for each string. If A and D are to be played consecutively and rapidly, the A string level chosen should be near the D string level. This is very important in the 3rd and 4th measures of example 3.

Recurring changes as found in example 3 may be played with the hand alone changing the position. The hand should not drop very low. Ex. 3 should be begun with the hand and forearm set on the A string, with the hand then raised to the D level.

Exercise 4. Beginning

The elbow should remain near the E string level.

Exercise 5: 5th measure

The elbow should remain near the A level.

Exercise 6: 2nd and 3rd measures

The elbow should follow the forearm as the bow moves to the G string level. The elbow drops first as the bow moves back to the E string level for the high G's.

Gavotte - Martini

"Elbow and middle finger of bow hand move together," is a favorite saying of Suzuki's. He likes to use pieces starting with an up-bow stroke to emphasize this point. The beginning of this Gavotte, with its two slurred staccato notes up-bow, lends itself well to elbow motion. Suzuki asks the student to start with the bow placed slightly above the middle and to raise the elbow with both up-bow strokes.

"The whole arm plays the violin," says Suzuki and jokingly asks the student to perform the following exercise. "Put down the bow. Start with the right arm at your side. Now reach up to touch the bridge with your right hand. Doesn't your elbow move up with your hand?"

The beginner should use small bows as he practices to learn the notes. Later Suzuki asks that different bow lengths be used for different dynamics. Rather than stressing greater weight on the bow for the loud passages, Suzuki asks the student to draw quick long bows. He also requests that the phrase endings be played with a pronounced diminuendo effected by a slower and lighter bow stroke.

Practicing this piece in this manner the student should become comfortable with marked changes in bow speeds.

Suzuki suggests review of the G minor tonalization as preparation for better intonation in the second phrase. Although almost all of the finger patterns in this piece have been encountered before, they should be practiced carefully at the very beginning. It is at this point, the beginning, that careless habits are formed. Intonation often suffers in pieces in which a number of different finger patterns alternate. There is often ambiguity in the placing of high and low first finger, and high and low second finger.

In the fourth measure of the 6th line, the first finger, moving back for the D sharp, may also pull the 2nd finger back, resulting in the B on the G string being played flat.

Many children have trouble remembering this piece because of the unusual number (5) of contrast sections played between repetitions of the first phrase. They might be helped by knowing the form is A B A C A D A E A F A. The first notes of the contrasting sections are: D, B, D, B, F. The teacher could ask the students to just start the contrast sections until they associated them with the letters in the form diagram. The teacher should point out the similarities and differences in phrases C and E.

Minuet - Bach

The student should be able to play the first portion of this minuet (Minuet No. 3 in Book I) with much greater facility in his bowing than the first time he studied it.

The new middle section, in the key of G minor, is played quite legato with a lighter sound. The intonation in this part is the main problem. Again, as in the Gavotte from Mignon, it is helpful to play the B flat major scale as a preliminary exercise to set the finger patterns for this piece.

The teacher should remind the student to lift the fingers ahead of time before they are put down in new positions, not to wait until the last note. (See line 5, last 2 measures: 2nd finger high, then low.)

There are many places in this piece where consecutive notes across strings are played with the 3rd finger. It may still be difficult for the small fingers to be able to cover both strings at one time, and yet there is little time or opportunity to lift the finger and rest it on the adjacent string. A compromise action may work satisfactorily. The two following examples are for illustration.

Exercise 1. (Second page, 2nd line, 2nd measure)

As the student places the 3rd finger on the E string for the note A, he should put the finger down on the A string side of the E string. To play 3rd on the A string for the note D, he moves the left hand and elbow to the right until the finger covers the A string enough to produce a clear tone. The hand returns to its original position on the next note on the E string, G.

Exercise 2. (Second page, 6th line, 2nd measure)

As the student places the 3rd finger on the D string for the note G, he should put the finger down on the A string side of the D string. To play 3rd on the A string for the note D, he moves the left hand and elbow to the left until the finger covers the A string enough to produce a clear tone.

In the same passage as Exercise 2 above (second page, 6th line, 2nd measure), the fingering printed in parentheses may be more difficult to learn at the beginning but may be a "cleaner" fingering and worth the extra practice.

Gavotte in G minor - Bach

Suzuki's edition of this Gavotte makes marked use of crescendo and diminuendo, dynamic contrasts that call for control of varying bow speeds. Suzuki says that the lengths of the bow strokes and the speed of the strokes should change continually as this piece is performed. He asks for very small bows for the phrase endings.

EXERCISE: 3rd and 4th measures

The passage of 8th notes starting in the first line and marked mf followed by a diminuendo is a difficult one for many students. After using short bow strokes for the preceding diminuendo, the student may have to be reminded to draw quick long strokes at the beginning of the next passage so that he can shorten the strokes to make the diminuendo. This one passage is excellent for calling attention to varying bow speeds. It should be repeated again and again.

The first four slurred notes of the piece make a fine study. Normally, the child will move his bow at the same speed during the stroke whereas he should be bowing slowly at the beginning and increasing speed gradually to effect the crescendo.

The lengths of the longest bow strokes to be used in this piece should be determined by the teacher. As the student becomes freer with his bow, longer bows should be used for the louder passages.

Intonation will most likely be a problem as the beginner learns this piece. In this regard, it might be well to practice the tonalization exercise (the G minor melodic scale) that follows at the same time the piece is studied. Also, the B flat major scale suggested for the Gavotte from Mignon and the preceding Bach minuet could be a helpful aid to acquiring good intonation in this piece because the finger patterns are similar.

Humoresque - Dvorak

Humoresque is another favorite of Suzuki's, a piece he uses often for review with more advanced students. The preliminary exercises given by Suzuki at the end of the piece are excellent for the development of fast finger action. They are, of course, closely related to the finger action of a trill. Suzuki says it is important to listen to the tone at the beginning of each bow stroke. " Don't let the bow slip here," he warns.

Particular attention should be paid to independent finger action as the two-note rhythmic figure (32nd note followed by 16th) is played again and again in this piece. For example, the 2nd and 3rd notes of the second measure should be fingered as follows: 2nd on the C sharp, 4th (without 3rd) on the E.

Beginners play the first section in the middle of the bow. This causes a problem when the child reaches the half-note E at the end of the line, a note which requires a long bow stroke. Suzuki asks for a very slow bow here, but still some children run all the way to the point. Some Suzuki teachers allow the student to pick up the bow after the up-bow stroke which precedes the half-note E and replace it near the middle for the long down-bow.

When Suzuki uses this for review with more advanced students, he asks the children to start below the middle and move the elbow up and down with the right hand on each bow stroke. The strokes are elongated considerably (particularly in the lower half of the bow) for the second and third measures which are played much louder. The bow is carried all the way to the frog on the up-bows. The two half-notes (at the ends of the 1st and 2nd lines) are played with very slow bows to produce an effective diminuendo.

Suzuki likes the next section (the next two lines) to be played with much more bow, except for the diminuendos at the ends of the lines, where the bow strokes are quite small. Advanced students start this section with full bows.

EXERCISE: Line 6, 3rd measure

rit. e dim.

A difficult fingering and bowing problem is found in the 3rd measure of line 6. It is good to practice this in this manner:
1. Play the Twinkle rhythm on each note, with stops in between.
2. Play each note with a short detached bow stroke.
3. Play slurred staccato.
4. Play as written. The string changes (from the E to the D string and reverse) should be made in silence, with the forearm. An alternate fingering frequently used is the use of the open A instead of 4th on the D.

Suzuki asks advanced students to play the middle section, (starting with the last line of the first page) with long bows. Beginners should try to play this section with as much bow as possible without losing control of the tone.

EXERCISE: 2nd page, 3rd line

Here is an alternate fingering given by teachers to avoid the long stretch and slide with the 4th finger (2nd page, 3rd line, last measure). The last two notes of the preceding measure are E and D. The E is played on the open E, at which time the student moves his first finger up to place it on the 3rd finger tape on the A string for the note D. The C, B flat, and A in the next measure are fingered 3, 2, 1.

Playing the very last phrase of the piece pianissimo (very softly) makes an effective ending.

Gavotte - Becker

Suzuki likes to stress phrasing in this piece, mentioning that there should be diminuendos at the ends of all the phrases. The student first studying this piece probably will play the first section in the upper part of the bow. The more advanced student uses small bows slightly below the middle except for the passage in the 3rd line marked "forte." It is played with full bows.

This piece begins as did the Martini Gavotte. Suzuki asks for light staccato on the 1st 2 notes, to be played with the elbow and bow hand moving up together.

Although there are dots above the G and A (the 3rd and 4th notes) in the 2nd measure, these are not usually played staccato.

EXERCISE: 3rd line, 3rd measure

EXERCISE: 4th line, 1st measure

The slurred staccato passages (3rd line, 3rd measure. and 4th line, 1st measure) are played in the same way as the similar passages in the Minuet in G of Beethoven. "Melodic staccato," Suzuki calls it. At first, the student articulates these notes without changing pressure on the bow stick. He merely stops between the notes. Later, Suzuki suggests that weight be applied to the bow stick by thumb pressure applied at the point of contact with the frog.

The 8th notes of the middle section (beginning in the 7th line, after the key change) may be played in the upper part of the bow at first, but Suzuki plays them below the middle with the elbow and bow hand moving up and down together. The second phrase of this section (9th line, 2nd measure) is played legato with long bows in marked contrast to the bow lengths used for most of this piece.

This Gavotte, in the key of G minor, presents intonation problems. It is helpful again for the student to practice the B flat major scale as suggested for the Gavotte from "Mignon." The finger patterns throughout this piece are identical to the pattern of the B flat major scale.

Examples: 1-1 Fingering

There are several examples (2nd line, last 2 notes, and top of 2nd page, 1st two notes) of the 1st finger being required to play two successive slurred notes a half-step apart (as in the Minuet in G of Beethoven). It is usually·still quite difficult for children to move the finger correctly at this stage. They should be taught to avoid bending the wrist with the finger movement, and to move the finger quickly with a jerk, a "staccato" finger action so to speak, rather than with a sliding action. These notes might be best played at first with a slurred staccato bow stroke.

Gavotte D - Bach

At the beginning, these Gavottes are bowed for the most part from the middle of the bow to the tip. Later, "as the children

become freer," Suzuki asks that the bow strokes be elongated, with increased use of the lower half of the bow. Advanced students were seen performing this music with long sweeping bows on the quarter notes. All of the 8th notes are played detaché (legato, no slurs) even though some are marked with dots indicating staccato articulation.

Suzuki asks advanced students to stop the half notes with the bow resting very lightly on the string.

The grace notes are difficult for small children. Many teachers omit these during the beginning study. These grace notes require strong and quick finger action, but the bow should move only a very short distance as they are played. Children often move the bow very quickly to accompany quick finger actions. As the children progress, they should gradually develop the ability to move the hands independently.

Several fingering problems deserve mention. Three of these involve the use of the low 1st finger on the A string to produce A sharp.

1. 4th line, 2nd measure

The low first finger for the A sharp should be moved back without bending the wrist inwards. The first finger, moved back, should not touch the side of the neck at a different place. The student should stretch the 2nd finger to play the C sharp in the same place as the preceding one.

2. 5th line, 2nd measure

As the student plays the 4th note (the C sharp) with the 2nd finger, he should lift the 1st to prepare it to move back for the. A sharp. The movement of the 1st finger up from A sharp to B should be done with a quick finger motion, not with a slide.

3. Gavotte II, 6th line, 3rd and 4th measures

Lift 1st as 2nd is played to prepare 1st to move back for the A sharp. Move the 1st finger up to B quickly.

EXERCISE: *Gavotte II,* 7th line

A bowing figure that will recur later is found in Gavotte II, 7th line, 2nd measure. The bow should be drawn down-bow very slowly for the three slurred notes, and then moved quickly and lightly up-bow so that the bow returns to the starting place.

Bourrée - Bach

This piece has for years been a milestone for the children in Talent Education. Until recently it was the first graduation piece, a point of arrival reflecting considerable growth in the child's development since his beginning with Twinkle. The tape recording required for graduation may not be made, however, until the child is well past this piece and can perform it with great refinement.

Although some teachers might require a staccato approach as the child learns the notes, by the time the child reaches this level he will be practicing rather soon the bow articulations of a finished performance.

The student should first practice Suzuki's trill and chord exercises given at the bottom of the second page. Playing on two strings at once is not done easily at first. Many children think that twice as much bow pressure or weight is needed to play on two strings. Suzuki asks that they place the bow lightly on the level of both strings as they would for tuning.

The three-note chords are actually performed with the first two notes sounding together, and then the single note on the top string sounding alone. At first, it is well to pause between these bow motions. As the 1st chord is approached the bow is on the E string. Suzuki keeps elbow and forearm on that level, moving the bow over to the low strings with only the hand. A similar procedure is followed for the second chord exercise.

This is a transcription for violin and piano of the Bourrée from the Suite in C major for solo cello. The music, copied from a well-known old edition, contains some 19th century editorial errors that should be acknowledged. Flats were placed on the Es in the 2nd full measure, last line, 1st page, and in the last measure of the 4th line on the second page. Although these are errors, most teachers live with them since they are on the present recordings most children are familiar with.

The first section is generally performed with stops after every quarter note, whether marked with a dot or not. The eight notes are connected. There is considerable variance in the lengths of the bow strokes, with bow strokes of gradually decreasing lengths used for all the marked diminuendos. This is accompanied by a lessening of the weight. Suzuki plays much of this section slightly below the middle with an active elbow motion.

Advanced students not only stop the bow after each quarter note but also release the weight at that same moment. The bow is put back "into the string" after each of these releases.

The 8th notes in the 2nd and 7th lines are played by the beginner detaché. Advanced students may play them with a brush stroke slightly below the middle of the bow.

The middle section is played somewhat slower and softer for a different quality. The crescendos and diminuendos indicated are produced by increasing or lessening the length of the bow strokes.

The motive consisting of the two staccato quarter notes up-bow (examples: the last two notes of the 2nd line; the two middle notes of the last measure of the 4th line, and the two middle notes of the last measure, 3rd line, 2nd page) is always played softly with very short bow strokes.

Here are instructions for the first measures of the piece given to a student by one of Suzuki's teachers, Kyoto Kawamoto. The notes are to be played fairly rapidly, but there are many stops called for.

EXERCISE: First measures

1. Put the bow on the A string slightly below the middle.
2. Play the 1st 3 notes without stopping, with a clear, strong tone. Short strokes. Stop the bow and release the weight, leaving the bow resting lightly on the A string.
3. Move the bow hand and 3rd finger to D string.
4. Play the next three notes quickly, without stopping, with a strong, clear tone. Stop the bow. Release the weight.
5. Drop the bow silently to the E string level. Prepare finger. Put the bow "into the string."
6. Play G on E string with elbow and hand moving up together as bow moves to frog. Stop the bow. Release weight.
7. Move bow hand to D-A level. Put bow back "into the string" but do not apply much weight.
8. Draw quick down-bow for chord as practiced in Suzuki's exercise. Stop bow. Release weight.
9. Play next 3 notes lightly, with bow strokes of decreasing length. Stop bow. Release weight.
10. Put bow back "into the string."
11. Play next 3 notes without stopping. Short strokes. Clear, strong tone. The directions continue in the manner as indicated above.

Book IV

In his instructions for this volume, Suzuki states that vibrato should be taught as the child commences his study of the Vivaldi A minor Concerto. All reference to vibrato study in this book will be found in the chapter entitled "Vibrato."

It has been suggested that reading music start about this time in the student's study. It is helpful for the student to look at the music as he learns the notes of these more difficult works. However, even though he does develop sufficient reading ability, he still should perform at lessons without music. See the chapter on "Reading" for additional suggestions concerning reading.

Up to this point in the Suzuki Violin School, the student's left hand has remained in one position at the fingerboard. This is called 1st position. In Book IV Suzuki presents, along with new pieces, the study of two new positions for the left hand, the 2nd and 3rd positions. These positions enable the student to play higher notes and to have more finger combinations available for melodic and technical passages.

At first Suzuki does not present shifting, that is, the movement of the hand in connecting two positions, but rather the positions themselves. The student's attention is brought to bear on the new fingering and the "feel" of the different stretches of the fingers. The familiar tonalization exercises are used to maintain good intonation. In fact, intonation becomes of primary importance here. The student should use more and more the device of checking his pitch with the open strings and other guide notes. See the chapter on "Intonation" for detailed suggestions.

As the student's hand moves up the fingerboard to higher and higher positions, the distances between pitches become smaller and smaller as the string lengths become shorter. Careful attention to the intonation is the guide to correct finger placement. Since the distances between pitches are largest in first position, the student may tend to over-stretch in higher positions, causing him to play sharp. He must gradually learn to "feel" the correct distances in each new position.

Study of the 2nd and 3rd positions should proceed concurrently with the study of the pieces in Book IV.

The first Seitz concerto should be practiced at the same time as the Tonalization exercises in the new positions. The Position Etudes that follow should be taught after the student becomes familiar with the Tonalization exercises.

In an older edition of the Suzuki Violin School, Suzuki had presented his Perpetual Motion transposed to different keys for position study. At first, it was presented in first position but transposed to B flat major. The piece started on B flat (low 1st finger) on the A string.

After the student became familiar with the new fingering for this version, he then proceeded to play it in 2nd and 3rd position. The 2nd position version begins with 1st finger placed on C (low 2nd finger in 1st position) on the A string. This version is in the key of C major.

The 3rd position version starts with 1st finger placed on D (3rd finger in 1st position) on the A string. This version is in the key of D major.

Many teachers still use Perpetual Motion in addition to the Tonalization exercises for position study. Some also use one and two octave major scales for additional work to establish the "feel" of the finger placements in the new positions. All of these examples are used because the student is familiar with their sound and should be able to know when he is playing out of tune.

Suzuki's brief two-line Position Etude for 2nd position contains four important elements:
1. Several notes are played in 1st position, including the pitch to which the 1st finger will move for the new position.
2. The first finger is then moved (shifted) to its place in 2nd position.
3. Several notes are played in the 2nd position for the "feel" of the position.
4. The 1st finger is then returned to its original place in 1st position.

The shift up and back is the new element. This should be practiced with care. It is not only important that the note of arrival should be correctly in tune but that the shifting motion should be done correctly. The shift in the lower positions has been described as a change of angle of the forearm as related to the upper arm. In other words, the forearm is moved as a unit. Neither wrist nor thumb nor shifting finger should change angle.

Suzuki begins the first shifts with a gliding motion connecting the two notes. Later the shift is performed silently. He says that each shift should be played accurately three times in succession to be good practice.

Here are pertinent instructions regarding the shift:
1. Be sure to articulate clearly the first note of the shift (note of departure).
2. Anticipate in the mind the distance to be covered with the shifting finger.
3. Release the weight on the shifting finger so that it will slide on the surface of the string during the shifting motion.
4. Shift forearm as a unit. Move slowly and evenly. Don't jump for the next note. (It is very helpful if the violin

neck is cradled between the bone at the base of the 1st finger and the ball of the thumb. If the neck is clutched by the hand, the shift is almost impossible. If the hand does not touch the neck as its moves, it is difficult to measure the shift.) Don't change the angle of the shifting finger. Don't bend wrist or thumb.

5. Stop at the 2nd note of the shift. Return the proper weight to the fingertip so that the note of arrival is clearly articulated. A tape on the fingerboard adds a visual aid to the ear to find the correct stopping point.

6. Do not move the finger, even if the top note of the shift is obviously out of tune. First, reflect on the motion made. Try to remember how the shift felt. If the shift was correct, after reflection on the motion, proceed with the notes in the new position. If the shift was incorrect, return to the 1st note and try again.

It is very important to have mental pictures of the shifting motion before and after the motion itself. This may be very difficult at the beginning but should become easier after the shift has been practiced several times.

Although the violin is cradled somewhat in the left hand, it is still held principally between chin and shoulder. This hold at the chin is noticeably strong for downward shifts.

After the student achieves some success in shifting accurately with a gliding motion, he should practice silent shifts. Each shift should be preceded by a pause of sufficient length for the student to conjure up in advance a mental picture of the motion. Students who have observed fine players at golf or archery have seen them pause for mental placement.

It cannot be said too often that work with shifting and positions should be done daily. It is better to practice shifting carefully only a few minutes a day than to do it erratically for longer periods. The student should realize that, after he begins his work with shifting, it will always be part of his daily practice from that time on.

Suzuki's Position Etudes for 3rd position are similar to those of the 2nd, however he does omit the notes in first position. Some teachers ask for the student to play the 2nd note in the exercise (the 1st note in 3rd position) at first in 1st position so that an aural image of the pitch can be made. This is followed by the shift. The rest of the shifting procedure is as given above for 2nd position.

Concerto No. 2 - Seitz

As mentioned earlier, far-sighted teachers introduce difficulties in advance of the actual study of the piece in which they are found. This movement of the Seitz Concerto in G is much longer than any piece previously studied since it contains so little actual repetition. In addition, it contains problems that may take some time to conquer. It is wrong to let the student become frustrated as his pace of learning new pieces slows.

In several ways, he should be prepared for this step into Book IV. First, the teacher should prepare both the parent and child for the slowing of the pace of learning new pieces. Second, the child should hear the recording for a very long period of time before attempting to study the piece. More repetitions are needed than were necessary for Book I pieces. Third, the teacher should introduce some of the difficult passage-work in this piece long before the student completes Book III. Of course, this must be done in small segments so that it does not take an appreciable amount of practice time.

One difficult spot is the slurred passages at the top of the 2nd page. The first measure might be adequate for the first segment.

EXERCISE: 2nd page, 1st measure

1. First, practice slowly with short separated bow strokes for each note. Put fingers down quickly and strongly.
2. Second, practice slurred staccato with short strokes. Put fingers down and raise them quickly.
3. Third, practice as written. Do not use much bow. Make sure all notes are clearly articulated, particularly those after string crossings.

Another difficult passage is found starting with the 5th line of the second page. This should be divided into many segments for practice. It is well to practice the double notes as directed by Suzuki for the double-note version of Perpetual Motion. Finger action, particularly the lifting of a finger which is to be moved to a new position, should be carefully taught.

EXERCISE: 1st measure, line 5

1. Put 1st down on A, then 3rd on D.
2. Play two quick short strokes on G (D3). Stop.
3. Play two quick short strokes on B (A1). Stop.
4. Put 3rd on A. Lift 1st at same time to prepare for move to low 1st on E.
5. Play two quick short strokes on D. Stop
6. Put low 1st on E. Lift 3rd. Continue as above.

Pupils beginning their study of this piece are generally not equipped to lift the bow off the string between the two up-bow strokes at the very beginning. Suzuki merely stops the first bow, leaving it resting lightly on the string. The 8th note B is thus separated from the preceding G. It is separated from the following D by short stop of the bow. If the beginner imitates very advanced players in lifting the bow off the string, the effect is usually quite rough.

Suzuki demonstrates all double stops and chords with a light bowing. Also, in his recording of this piece, he does not use a bouncing bow at all for the 16th notes on the second page. (This should be reserved for the review of very advanced students who have been taught this bowing.) Although he does not use a bouncing bow, he does perform the stroke with the hand relaxed at the wrist.

Concerto No. 5, 1st Movement - Seitz

By the time the student studies this piece, he should be able to use quite long bow strokes as they are called for, as in the very opening phrases. Suzuki asks again and again for slower bow strokes to end the phrases. "Bow speed control is so important for phrasing," he remarks.

EXERCISE: 5th line, 3rd measure

The triplets (5th line, 3rd measure) are to be played with very short light strokes. Advanced students often play these with a short brush stroke slightly below the middle of the bow.

Suzuki points out a passage that is often a problem for clarity since it involves irregular string crossings with slurs: the triplets of the 2nd measure of the last line of the first page. He asks that this passage be practiced slurred staccato with careful attention to uniform volume, particularly as the bow crosses the string.

EXERCISE: 1st page, last line

EXERCISE: 2nd line, 2nd page

This slow passage (2nd line, 2nd page) calls for expressiveness produced by varying bow speeds. The crescendo is effected by a fast bow stroke, which slows for the diminuendo in the next measure. Care is taken not to accent the quarter-note up-bow strokes that start the new phrases (example: 2nd page, 2nd line, 4th measure).

At this time the student learning new passage-work should be able to put the fingers down and lift them quickly. This does not mean the passage should be practiced rapidly. On the contrary, there should be a stop for preparation before each quick finger action. This takes great self-control, yet produces results much more quickly than the student going straight through the passage with sluggish finger action, and no time for preparation. If the passages are practiced with staccato bowing, it is more likely that the finger action will be quick and decisive.

The long 16th-note passage (starting on the 2nd page, 4th line, last measure) should be broken into many parts, preferably four notes at a time. Although practiced slowly at first, the bow strokes should always be short. Each four-note segment should be repeated until the student can play it fairly rapidly. After he has done four of these in this fashion, he then should put them together, starting with 8 notes at a time. If he is not ready, the accumulated problems will cause his mind to "jam." He must then rest or practice smaller segments.

Many students start the passage off too rapidly only to find that they cannot play its second measure, which is much more difficult than the first.

EXERCISE: 2nd page, 8th line, 2nd measure

cresc.

. The rapid string crossings (8th line, 2nd measure and 9th line, 1st measure) cause a great deal of difficulty if there is a wide arm motion. Some teachers teach a hand motion here. The forearm and elbow are kept on the E string level throughout. Only the hand is raised for the notes on the A. This may be too refined for some small students who are then allowed to change strings with the forearm, provided the motion is very small. The E string level used should be very close to that of the A.

Suzuki points out that the elbow should not be raised for the string crossings for the chords at the end of the piece.

Concerto, No. 5, 3rd Movement - Seitz

This is the most difficult of the three Seitz concerto movements. Because of its many ritards and fermatas, it is not frequently heard in group performances. Some teachers omit this piece and return to it later because of the difficulty of the double stops. This may be also due to the persistent requests of a child for the Vivaldi concerto that follows. Group performance is supposed to be a motivating factor, and since the Vivaldi concerto is one of the most prominent group selections and this Seitz is not used in large groups, the child may understandably ask the teacher if he can go directly to the Vivaldi.

Suzuki encourages the use of small bow strokes for the main melody of this piece, often asking students to play the first variation of Twinkle before they start to play this melody.

The contrasting melody (end of 7th line) is to be played with long bow strokes.

The first of two difficult technical problems in this piece is found beginning at the last measure of the first page. It is very difficult for the student at this stage to play the six slurred 16th notes with a slow enough up-bow so that the single 8th doesn't leap out because of its being played with a fast down-bow one-third the duration of the preceding up-bow. It is marked with an accent, but an accent however that is often played all out of proportion to the volume of the other notes.

EXERCISE: 1st page, last measure

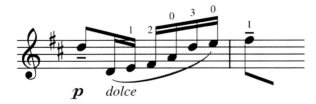

The student should draw the first 8th of the passage (1st page, last measure, 1st note) quickly and lightly to the point of the bow. The next six notes should be played slurred staccato, with as little bow as possible.

The next 8th should return the bow to the point, and so on. After this has been practiced a number of times, the student should try to play the slur as written, with a very slow up-bow, but not drawn so slowly that one cannot hear the notes.

Suzuki says that one of the main problems of the double stops is that students press the bow into the strings crushing the tone and changing the pitch. He feels that the bow weight should be lighter than usual to offset the urge to lean too heavily. The first eight measures of this long double-stop passage are alike in that one of the double notes is always an open string.

A different problem occurs in the ninth measure when both of the strings are fingered.

EXERCISE: 9th and 10th measures of double stops

Instructions for the 9th to the 11th measures:
1. Moving the 1st finger back from E to D sharp may cause the student difficulty in finding the C natural on the A (low 2nd) to match the 1st finger correctly. It would be helpful to practice putting the low 2nd on C and play with the 1st at E before it moves back. The 2nd finger could then lift and remain in position as the D sharp is played with the open A. This would help the low 2nd find its position.
2. After the bow moves to the two top notes, the C on the A string and the A on the E string, the 1st finger is no longer needed and should be lifted to find its new location on the A one half-step behind the low 2nd.
3. After the last note in the 10th measure, the 1st finger must be raised quickly and moved back a half step to the D sharp on the D.

Suzuki plays the double-stop passage slightly below the middle of the bow with the elbow moving up and down with the bow hand. The bow leaves the string slightly between strokes. This is the bowing for advanced players.

Concerto in A Minor, 1st Movement - Vivaldi

This is one of the most frequently programmed selections in the Suzuki literature. Suzuki regards it as an ideal vehicle for the development of bowing, using it again and again with advanced students to make them freer with their use of the bow, particularly the lower half. When Suzuki visited our program in Knoxville in 1968, we had twenty-six youngsters greet him with a performance of this piece. "Very good," he said, "now let's play it again, playing all of the 8th notes in the lower half of the bow." This wasn't the easiest thing for most of the children to do at once, so later we used this piece to develop that neglected lower half.

Students just learning this piece may play with short bows above the middle, but Suzuki's goal for the students is to start the beginning in the middle of the bow, and play all of the 8ths with the lower half. In fact, for more advanced players he broadens the strokes. Japanese tour children have been seen playing the 8th notes with full bows.

Suzuki urges teachers to use his Allegro as a warm-up for the long, sweeping strokes he wants here.

This is the first piece that requires the use of third position. These passages should be practiced carefully for correct intonation. There are four of these passages.

EXERCISE: Beginning

1. 1st and 2nd measures. Starting in 3rd position is not difficult, but getting back down to 1st is difficult. After the notes C B A are played three times, the student should stop long enough to move his hand back to 1st position and to place the 1st and the 2nd fingers in the correct places. This pause should become shorter as he progresses.

EXERCISE: Top of 2nd page

2. 9th line, last two 8ths on to the 1st measure of the next line. This is a difficult shift and should be practiced many times slowly.

All of the notes of this passage should be practiced with the rhythm of the first variation of Twinkle. This slows the practice pace and enables the player to hear all of the pitches clearly.

   a. Put low first on E string (F natural). Play rhythm.
   b. Slide 1st lightly, slowly and evenly to its place in 3rd position, the note A on the E. Play rhythm. (This is the guide finger for the shift and will later be inaudible.)
   c. Put the 4th finger on E in 3rd position. Play the rhythm. (The 4th finger is often too high causing the note to sound sharp. To test, play the rhythm on open D, or listen to the relationship between 1st and 4th fingers. This interval should have the same sound as the opening interval of the piece.)
   d. Play the rhythm on all of the descending notes. There is a whole step between 4th and 3rd, a half step between 3rd and 2nd, then another whole step between 2nd and 1st. This pattern is repeated for the notes on the A string.

Some teachers put tapes on the E string to guide the student first practicing this passage. The above exercise should be repeated later with a single short bow stroke for each note, rather than the rhythm. Finally, the passage is to be played as written.

EXERCISE: 2nd page, 3rd line

3. 2nd page, 3rd line, 1st measure. The Twinkle rhythm should be used here also.
   a. Put 2nd finger on A string in 3rd position. This is the last note (E) of the preceding measure. Play rhythm.
   b. Keep the 2nd down. Place 3rd next to it (a half step above) on the E string. This is the note C. Play rhythm on C.
   c. Place 1st on A close behind 2nd (a half step lower). Lift 2nd and 3rd. Play rhythm on D sharp.
   d. Place 2nd above 1st on A string (one half step above) in the same place as before. Lift 1st. Play rhythm on the note E.
   e. Place 1st on D string, one whole step behind 2nd. Lift 2nd. Play rhythm on note G on D string.
   f. Play rhythm on open A as left hand moves back to 1st position.
   g. Put 4th on A for the note E. Play rhythm.
   h. Put high 2nd on G. Lift 4th. Play rhythm on B on G string.
   i. Lift 2nd. Stretch 3rd to high 3rd for D sharp on A string. Play rhythm.
   j. Put 4th next to 3rd. Test to see if pitch is the same as open E. Play rhythm.

4. 2nd page, 6th line, last measure. This is the beginning of a passage of several measures in length in which are found shifts from 1st to 3rd and down again. None of the shifts are the gliding ones that use guide fingers. Careful attention must be paid to the first note in each new position. The student should know how it should sound and should form mental pictures of the motions involved. If he misses a shift, he should try it again rather than adjust the wrong note. The violin should be held tightly between chin and shoulder as these shifts are undertaken.

Suzuki finds many children taking too much bow on the middle notes of the 16th note passages such as the one found starting in the last measure of the 8th line. He asks that the passage be practiced in the following manner: "Play the first note with a fairly long bow stroke (a quarter or third of the bow). Stop, then play the next three 16ths with very short bows." Later the stop is omitted. He points out that the principal notes are the first of every group of four, and that they should be brought out by the use of a longer bow stroke.

This passage gives trouble to some children as they try to perform it from memory. It may help if the instructor points out the pattern found in the first notes of every four. This kind of information might also help with the long passage on the third page.

Concerto in A Minor,
3rd Movement - Vivaldi

As has been stated before, it is well to anticipate the complete study of these pieces with an introduction to some of the most difficult problems the student will face in the piece. Suzuki feels that study of this selection should begin with the long string-crossing passage starting on the 2nd page, line 5, 2nd measure. He suggests that the slurs be at first played slurred staccato, with careful attention to the volume as the many string crossings are encountered. As the slurs are later played as written, without the staccato, the bow strokes should remain slow on the slurs.

As the large leaps across strings are made, the elbow should remain pretty much in position, certainly not moving farther up than the A string level. The bow should remain in the upper half. At first, the notes should all be played staccato. The many string crossings cause a "slip tone" to appear, with corresponding lack of clarity. The passage is also best practiced in fragments. Careful attention must be paid to the intonation, particularly in the 3rd measure of the passage and the 7th measure.

EXERCISE: 3rd measure

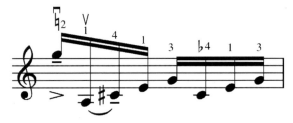

In the first example, the low 4th on the G (C sharp) and the 3rd (G) on the D need to be placed close together.

EXERCISE: 7th measure

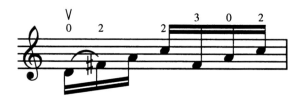

In the second example, the low 3rd (F sharp) and the low 2nd on the A (C natural) should be close together.

Two passages in 2nd position (second page) have been chosen for illustrative instructions: (It is helpful to play Suzuki's Twinkle rhythm on each note at the beginning.)

EXERCISE: 2nd page, line 7

a. Place low 1st on E for F. Play rhythm.
b. Place low 2nd on E for G. Lift 1st and move to high 1st on A string, covering B natural. Play rhythm on G on E string.
c. Slide 1st one half-step up to C which should be directly opposite the former position of low 2nd playing G on E string. Play rhythm.

The next notes continuing in 2nd position sound a C major scale.

EXERCISE: 2nd page, line 8

a. Place low 2nd on A string for the note C natural. Play rhythm.
b. Lift 2nd. Remember its position. Play rhythm on open E.
c. Move 1st finger on E to the note G, opposite the position just played by low 2nd on A. Play rhythm. Be sure forearm has moved forward as a unit.

Suzuki's students play the beginning theme of this movement vigorously with long, strong bow strokes. Suzuki asks students to think of moving the bow hand vertically as well as horizontally so that the bow will stay well "in the string." He says that if the hand moves horizontally without sufficient application of weight the bow tends to leave the string, causing a small tone.

All passages involving string crossings are to be played with small bow strokes and with a minimum change of arm level.

The student should stop before each shift. Each shift should be anticipated mentally, then executed unhurriedly. If the shift note is out of tune, the student should stop and practice the shift slowly for accuracy several times before continuing. It is very important that the first note in each new position be in tune, since all of the notes following are dependent upon it. If the hand is in the wrong position, the whole passage suffers. There are many more shifts in this movement that there were in the 1st movement. These many shifts constitute the main problem for the student. Even though study of this piece had been preceded by practice of Suzuki's Positions Etudes, these shifts are still difficult. If the student rushes through the shifts without care, his intonation will deteriorate rapidly. Parents often wonder what has happened to their children who seemed to "play so well in tune until the Vivaldi Concerto in Book IV." It is impossible to give too much emphasis to this problem. It is almost as though the student were embarking on a new plane of activity as he begins to employ frequent use of shifts.

A new symbol for fingering is found in the 4th line, 2nd measure. Above the high E, the last note of the measure, is found both on a 4 and a 0. This means that the 4th finger is moved up to the place where E sounds, yet touches the string only lightly on the surface, producing what is called a harmonic. If the finger is in the right place, the tone rings clearly with a more resonant sound than that of the notes played with fingers placed firmly on the string.

EXERCISE: 4th line, 2nd measure

It may be difficult for some children to perform this quick extension of the 4th finger. An alternate fingering may be helpful: the first note of the 2nd measure of line 4 is C, played with the 3rd finger. For the repeated C, move the 2nd finger up to C, and play the D with 3rd finger, and the E with the 4th finger. This particular pattern is found several times in the selection.

Concerto for Two Violins- Bach 1st Movement - 2nd Violin

Some violinists have objected to this piece being introduced to youngsters at this stage in their development, saying that they are too young and immature to appreciate its inherent worth that they will play it as a "motor" piece and therefore will never be able to change their evaluation of it. Suzuki teachers who have taught long enough to see changes in their students' performances of this work as they mature overrule this objection. Almost all of the children come to love the music of Bach through intimate contact with this great work. It is a recognized fact that they appreciate it first as a "motor" piece, liking the rhythm and the wonderful interaction of the melodic lines. Ten years later these same children perform it much more sensitively, with no evidence of harm done by the early exposure. This same observation can be made with the Bach A Minor Concerto in Book VII. It is difficult to imagine Johann Sebastian Bach wanting to withhold his music from youngsters until "they are mature enough to appreciate its greatness!"

Some teachers with older beginners first teach them the first violin part to this concerto, so that they will more readily have a group to perform both parts together. These students later are taught this part (second violin). Some students know both parts so well that they are able to change from one to another in performance, without a pause. Japanese tour groups have demonstrated this ability many times.

At the student's arrival at this work, it is well to sound again a clarion call for increased attention to intonation. It is understood that the student should have heard the recording many times before studying the work. If the child does not have access to a stereo set where he can hear the second part alone with the accompaniment, the teacher should make a recording of the sec-

ond part with piano so that he can hear the intricacies clearly. Not only do the many shifts contribute to the intonation problems, but also the complex melodic patterns. The child is climbing fast now in his growth. One needs only to glance back at the music of Book III to see how the ascent has accelerated.

It is here that good practice habits must be upheld. The most important habit to have instilled is that of practicing slowly and carefully in very small sections. Some teachers number every measure and assign the piece measure by measure.

As the children advance, the bowings used as they learn the notes of a piece more nearly approximate the bowings used in performance. Suzuki demonstrates with bow strokes extending both above and below the middle of the bow, with noticeable elbow action on the 8th notes and those of longer duration. The student is advised against getting "trapped " at the point of the bow.

At times the students are asked to move the bow gradually nearer the frog as they play a series of 16th notes (as in the 1st and 2nd measures of the 2nd line, and the 1st measure of the 3rd line.) This is in preparation for a long down-bow that follows.

The bow must be particularly controlled at the places where the bow crosses two strings at once. These crossings should be done quite slowly at first with great attention paid to the position of the elbow and forearm. The elbow should move only slightly as these crossings are executed and preferably remain near the level of the top string.

EXERCISE: After "A"

For example, to play the passage immediately after A, the bow should be at first set on the E string level. Then the bow hand should be raised to the D string level. The string crossings should then be made with the bow hand and forearm, with the elbow moving only slightly. Another example: before the crossings at B, the elbow should remain on the A level as the descending passage before B is played.

The student should stop before each shift, prepare mentally, then shift unhurriedly with care. There are many shifts indicated in the fingerings. Suggested exercises for five of the most difficult passages are given below. These passages should be practiced first with the Twinkle rhythm; second, with separated single short bow strokes; third, as written.

1. EXERCISE: 7th line, 1st measure

a. Put low 1st on A for B flat. Play rhythm.
b. Put 3rd on A for D. Play rhythm.
c. Lift 3rd. Try to remember its pitch and location.
d. Release weight on 1st. Slide 1st finger slowly and evenly up to its place in 3rd position (the D just played with 3rd finger.)
e. Return weight to tip of 1st finger. Play rhythm. Is pitch correct? If not, return to low 1st and repeat preceding steps.
f. Keep 1st down. Put 4th on E for high D. Play rhythm. Is pitch correct? If not, lift 4th and replace, after sounding lower D (1st finger on A). Try again.
g. Lift 1st finger, keeping it in position.
h. Play rhythm on open A.
i. Place 3rd a whole step behind 4th on E string. Lift 4th. Play rhythm. Keep 3rd down. Lift bow hand to D level.
j. Move 1st directly across to D string and place for note G. Play rhythm.
k. Move bow hand to E level. Play rhythm on C (3rd finger).
   Repeat above, placing but not sounding the guide finger for 3rd position. (Omit steps b and c.)

2. EXERCISE: 7th line, 3rd measure

a. Put high 2nd on A for C sharp. Play rhythm.
b. Play rhythm on open E.
c. Release weight on 2nd. Slide 2nd finger slowly and evenly up to its place in 3rd position (the note E which has just been played on the open string). This note is the guide note and will later be inaudible.
d. Return weight to tip of 2nd finger. Play rhythm. Is pitch correct? If not, return and repeat preceding steps. Keep 2nd down for the following steps.
e. Place 4th on A string for the note G. Play rhythm.
f. Lift 4th. Place 3rd next to the 2nd for the note F natural. Play rhythm.
   Repeat above, placing but not sounding guide finger. (Omit step d.)

3. EXERCISE: 2nd page, 1st measure

2nd page, 1st line, 1st measure. This should be practiced as example 2, the guide finger in this case being the 1st finger.

4. EXERCISE: 2nd page, 6th line starting in the 3rd measure and continuing.

a. Play the preceding 8th note passage to be sure the last 8th note (G, played with the 2nd finger on the D) is in tune. Check its pitch with that of the open G string.
b. Place 3rd on the A string next to the 2nd (one half-step above). This is the note E flat. Play rhythm.
c. Place 4th on A one whole step above 3rd. This is F. Play rhythm.
d. Lift 4th. Play rhythm on 3rd.
e. Lift 2nd. Place directly across on A string behind 3rd.
f. Lift 3rd. Play rhythm.
g. Place 1st a whole step behind 2nd for C. Lift 2nd. Play rhythm. Continue as above until the C natural, the 5th note from the end of the measure.
h. Move 1st back lightly to 1st position. Return weight on tip. Play rhythm on B natural.
i. Place 3rd on A for D. Lift 1st at same time to prepare for move to low 1st on E for F natural. Play rhythm.
j. Place low 1st on E. Play rhythm.
k. Place low 2nd on E for G, then lift 1st and move to a position above the A string to prepare for 1st finger to move up to the note C in 2nd position. Play rhythm on 2nd on E.
   Move 1st in position directly opposite 2nd on E just played. Play rhythm. Continue as above.

5. EXERCISE: E, 1st measure

After the note G (5th note) is played after the shift, lift the 1st finger as A and B flat are played with the 2nd and 3rd fingers. Replace the 1st finger in the same position, but try to cover both the G and D strings with the fingertip. (In a rapid tempo it will be difficult to lift the 1st and move it back and forth.) Rocking the fingertip sideways slightly as one plays may be helpful.

Alternate fingering: It is easier to perform the two measures before F in 1st position throughout.

Trill Study

The student has encountered trills before in his study but this is the first time Suzuki has inserted trill exercises for continuous study. He feels that by this time the child's hand and fingers are strong enough for fine trill action. These studies are intended to become part of daily study for a long time, until the teacher determines that their goals have been achieved.

At the very first, Suzuki reminds his students that the bow strokes are of paramount importance. He asks for a strong tone, with clear articulations, and says that many children first accompany the fingering of the trills with correspondingly fast bow strokes that skip over the strings making the trill barely audible. "Use short bow strokes. Keep the weight on the bow," he often remarks.

In addition to the mistake of drawing light bows, many children press the trilling finger into the string, slowing the trill action noticeably. Their fingers should strike the string as little hammers, with no pressure. The fingers should then spring up quickly. "Trill as rapidly as you can, but take plenty of time between trills. I call this deliberate fast practicing. Many children play slow trills one after another quickly without preparation. This is slow practice being done too rapidly and does not develop speed."

Suzuki cautions students against lifting the fingers too high or out of their positions above the strings. He calls attention to the two motions of the fingers, the putting down and raising. Both should be done quickly.

The student should not only develop speed with these exercises, but also strength and endurance.

Judith Starr studying...

...in Matsumoto.

Book V

Tonalization

Suzuki indicates that these Tonalization Exercises are to be practiced with vibrato. Also there is an indication that they should be practiced forte and piano. In this book, all references to vibrato study are in the chapter entitled "Vibrato" and further references to Suzuki's tonalization are in the chapter entitled "Tonalization."

Position Etudes

Suzuki here extends the range of the student's playing by the presentation of the 4th position. The exercises are similar to those used for the study of the 2nd and 3rd positions and should be practiced accordingly. The studies presenting the 5th position are given three pages later. The 5th position is presented from the 2nd in these exercises. Therefore, the student has the same melodic interval from the 2nd to the 5th position as he had from the 1st to the 4th. This helps his intonation in the 2nd to 5th position exercises. In these exercises, it is helpful for the student to play the second note first with the 4th finger in the old position and then shift to that pitch with the first finger.

Gavotte - Bach

Suzuki mentions three important points for study in this Gavotte. The first is at the very beginning. The student should put the bow on the strings before starting to play the chord. The elbow should be on the E string level. The bow should not move past the middle on this first chord. The rest of the up bow should be used for the next quarter note, which should be of equal volume to the chord.

The second bowing problem is found at the beginning of Gavotte II, the group of repeated up-bows. For most students it is best for the notes to be spread over the entire length of the up-bow, a kind of slurred staccato with more tone on each note than is usually given for slurred staccato passages. This means that the passage should start at the point. Very advanced students who are able to retake the bow quickly and replace on the string with no trouble may play the passage in the lower half, lifting the bow after each note and moving it back to be placed on the string in the same place each time. In order to do this, the player must have a firm but relaxed hold of the bow. The tip of the bow should not wobble, nor should the bow strike the strings roughly. Finger flexibility provides a considerable advantage.

The string crossings in the 6th, 7th, and 8th lines of the 2nd page should be performed mostly by the hand with very little motion up and down. Usually students start with a modest motion which grows bigger and bigger as the passage progresses. There should be no change. The student must remember to start on the level of the E string that is close to the A.

Concerto in A Minor - Vivaldi
2nd Movement

Suzuki delayed the presentation of this second movement until the student had some chance to develop a vibrato which could be used here. Teachers whose students are not ready with vibrato at this time may delay the study of this piece until even later. Vibrato on notes of such short duration may still be a real problem for many students.

Bowing with the correct weight for the variation in dynamics is a real challenge. Suzuki asks for clarity in all the passages, with neither a 'slip tone' nor a 'crushed tone.' The piece is also an excellent vehicle for interpretive work.

Etude for Changing Strings

This etude, with its variations, is self-explanatory. Care must be taken that the intervening string remains silent, and that the volume remains the same for each note.

Concerto in G Minor - Vivaldi
1st movement

The first movement of the Concerto in G Minor of Vivaldi is another graduation piece of Suzuki's, a piece that represents another milestone in the development of the musical abilities of thousands upon thousands of Suzuki-trained children.

Suzuki asks for long, sweeping bow strokes for the opening melody. He reminds teachers that there are very few bowing studies in his books, and that the teachers should use the pieces to develop freedom in their students' bowing.

The student about to learn the notes of this piece should have heard the recording many times, not only as an aid to his memory but also as a guide for his intonation. This concerto is in a difficult key, and considerable attention must be given to the intonation problems. Many notes should be tested for pitch. (See the chapter on Intonation for specific suggestions.)

The movement should be divided into many sections by the teacher for the student's home practice. The student will learn the fingerings much more rapidly if he looks at the music as he learns the notes.

The shifts should be prepared. By this time the student should have developed the habit of stopping to prepare each shift. Guide fingers should be used wherever possible.

There are two passages involving difficult string crossings. (1st page, 8th line, 2nd and 3rd measures: 3rd page, 8th line, 3rd, 4th, and 5th measure). It is recommended that the original bowing, given below, be used.

EXERCISE: 1st page, 8th line
Original bowing, no slurs

EXERCISE: 3rd page, 3rd line
Another very difficult passage involves a shift to 5th position, (3rd page, 3rd line, 5th and 6th measures). It is important to use a guide finger. Suggested instructions follow.

1. Play Twinkle rhythm on D, 1st finger on A, 3rd position.
2. Place 2nd on A for note E. Play rhythm.
3. Place 3rd close to 2nd for F natural. (One half step above E.) Play rhythm. This will be the pitch of the 1st finger after it has moved up into 5th position.
4. Try to remember the sound and location of the 3rd finger.
5. Lift 2nd and 3rd. Release weight on 1st finger and move it up slowly and evenly to F natural, the pitch just played by the 3rd finger. Play rhythm.
6. Place 3rd finger for note A. Play rhythm. Lift both fingers slightly above the string, and play open A to check the pitch on the top A. Put fingers down again.
7. Lift 3rd. Keep 1st down. Place 2nd on E string for the note D. Play rhythm. Test pitch of D by playing rhythm on open D. If these first notes are tested carefully, the rest of the passage in 5th position is not so difficult.

The trills on the 8th notes in the 7th line of the second page should be very short, not more than two turns. Since trills in music such as this written in the Baroque period were usually started on the note above the written one, these trills would consist of four notes, starting on the note above.

EXERCISE: 3rd page, 7th line

Another difficult intonation problem bears mentioning (3rd page, 7th line, 4th and 5th measures). A new interval appears prominently in this passage, the interval between the notes F sharp played by 4th finger, and E flat, played by the 3rd finger. It is called an augmented second, and requires quite a stretch for the 4th finger while the 3rd finger must remain back near the 2nd. This passage should be practiced very slowly with stops between each note.

Concerto in G Minor - Vivaldi
2nd Movement

This slow movement is a favorite of Suzuki's. It gives the performer ample opportunity to demonstrate the results of his work with tonalization. This is a required solo on the graduation recital of all of Suzuki's teacher-trainees.

The long sustained bow strokes are a real challenge to the student. The bow distribution should be carefully determined so that the student doesn't "run out of bow." Some teachers lead their students through this piece for the first time with careful attention to the tone produced by the bow, but with little regard for the vibrato. The piece is reviewed later after the vibrato is thoroughly developed.

For maximum effectiveness in performance of this piece, the vibrato should be very well developed, both the vibrato used for long sustained tones and that used for notes of short duration, notes such as the 16th notes of this piece. It is difficult to "learn" a vibrato with such a piece as this. The student should approach the piece with a well-developed vibrato.

Several of the melodic shifts on the A string are very difficult. They should be practiced with a guide finger, the last finger playing in the 1st position. Suggestions for three of the shifts follow:

EXERCISE: 7th line, 2nd measure

1. The last note before the shift is B natural, played by the 1st finger. Slide this finger to the D that has just been played two notes earlier by the 3rd finger. The 4th finger A flat following will be a half-step extension for the 4th finger, a stretch that should not be difficult.

EXERCISE: 8th line, 1st measure

2. The last note before the shift is C sharp, played by the 1st finger. Slide this finger to the E natural that has just been played two notes earlier by the 3rd finger. The 4th finger B flat following will be a half-step extension for the 4th finger, as above.

EXERCISE: 10th line, 3rd measure

3. Slide the 2nd finger from C sharp to the note G in 5th position. The G should match the one just heard in the previous measure.

Concerto in G Minor- Vivaldi
3rd Movement

Infrequently heard in Japan, this movement presents no particularly new problems although good intonation is hard to achieve in this difficult key. Suzuki asks for free use of the bow, with many long bow strokes and considerable use of the lower half of the bow. Along with the elongation of the bow strokes, Suzuki insists upon a strong tone well "into the string."

The student should approach all shifts carefully, making sure that the first notes in new positions are well in tune so that the hand is placed correctly. Notes should be tested for pitch throughout this movement. A particularly difficult shift interval is found on the 2nd page, line 8, last measure. (The 2nd finger C on the A string to the 3rd finger high D flat on the E string.) This is not so difficult if practiced this way:

EXERCISE: Page 2, line 8

1. Play low 1st finger on E for the F natural at beginning of measure. Try to remember the sound of this pitch. Lift 1st.
2. Play low 2nd on A for note C.
3. Move 2nd finger up on A to F natural, the same pitch just produced by low 1st on E. Keep 2nd down.
4. For D flat, place 3rd on E next to (one half step above) 2nd on A.

Alternate fingering: 3rd page, 10th line, 5th measure. Move 1st up from preceding A to B flat. G then is played with 3rd on the A, and the high E flat is played with the 4th placed next to the 3rd on the A string.

Country Dance -Weber

Another favorite of Suzuki's students, this piece is frequently used as a solo but much less frequently in group work, although it has been played by the Japanese tour groups, which are small and manageable ensembles.

The staccato used throughout this piece is played in either of two ways. Some students produce the staccato by just stopping the bow between each note. No particular effort is made to pinch the string as the bow arm moves, but there is considerable weight applied to the bow. The main difficulty is to save the bow, and not squander it on the first notes of the slurred staccato.

Suzuki demonstrates a staccato produced by application of pressure between thumb and middle fingers to articulate each note. In either case, the up-bows should start as near the tip as possible, and should move only a very short distance for each staccato note. Quick down-bows are often needed to return the bow to the tip to prepare for the up-bow staccato passages.

The energetic two-note rhythmic figure (starting in the 4th line, 4th measure) provides a fine opportunity for fast finger action. Suzuki plays these quite rapidly, stopping the bow after each two-note figure. The student practicing these should play them rapidly as soon as possible, but should stop between each figure to prepare the next fast motion.

Some teachers encourage their advanced students, in reviewing this piece, to play with a bouncing bow rather than staccato. This is very difficult to do well.

German Dance - von Dittersdorf

These short pieces, inserted after the long Vivaldi Concerto, give the student a sense of coasting instead of climbing. This German Dance is technically quite easy compared to the selections immediately preceding. The key of E flat is not an easy one for the violinist, however, and considerable attention must be paid to the intonation. Shifts should be prepared as usual. The bowing is light, mostly in the lower half of the bow.

One particular shifting difficulty is made easier by the use of the guide finger. (See 2nd line, 2nd measure.) After the open D is sounded, the 1st finger should be moved up to the D an octave higher on the A string, in 3rd position. After this finger is placed, the A flat played by the 4th finger is found by extending the 4th up one half step above its normal 3rd position note G. This stretch should not be difficult . At first, the 1st finger D should be played, then later it will be placed inaudibly.

Gigue from Sonata in D Minor - Veracini

This gigue is played throughout with the bow remaining on the strings. Suzuki's students use quite long bow strokes for the forte passages, giving the performance a robust quality.

The slurred scale fragments are the main problems. These are often played rhythmically erratically with lack of clarity. The fingers have a tendency to go down together in "clumps," and the bow tends to come off the strings. These passages should be at first practiced with slurred staccato with strong well-articulated finger action. When the slurs are then played, care should be made to keep the bow "into the string." The fingers should come down rhythmically with the same strong 'staccato' action used with the slurred staccato bow stroke. The bow strokes should be small and firm. The bow should be stopped after each group of notes.

These ascending and descending scale fragments provide a wonderful opportunity for finger and bow development. They should be practiced carefully, not with the attitude that the child will learn to play them better later on.

An unusually difficult chord is found in the 1st measure of the last line of the first page. A suggested procedure for practice follows.

EXERCISE: 1st page, last line

1. After the open A (the second note in the measure) move the hand into 2nd position to play the F natural with 1st finger.
2. Upon arriving at the chord, stop the bow to place the fingers.
3. Move the 1st up one half step to the note F sharp on the D.
4. Place the 2nd finger on the E string for the note A. It will be a half step above the F sharp covered with 1st finger.
5. Rapidly place 3rd on the A string, one half step above the 2nd finger A, for the E flat.
6. After playing the chord, slide 3rd back one half step to the note D. Lift the other fingers.

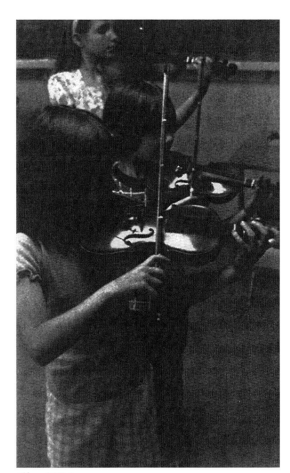

Thursday afternoon group lesson in Knoxville, 1976.

Concerto for Two Violins - Bach
1st movement - Violin I

Many of the passages in this first violin part are identical to those of the second part. This will come as a welcome bonus to the student. The bowing technique used is identical. Although there are contrasting passages, the problem with intonation remains the same. As was suggested for the study of the second violin part, this part should be divided into many sections for study. It might be well to number the measures and teach it measure by measure. The student should check pitches with the open strings as often as possible. (See the chapter on Intonation for details.) There should always be a pause before each shift for mental placement. Another pause should follow the shift, to give the student an opportunity to check the pitch of the first note in the new position and to reflect on the 'feel' of the shift, whether it was correct or not.

Some teachers use an alternate fingering for the passage at D. They guide the student into 1st position for the descending scale before D. The hand then remains in first position throughout the 16th note passages.

As the children's bowing becomes better controlled they may use quick, long bow strokes frequently, particularly on the short 8th-note up-bows that precede long down-bows.

Books VI - X

Up to this point the pieces have been presented individually with general recommendations for study and suggested exercises given for particular difficulties in each piece. This has brought about much repetition. It was felt that this repetition was necessary in order to drive home salient features of the Suzuki approach. I hope that the repetitions have not been regarded merely as redundancies.

In looking at the problems in the following books I saw a number of repetitions of newer problems in the various pieces, plus a vast number of repetitions of the old problems for which numerous suggestions had already been given. In lieu of continuing to cover problems in a "piece-by-piece" fashion, I have chosen to group related problems together in chapters, feeling that it would be not too difficult for the contents of these chapters to be related to the individual pieces. Also, by this time, practice procedures should have been well set through the instructions and suggestions given in the early books. All kinds of technical problems have been grouped into chapters on Tonalization, Vibrato, Shifting, Intonation, Practice, Relaxation, and Memorization. Technical problems beyond Book X are presented in these chapters with the exception of several virtuoso

bowings, and left hand pizzicati, artificial harmonics, and glissandi.

Suzuki, in volumes VII-X, has chosen to present many specific instructions for practice. These should be of great value to the teacher and student, not only in themselves, but also as guides to similar problems.

I hope that the principles covered in the earlier chapters and those covered in the chapters listed above will be sufficient to guide the Suzuki violinist for a considerable length of time.

One is often asked, "When do you quit teaching 'Suzuki'?", as though it were not 'violin' teaching. Most of the differences between Suzuki's teaching and traditional forms are found in the early years of development. The advanced Suzuki player does not 'look' different from an advanced player trained according to certain traditional methods. The best answer to the above question is that the student ceases to study Suzuki literature when he completes the ten b o o k s of the Suzuki Violin School. It is hoped that teacher and student will continue to be inspired by the Suzuki pedagogy under which they worked together during the study of Suzuki's ten volumes.

Suzuki listens carefully . . .

Tonalization - Bowing

(See the 'Introduction to Tonalization' on page 39)

An attempt is made in this chapter to state and explain the principles of Tonalization, and to present a number of suggestions and exercises for the development of a beautiful tone. The violinist produces tone by contacting the strings in two places: the bow contact (discussed in this chapter) and the finger contact (discussed in the chapters on Intonation and Vibrato). As the student progresses in his study, he should become more and more sensitive to the manner in which he touches the strings at these two points. His ear will be his best guide. The goal is a beautiful sound.

I The Bow Hold

A. *Thumb*

As explained earlier, the beginner's bow hold developed by Suzuki involves the placement of the thumb under the frog. Since 'thumb power' is so important in Suzuki's concept of tone production, the placement of the thumb in the 'regular' or 'normal' bow hold is of paramount importance. The teacher should set the thumb in position and check it many times. It may be uncomfortable for the child, and thus he may move it to a more comfortable position but one that will hamper his bowing in the future. The right corner of the thumb should contact both the stick and the frog. Many children adjust the thumb so that it is not placed on the frog itself, but merely touches the frog. Pressure applied by the thumb should be made at an angle toward the frog, not at a right angle toward the stick. The thumb is not flexed at the beginning, but the advanced student learns to flex the thumb and fingers later. If the thumb is stiff, it cannot be flexible.

B. *Middle Fingers*

These fingers should be placed opposite the thumb. For a powerful tone, they literally 'hang' on the bow, applying weight to which the thumb applies counterpressure.

C. *Little Finger*

At first, for the very small child, this 4th finger may be placed on top of the bow, but it should eventually find itself placed near the top but on the side of the stick toward the hand. This is to prevent its sliding over the stick when it is flexed. Its strength is developed by Suzuki's early preliminary bowing exercises, however, it should not become stiff. The teacher can check for stiffness by massaging the bow hand gently as it is placed in position.

D. *First Finger*

Much of what Suzuki says about the first finger is negative. "Don't press with the first finger", is a common refrain. He has seen so many players producing harsh tones by this means. The first finger is quite forward of the thumb on the bow stick, and thus has an advantage over the thumb for counterpressure.

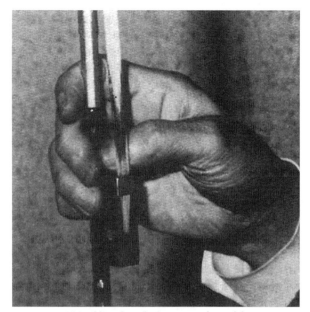

Suzuki's thumb in normal position

Teacher-trainee's thumb in normal position

Pressure on the first finger is very easily too excessive, causing a crushed or forced tone. The middle fingers, however, being opposite the thumb on the bow, can press strongly to produce a big tone without scratch.

Many times Suzuki asks his students to bow with the first finger lifted off the stick so that they will feel the middle fingers and thumb as the center of the bow hold.

Suzuki does have some use for the first finger. "With your first finger you can control the tip of the bow. With it, you can bring the tip of the bow closer to the bridge. At the point, it can help keep the bow 'in the string'."

II Moving the Bow Up and Down

A. *Whole Arm*

"The whole arm plays the violin," says Suzuki. He doesn't want the student to compartmentalize his bow strokes, i.e., finger action, hand action, forearm action, upper arm action, etc., even though he realizes that at different times each of these motions may be the most important for certain bow strokes. He wants the student to feel that they are used in different proportions at different times.

B. *Elbow*

When one speaks of elbow motion, this is the same as referring to motion of the upper arm. Suzuki feels this to be the most neglected and undeveloped motion. He constantly talks about activating the elbow, even in the very early stages with the first variation of Twinkle. However, his ideas on elbow motion come to the fore as he demonstrates bowing in the lower half. Suzuki's typical full bow strokes could be described in the following manner: The bow is placed on the string at the tip to start an up-bow. As the bow hand reaches the position of the "square" the elbow then moves up with it to the frog. (Overzealous students often move the elbow out as it rises, but this is not what is meant.) The down bow stroke starts with the elbow leading down immediately and not stopping until it reaches its first position. For forte passages, the elbow is kept lower and closer to the body. "Elbow and middle finger together" is another oft-repeated phrase of Suzuki's.

Advanced students find that the ability to lead with the elbow facilitates quick up-bow strokes. They move almost effortlessly at great speed to the frog.

Elbow motion at the frog reduces the noise of bow changes at the frog, as the elbow carries the bow through the changes.

Suzuki demonstrates . . .

elbow action . . .

with full up-bow

C. *Forearm*

Motion of the forearm is almost always present. Students don't need to be reminded to move the forearm, except when they play short fast bow strokes either tremolo or sautillé. Many students play these strokes with the hand only, causing loss of tone and control. For these short, rapid bow strokes, the impulse should come from the forearm as it does for longer strokes, with the hand moving freely a greater distance but not too wide. Suzuki demonstrates this action when he pretends to bounce a ball with his hand.

D. *Shoulder*

The shoulder joint should be completely relaxed at all times. The shoulder moves only slightly up and down as the result of the elbow motion in the lower half. It should never be raised and pushed into the neck.

E. *Hand and Fingers*

The beginners are taught to move the hand, fingers, and forearm as one unit. The teachers, however, demonstrate with flexible motion in the wrist and fingers. Gradually, with many repetitions of pieces like the 16th-note variation of Twinkle, many of the students become more flexible in the wrist and finger joints. Others need careful guidance for proper relaxation. It is quite possible to relax too much, with a consequent loss of control and tone. Suzuki says that Japanese children have acquired previous experience flexing their fingers through their use of chopsticks. Western parents might find eating with chopsticks an attractive exercise for their children.

A string at tip

Suzuki demonstrates finger flexibility with a pencil. Holding the pencil vertically with the normal bowing hold, he moves it straight up and down with the fingers and hand. The thumb must bend with this action. The little finger must not slip off the pencil. At first this is very difficult for some students, but gradually they find the way to do it. The finger action should be accompanied by lifting and lowering the back of the hand. It is better to emphasize the lifting motion since the motion from normal to high will be incorporated into the complete bow stroke much easier than the low position with the fingers straightened out and the wrist high. Japanese teachers were seen asking the children to do this exercise while seated at a desk, and resting the pencil tip on the desk top. Only the higher motion was possible.

Here is another exercise for finger and hand action. It is to be practiced with the bow. Put the bow on the string in the middle of the bow. Push the bow upwards an inch or so with the hand and fingers, without moving the forearm. If necessary, hold the forearm with the other hand. The bow should remain in correct position on the string as the hand and fingers move the bow

A string at frog

upward. Next, the bow should be returned to the original place by means of hand and fingers. This bowing action is never used without some forearm motion, but it is well to practice it without the forearm so that the forearm will not take over the entire motion. The fingers and thumb should all bend and straighten without tension.

A third exercise to develop finger and hand action involves flexing of the wrist with an accompanying flexing of the fingers. In the first step of this exercise, put the bow on the string in the middle. Lower the wrist without moving the bow. The fingers and thumb should be bent. Return the wrist to its normal position. The second step follows. Lower the wrist as above. Keep it lowered while drawing a short down bow. Stop. Return the wrist to its normal position. Raise it slightly. Keep it raised while drawing a short up-bow. Stop. Return the wrist to its lowered position. Keep it lowered while drawing another down bow. Stop. Return it to its raised position. Draw short up-bow stroke. Continue as above. The third step is like the second except that all of the stops are omitted. It is important that the timing of the lowering and raising of the wrist be correct, otherwise it could work backwards. *This wrist action is purposely exaggerated for practice purposes,* and is not used independently. In actual playing, the wrist moves much less than this, and almost negligibly with fast strokes.

Some students become depressed by the temporary lack of control. Finger flexibility should be developed gradually.

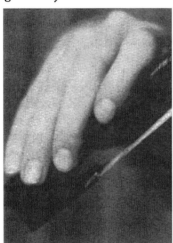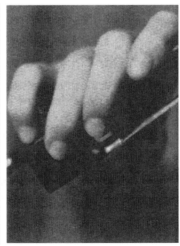

Horizontal finger motion

III Moving the Bow — Changing Strings.

A. *Without Slurs*

Changing strings by means of the forearm has been discussed many times throughout this book. (See Changing String Levels). The forearm motion should be refined as the child progresses, and should become quite small when used for two adjacent strings.

When moving from the E string down, the hand should lead and the elbow follow. When moving toward the E string, the elbow should drop first.

For rapid changes of string, the hand motion should be developed. The forearm should be set on the higher-pitched string, then the hand should be raised to the level of the lower string. The student should at first practice raising and lowering the hand vertically without drawing the bow and without moving the forearm. Instructions for the next exercise follow.

1. Place the bow on the A string, on the level nearest the D string.

2. Raise the hand until the bow rests on the D nearest the A level.

3. Draw a short down bow with the forearm, keeping the hand raised. Stop.

4. Lower the hand to the A string level.

5. Draw a short up bow with the forearm, keeping the hand on the same level. Stop. Continue as above. Later reverse the bow directions, starting on an up bow, and/or starting on the higher string.

Changing strings . . .

String changes at the frog are difficult, and should be made with little motion. Suzuki demonstrates with string changes at the frog being executed with only the fingers.

For all string changes, the arm and wrist should be relaxed and flexible. Another Suzuki exercise for string changes: Rest the bow on the strings. Without making a sound, arpeggiate the EADG strings with a minimum of motion. Start this exercise on the E, and then on the G. Be sure that the forearm and elbow are in the correct position before starting.

B. *With Slurs*

Suzuki suggests that all slurs involving string changes should at first be practiced slurred staccato, that is, the bow should stop between each note of the slur. The student should move the bow carefully onto the new string and should strive to continue playing on the new string with the same volume. A "slip tone" often occurs because the bow does not engage the new string at the beginning.

IV Volume

Three ways of producing tones of different volume are discussed in the "Introduction to Tonalization".

At first Suzuki's Tonalization Exercises are to be performed with a full, round tone with no change of volume. At the beginning of Book V, he shows the paths for forte and piano.

Advanced students are also asked to play the tonalization exercises forte with full bows, then the same volume with only half bow, and finally, the same volume with quarter-bow strokes. He points out that the bow should move closer to the bridge with the slower bow stroke, and that the elbow should be lower for increased weight.

The Tonalization Exercises are also used for the practice of crescendo and diminuendo, with all three techniques for change of volume utilized—bow weight, path of bow, and speed of bow. At times Suzuki isolates one of these to develop it to the utmost.

Maintaining a constant volume level with bow strokes of unequal duration is a problem Suzuki works with often. He asks for fast, light bows to match slower, heavier strokes. This technique is called for many times when there are slurs of unequal duration and no changes of volume indicated.

V Application of Weight to the Bow

Suzuki tells the story of a conversation with Mischa Elman, the renowned virtuoso, about the source of the big tone Elman was famous for. "I asked him to tell me briefly what he regarded as the most important cause of his big tone. He didn't say a word, but stuck his right thumb up toward my face. Since that meeting I have been convinced of the importance of what I call 'thumb power' in the production of a big unforced tone."

In order to keep the bow 'into the string', Suzuki feels that it is good for the student to picture bow motion as vertical, not horizontal or lateral. The student should feel the arm weight as helping to keep the bow 'in the string'. "Put the bow on the string. Feel the weight on the bow as applied through the thumb and the middle fingers. The thumb and middle fingers are the center of the bow hold". "Put the bow on the string. With thumb and 2nd finger increase and decrease the bow hair's elastic power, without making a sound."

Suzuki has conjured up a number of exercises to point up the arm's relation to the bow. These are listed under "Exercises for Tone". He uses unusual approaches to drive home the fact that the unsupported bow has a different weight at every point of contact with the string, too heavy at the frog, and too light at the tip. The student playing a long bow stroke of uniform volume should add weight constantly as he moves to the tip away from the frog.

Suzuki mentions weight of bow and arm every time anything arises to keep the bow from remaining 'in the string', i.e., fast bow stroke, percussive fingering, as in trills, change of string, vibrato, and shifting.

Suzuki avoids using the word "pressure" because it has the connotation of tension. "Put the bow on the string with the proper weight, then play. Don't press!"

Only after the student can produce a full powerful tone and a full soft tone as well does Suzuki mention the production of a light, transparent sound.

VI Staccato

A. *One Note per Bow*

With regard to volume, there are three basic kinds of articulations for any single note: 1) the beginning and the end of the tone may be louder or more forceful than the main body of the tone, 2) the beginning and the end of the tone may be softer than the main body of the tone, or 3) the beginning and the end of the tone may be the same volume as the main body of tone. Of course, Suzuki desires his students to master the last type of articulation, which is by far the most difficult. However, in his long years of experience working with small children, he found that it was best to start with the first kind of articulation. So the children are taught in the Twinkle variations to give each tone a definite beginning and ending. Suzuki found that the habit of producing tones "slipped into and slipped out of" was very difficult to overcome. He found it easier to ask for heavier tones 'gradually lighter'.

As he develops control of the bow, the student is taught not to attack the beginning of every separated note, or to 'brake' its ending, but to put the bow on the string and start the tone with the same kind of feeling one has as one lowers one's hand into the water from a boat, not the kind of feeling of keeping the hand on the surface. The weight is to be released at the end of the bow stroke, and the bow allowed to rest lightly on the strings. The bow is to be put back 'into' the string for the next tone.

Suzuki says that the quality of tone of separate notes should be the same as that of legato, but with stops between the notes. The tone quality of a note of even short duration should be the same as that of a long sustained tone. It should not be of different character because it is short.

If the separated note is to be accented, Suzuki feels that this should be done with fine quality. The accent, whether made by thumb pressure or by a quicker movement of the bow, should not be dry or harsh and the rest of the tone after the accent should not be pale and colorless.

B. *Slurred Staccato*

There are two basic types here, the first of melodic quality in which each tone is fairly long. The bow sinks into the string without pinching the string. One thinks of the opening of Kreisler's "Schon Rosmarin" in this case. The second type is the rapid kind. Suzuki advocates pinching the bow between thumb and middle finger. The sound is percussive.

VII   Legato

Suzuki regards legato tones as the same as long staccato, the difference being that in the legato passages the tones follow consecutively without a pause.

VIII   Double Stops and Chords

A. *Double Stops*

Suzuki feels that tuning the strings is the best possible practice for double stop tonalization. For Suzuki, playing on double strings does not mean double power or pressure. The bow should rest evenly on both strings. The double notes should resonate as clearly as single notes.

B. *Chords*

Chords should not be played too heavily. The bow should cross over the strings smoothly with even weight. "Try to change string level for chords with thumb and middle finger only". If three notes are to be played simultaneously, the bow should be moving near the fingerboard with not too much pressure.

IX   Tremolo / Detache / Bouncing Bow
Brush Stroke

These bow strokes sound quite different and yet there is a relationship between them. Suzuki feels that always there should be tone of good quality, no matter how short the duration of each tone.

A. *Tremolo and Détaché*

Tremolo and détaché are produced in nearly the same manner. The tremolo stroke is usually much faster, and yet there should not be a substantial difference in the production of the two bow strokes. They differ primarily in speed and breadth. How often students playing tremolo passages in orchestra are seen stiffening the whole arm and raising a tightened shoulder! The tone becomes weaker as this is done. Actually, the impulse for these bow strokes should come from the forearm, not the hand. The hand should move a greater distance than the forearm. The wrist, flexible, should be slightly lower than the hand when the bowing is executed in the upper portion of the bow. The forearm needn't tighten or stiffen. It's the same action as Suzuki's bouncing ball action.

The player will find the right side of his body shaking if he is moving his forearm with a relaxed, rapid, small motion. The breadth of the stroke should be determined by the breadth of the forearm motion, not the hand motion, since the hand motion should not change breadth appreciably. It should always move just an inch or two farther than the distance covered by the forearm. A wide hand action tends to get out of control.

B. *Bouncing Bow*

The natural bouncing bow, or sautillé stroke, is related to the tremolo. To experience this relationship, the student playing a tremolo (on the note D on the A string, for example) with fairly rapid, short bow strokes should move gradually to the lower part of the bow. He should lighten the weight as he moves, and should eventually come to a point where the bow will bounce off the string naturally. He may have to turn the bow stick slightly outward by rotating the wrist to produce this natural bounce. If the bow does not bounce, he should continue to move around the middle of the bow until he finds the bow's natural bouncing place. If he is unable to do so, he should return to the upper part to try a faster or slower tremolo stroke. As the bow moves down toward the middle, the forearm should continue to initiate the bow stroke. The hand motion may be varied in breadth slightly if the bounce does not occur. This kind of natural bounce may be impossible to achieve with badly constructed bows.

C. *Brush Stroke*

The brush stroke or controlled spiccato is related to the natural bouncing bow described above. To experience this relationship, the student should continue the bouncing bow, all the while making a very gradual ritardando. He will find that he will have to use more forearm to keep the bounce which is no longer occurring naturally. Gradually as he slows down, the elbow begins to participate more and more as long brush strokes are made. The bow should stroke the string smoothly. A flexible finger action should accompany the upper arm and forearm motion. The hand and finger motion should not widen as the tempo slows, rather the upper arm and forearm participate more and more.

If a more percussive sound is desired, the finger and hand action can produce this. Instead of moving back and forth in a brushing stroke, the hand and fingers can spring back and forth, the bow being dropped on the string and sprung off by the finger action.

X   Exercises to Improve Tone Production

1. Play open strings, full bow strokes. Listen to the sound of the freely vibrating strings, particularly at the ends of the strokes. Try to imitate this sound with fingered notes of the same pitches.

2. Perform the 'Casals' exercise. Draw long sustained bows, sinking deeply into the string, with elbow weight and thumb pressure, and then out again. Try to do this three or four times on one bow stroke. The tone should be continuous. The effect is that of a pulsating tone. This bowing is sometimes referred to as a portato stroke.

3. Tap strings with bow in the same place. Move the bow with thumb and fingers, not hand.

4. Play harmonics with bow near bridge. Try to get the same volume and clear tone from fingered notes of the same pitch.

5. Play tonalization exercises with full, then half, then quarter bows. Try to maintain same volume throughout.

6. Play tonalization exercises and Twinkle rhythm with bow held at tip to feel weight of frog.

7. Play tonalization exercises with bow hold on hair of bow near frog. The thumb and fingers transmit pressure directly to the horsehair.

8. Try bowing with different combinations of fingers on bow. First, play with 1st finger lifted. Second, use middle fingers only. Third, use 1st and 3rd fingers to play piano.

9. Play Twinkle rhythm at all parts of the bow, same volume.

10. Play 16th-note variation of Twinkle at frog with elbow motion. Try to avoid making noise with the bow.

11. Place bow on string at tip. Lift tip and frog together and replace again and again.

12. Play repeated down or up bows at all places in the bow. Take the bow off the string and return with a round motion. Replace bow on string carefully.

Suzuki raising the elbow with the left hand

Suzuki reaching over the violin

Hitomi Kasuya, frequent tour soloist. E string posture.

A string

D string

G string

Shifting

Mental anticipation of the 'feel' of shifts to be made and mental reflection on the 'feel' of shifts that have been made are of crucial importance in the development of a fine technique of shifting. When first practicing any shift, the student should not adjust an incorrect pitch by moving or bending the finger, but rather make a mental note of the 'feel' of the incorrect motion, and then repeat the shift. As a performance nears, however, he must learn to adjust errors quickly, but this should be avoided in the early stages. Many children adjust or miss most of their early shifts, consequently not developing any security in shifting. They persist in adjusting because it is so easy to do. In order for an archer to 'adjust' his error the way the violinist does, he would have to run to the target and move his errant arrow into the bullseye!

I. **Shifts: 1st to 4th positions (the hand remains in contact with the neck on both sides.)**

   A. The shift from a finger to the same finger in a new position.
   (See the discussion of Suzuki's Position Etudes, beginning of Book IV.)

   B. The shift from a finger to another finger in a new position, with the first finger used as a guide finger.

   (See the discussion of the 1st movement of the Concerto in A Minor of Vivaldi, Book IV.)

   C. The shift executed as an open string is played. If the violin neck is 'cradled" lightly between the ball of the thumb and the bone at the base of the first finger, this shift should be easy. Of course, the violin should be held principally between chin and shoulder. The shift should be preceded by a mental image of the 'feel' of the distance to be covered and an aural image of the correct pitch of the arrival note. If the shift is missed, a mental note should be made of the error and the shift should be repeated.

   D. The shift from a finger on one string to another finger on another string. If the strings are adjacent, a guide finger should be used. If not, the player should stop the bow for the string change, and shift as though from an open string.

   E. The shift to the same pitch, with a different finger replacing the first one. In this shift, the second finger to be used is the one that should make the shift.

   F. The half shift, so-called because the thumb re-remains in the same position as the fingers move back and forth. For example: A string,

A sharp, played by 1st finger, then B by 2nd. The 1st finger moves up to play C natural, the 2nd C sharp, the 3rd D. The thumb remains in the original position. In many of the uses of this half shift, the fingers return to their original positions. This shift is used extensively with chromatic passages (passages with many consecutive half steps).

   G. The glissando melodic shift. The shift from one finger to another in a new position. The first finger used is not the guide finger, rather the 'arrival' finger slides audibly into its place for musical effect.

   H. The delayed shift. The player stretches a finger into a new position. The hand follows later. Used for adjacent positions, such as 1st to 2nd.

II. **Shifts that involve a change in the basic hand position.**

In the previous category of shifts up to the 4th position, the hand could remain in the same position touching the neck of the violin on both sides. In shifts involving movement of the hand away from the neck and involving the thumb at the end of the neck, each player must determine when and how far his hand should move away.

   A. If the shift is a long one from 1st position to a very high position, the hand should move out at the outset so that there can be one smooth movement of the hand and arm together.

   B. If the shifts are consecutive, as in an arpeggio, the hand should move out to prepare for each higher shift as the notes are being played in the old position. This may seem awkward to the student at first but will facilitate the acquisition of speed.

Fast shifting, as found in rapid arpeggios, is a real stumbling block for many students. The slow practice must resemble the fast performance. The shifts should be rhythmically correct and unhurried. The forearm should move as a unit. Here is a suggested practice procedure for the ascending E Major 3 octave arpeggio.

   E (1st on D string) Establish a steady slow beat for each note.

   G Sharp (3rd on D)

   B (1st on A) Immediately after articulating B, release weight from tip and move 1st unhurriedly to E. Don't arrive at this E before the beat. Move the bow slowly and relax bow pressure.

   E (1st on A) Return weight to fingertip to articulate E clearly. Return bow pressure.

G sharp (3rd on A) While playing this note, move thumb and hand around for next shift.

B (1st on E) Immediately after articulating B, release weight from tip and move unhurriedly to E. Don't arrive before the beat. Move the bow slowly and relax bow pressure.

E (1st on E) Return weight to fingertip to articulate this E clearly. Return bow pressure.

G sharp (3 on E)

B (4th on E) Slide finger up to the harmonic E.

E (4th on E, harmonic)

Premature fast execution of an arpeggio like this one can be disastrous. Students reaching the Book IX level might do well to practice short arpeggios like this for a few minutes a day for a year or two with only a very gradual increase in speed. This will prepare them for the arpeggios found in concertos such as the Mendelssohn and the Bruch G minor.

 C. Descending shifts found in scales and arpeggios are quite difficult and must be prepared with care. As the guide finger, the 1st finger, moves down to the lower position, the finger playing the first note of the new position should assume the approximate distance from the guide finger as the shift takes place. The hand should not contract for the shift and then expand to place the finger properly.

 D. The half shift action, in which the thumb remains in place as the fingers and hand move, is used commonly for descending shifts out of the high positions. In fact, the thumb may seem to crawl around the neck and down, moving after the hand and fingers have already moved down to the new position.

 E. Shifting with double stops is particularly difficult. The sliding glissando shift should be used at first so that the ear can hear the approaching pitches. The student should be conscious of the varying distances covered by the fingers shifting in double stops. For instance, in octaves, the 4th always travels less distance than the 1st. In scale passages in 3rds and 10ths, the student should always be aware which finger is moving a whole step and which one a half step.

In very high positions, the fingers can reach easily into several positions without the player having to move the thumb or hand. Students with very small hands may not be able to keep the thumb pressed against the neck as they move into the very high positions, but may have to move it around on the side of the instrument. It should be pressed firmly against the body of the violin. The violin should be held quite firmly at the chin.

The thumb must remain secure

Intonation - Playing In Tune

Teachers entering the Suzuki movement often naively assumed that rote learning with its heavy emphasis on listening guaranteed success with intonation problems. In addition, tapes on the fingerboard were there to guide the child during the early stages. Fortunately, there was some truth in the assumption. Beginners did seem to play better in tune than one expected, but later on, as the melodic patterns became more complex, the problem of playing in tune asserted itself forcefully. Many teachers reacted in one of three ways. "He isn't listening enough!" "He's been listening to the records for years, but he's not playing in tune. He just doesn't have an ear." "He doesn't care whether it's in tune or not."

Some children seem to have a direct line from the ear to the finger. If they hear an out-of-tune note, the offending finger adjusts immediately. If a child does not do this readily, however, it is wrong to assume that his hearing is incorrigible. Sometimes the child simply does not hear what he is doing. He is so absorbed with the actual performing that it seems as though his ears are detached.

The first requisite for playing in tune is to know how the pitches should sound. Listening to the pieces one is to study certainly helps develop aural images of the pitches, but experienced teachers, including Suzuki, know that this is not enough. Suzuki himself said, "It takes almost two years for a small child to play the first three notes of my tonalization exercise well in tune". So it follows that we teachers and parents must help the child to develop his pitch perception.

Parents and teachers assisting students with intonation should have a firm belief that the students can improve, that their pitch discrimination can be refined. One must expect children to develop this ability at different speeds as they do in learning everything else, and one must expect that they will never reach the limit of their capability in this regard. This belief, this faith in each child's capabilities, must shine through to convince those children who perceive pitch differences only slowly and imperfectly at the beginning and lose confidence in their ability to improve. It is difficult for the teacher, however well-intentioned, to conceal from the child the fact that he regards him as hopeless.

It might be mentioned here that, while the tapes are a valuable visual aid to the correct placement of fingers, if pitch is never mentioned in the lessons, the child may simply rely on the tapes and actually not listen to his own playing.

The first step to be taken to guide a child with intonation is to give him a model to imitate. This is of course provided by the recordings but at performance tempo, which is often too rapid. Some teachers make practice tapes for their students, playing difficult passages very slowly and separated so that the child has an opportunity to match the pitches.

It is helpful to ask the child playing out of tune to try to sing the melody and then try to play the same pitches he sang.

Following Suzuki's policy of playing games to illustrate points, the teacher could play a passage and ask the child to identify a wrong note, then tell whether it was too high or too low. At first, the wrong note should be quite wide of the mark, then gradually closer. This leads naturally into a game of matching pitches. This distresses some youngsters who feel that they should be able to do it immediately without fail. "Don't be afraid to try different pitches", the teacher should say encouragingly. Easily distracted children might do this better with their eyes closed. It is well to use the Twinkle rhythm, since a single note may be difficult to remember.

Matching pitches played by the teacher leads to the student matching pitches played by himself. Unisons (the same pitch) are the easiest except for the fact that this involves the use of 4th finger in first position. Example: Student plays Twinkle rhythm on open E, then places 4th on A and tries to match the pitch.

Suzuki teaches octave matching first, matching pitches that are octaves of the open strings. These are particularly resonant tones. The resonance aids the ear in evaluating the pitch. It is difficult to explain the alikeness of octaves to small children. Some children are content when the teacher says, "Listen, this G sounds just like the low G, only higher." Enterprising teachers have come up with all sorts of explanations for octaves, including the statement that notes an octave higher are like the same people riding in an elevator and having gone up one floor, or the statement that the octave notes are the same people dressed differently.

There are nine notes in first position that can be matched with the open strings in unisons and octaves. Not only are these notes often principal pitches in the keys the student will be hearing, but they are valuable reference notes for gauging the correct pitches of other notes. The student who can play these nine notes with reasonable accuracy has come a long way in the development of his intonation.

The nine notes described are:
G string: A, 1st finger; D, 4th finger
D string: E, 1st finger; G, 3rd finger; A, 4th finger
A string: D, 3rd finger; E, 4th finger
E string: G, low 2nd finger; A, 3rd finger

From this point, it is difficult to be dogmatic about pitch. From the study of physics of sound, we know that there is a natural tuning related to the essence of the various pitches. This is no place for a discourse on natural and 'tempered' tuning, but a few points must be made to avoid complete oversimplification of the problem. For instance, a vibrating string vibrates not only as a whole which produces the tone we hear (the fundamental) but also vibrates in parts which produce tones called partials or harmonics. The vibrations of the open G string produce an infinite number of partials, some of which can be clearly heard by the discerning ear. The notes of the strongest partials are G, B, D. The vibrations of the E string produce these strong partials: E, G sharp, B. The B naturals in both cases are naturally in tune with the fundamental tones. The catch is that the notes we call B in both cases differ slightly in pitch. The B produced as a partial of the open E is slightly higher than the B produced as a partial of the open G.

In the past, this created a real problem with the tuning of keyboard instruments. The proposal was made to adopt a tuning called 'tempered' in which these differences would be ironed out by choosing pitches that divided the octave into twelve equal parts. This is the way pianos are tuned today. So a violinist playing with piano accompaniment adjusts his tuning slightly to match the piano pitches. "Natural" tuning is found when strings play together as in a string quartet. Incidentally, J. S. Bach was a champion of the tempered tuning for keyboard instruments, writing a set of pieces in all keys he called "The Well Tempered Clavier".

What does all this have to do with helping the student with his intonation? Simply this, the following suggestions for locating pitches are somewhat oversimplified, and yet should provide pitches that are acceptable. As the student matures and becomes more and more conscious of pitch, he will learn to make choices of pitches depending upon factors such as the accompaniment and the key and harmonic structure of the music. The guides given here should prevent gross errors, errors offensive even to the untrained ear.

One of the most helpful guides to intonation is a secure aural image of the major scale. Suzuki talks frequently about this natural way to relate pitches. The A, D, and G major scales should be familiar from the study of Book I. After these are well in the ear, it is not so difficult for the student to play scales starting on other pitches, although these scales are not as resonant on the violin as the ones mentioned above. One of the most characteristic intervals in the major scale is the half step interval from the 7th tone (the leading tone) to the 8th tone (the tonic). The tonic, also the 1st tone, is the note on which the scale is constructed. Its name is the name of the scale and the key.

The characteristic leading tone-tonic relationship, ingrained in the student's ear, can be used effectively with the nine notes which are octaves or unisons of the open strings to tune additional pitches.

Example: To find the pitch of G sharp, high 3rd on D, don't play G and then move the finger higher. G and G sharp are not in the same key and are difficult to identify next to each other. Rather, play A with 4th

finger. Check its pitch with the open A, then proceed to imagine it as the tonic note of the A major scale. Then play the high 3rd, G sharp close to the A, thinking of it as the leading tone of the A scale.

The leading tone-tonic relationship can be reversed to locate other pitches. In this case, one of the nine notes mentioned above may be conceived as a temporary leading-tone in a scale, with the notes one half-step above as its tonic.

Example: To find the pitch of A flat, low 4th on the D, don't play A and then move the finger back. A and A flat are not in the same key and are difficult to identify next to each other. Rather, play G with the 3rd finger. Check its pitch with the open G, then proceed to imagine it as the leading tone of a major scale. Then play the low 4th finger, A flat, close to the G, thinking of the A flat as the tonic of the scale.

This principle of thinking the leading tone-tonic relationship gives the student a guide to checking a great number of pitches, nineteen in the first position alone.

Other portions of the major scale can be used to locate additional pitches.

Example: To find the pitch of B, high 2nd on the G, play up from the open string the first three notes of the G scale. Then play G - B. This interval, 1 - 3 in the scale, is called a major third. It is very prominent and very frequently used.

Suzuki also asks teachers to teach double stops with open strings for the development of correct intonation. "Please teach perfect intonation of octaves, thirds, fourths, etc. All of these intervals have a characteristic resonance. Beautiful intervals are perfectly in tune and one can hear their resonance."

Example: A perfect 4th is the interval 1 - 4 in the major scale.
Play A, 1st on G, as a perfect 4th with open D. Listen for the resonance.

Example: A major 3rd is the interval 1 - 3 in the major scale.
Play F on D, low 2nd, as a major 3rd with open A. Listen for the resonance.

Example: A minor 3rd (one half step smaller than a major 3rd) is the interval 3 - 5 in the major scale.
Play C sharp on A, high 2nd, as a minor 3rd with open E. Listen for the resonance.

Example: A major 6th is the interval 1 - 6 in the major scale.
Play F sharp on the E, 1st, as a major 6th with open A. Listen for the resonance.

Example: A minor 6th (one half step smaller than the major 6th) is the interval 3 - 8 in the major scale.
Play F on E, low 1st, as a minor 6th with the open A. Listen for the resonance.

Below is a list of the notes of first position in chromatic order from the G string to the E. (Rare pitches like B sharp and C flat are omitted.) The fingering is given with a guide to determining the correct pitch.

G string

G sharp: Low 1st. This is the leading tone of A, 1st.

A flat: Low 1st. Open G is the leading tone of this note.

A : 1st. Octave of open A.

A sharp: High 1st. This is the leading tone of B, high 2nd.

B flat: Low 2nd. A, 1st, is the leading tone of this note.
(M a j o r 3rd: B flat with open D.)

B : High 2nd. Major 3rd above open G. 1 - 3 interval in major scale. (Minor 3rd: B with open D.)

C : Perfect 4th above open G. 1 - 4 interval in major scale.

C sharp: High 3rd. This is the leading tone of D, 4th.

D flat: Low 4th. C, 3rd, is the leading tone of this note.

D : 4th. Unison with open D.

D string

D sharp: Low 1st. This is the leading tone of E, 1st.

E flat: Low 1st. Open D is the leading tone of this note.

E : 1st. Octave of open E.

E sharp: High 1st. This is the leading tone of F sharp, high 2nd.

F : Low 2nd. E, 1st, is the leading tone of this note.
(Major 3rd: F with open A.)

F sharp: High 2nd. This is the leading tone of G, 3rd.
(Minor 3rd: F sharp with open A.)

G flat: Low 3rd. F, low 2nd, is the leading tone of this note.

G : 3rd. Octave of open G.

G sharp: High 3rd. This is the leading tone of A, 4th.

A flat: Low 4th. G, 3rd, is the leading tone of this note.

A : 4th. Unison of open A.

A string

A sharp: Low 1st. This is the leading tone of B, 1st.

B flat: Low 1st. Open A is this note's leading tone.

B : 1st. 7th degree of the C major scale. 6-7-8. Open A, B, C.
(Perfect 4th: B with open E.)

C : Low 2nd. Tonic of C major scale. 6-7-8. Open A, B, C.
(Major 3rd: C with open E.)

C sharp: High 2nd. This is the leading tone of D, 3rd.
(Minor 3rd: C sharp with open E.)

D flat: Low 3rd. C, low 2nd, is this note's leading tone.

D : 3rd, Octave of open D.

D sharp: High 3rd. This is the leading tone of E, 4th.

E flat: Low 4th. D, 3rd, is this note's leading tone.

E : 4th. Unison of open E.

E String

E sharp: Low 1st. This is the leading tone of F sharp, 1st.

F : Low 1st. Open E, is this note's leading tone.
(Minor 6th: F with open A.)

F sharp: 1st. This is the leading tone of G, low 2nd.
(Major 6th: F sharp with open A.)

G flat: Low 2nd. F, low 1st, is this note's leading tone.

G : Low 2nd. Octave of open G.

G sharp: High 2nd. This is the leading tone of A, 3rd.

A flat: Low 3rd. G, low 2nd is this note's leading tone.

A : 3rd. Octave of open A.

A sharp: High 3rd. This is the leading tone of B, 4th.

B flat: Low 4th. A, 3rd, is this note's leading tone.

B : Perfect 5th above open E. Interval 1-5 in major scale.

The students should remember that the open strings are their best guides for pitch reference. It is a good practice habit to brush an open string lightly to check its unison or octave as it occurs in the music.

Examples of practical application of these principles:

1. Book I: Minuet No. 2, Bach
(6th line, 3rd measure, critical note: D sharp to be played with high 3rd)

a) Play B, 1st finger on A.

b) Play E, 4th finger, as tonic.

c) Play D sharp, high 3rd, as leading tone.

d) Play B again.

e) Play D sharp, high 3rd, remembering pitch and location of step (c).

2. Book I: Gavotte, Gossec. (2nd line, 3rd measure, critical note: C sharp to be played with high 3rd)

a) Play E, 1st finger on D.

b) Play D, 4th finger on G, as tonic.

c) Play C sharp, high 3rd, as the leading tone.

d) Play E, 1st finger again

e) Play C sharp, high 3rd, with same pitch as step (c).

3. Book II: Two Grenadiers, Schumann (1st full measure: critical note is F natural to be played with low 1st)

a) Play F, low 1st as double stop with open A. This is a minor 6th interval. Listen for the resonance.

Developing the ability to know and find the correct pitch is of paramount importance in performing with good intonation but the student is lost if he does not develop the kinesthetic sense, or motor memory. The fingers need to be trained to "feel" the correct pitches and remember their distance and location. Suzuki's first pieces utilize only one finger pattern so that the child can develop a good basic hand position and remember the "feel" of the relationships of the fingers in this pattern.

As the child is introduced to new finger patterns, the teacher should call his attention to the 'natural' errors that may occur due to the slight changes in the frame of the hand. For example, when the low 2nd finger is first used, it has a tendency to pull the 3rd back, causing its note to be flat. A colorful way to express this to a small child could be "Your 2nd and 3rd fingers have been together for so long that when 2nd moves down to be with 1st, the 3rd wants to follow."

The ear tells the player where the finger should be placed the first time. The kinesthetic sense tells where it should go after that. Fortunately this motor memory develops naturally as the children learn to play, but the teacher can help immeasurably by playing games with the children to see if they are building the ability to 'know' where pitches are on the fingerboard without hearing them first. (See Suzuki's placement games at the end of Book IV.)

Some children persist in sliding into a correct pitch. The teacher should ask if they can anticipate the correction and put the finger down correctly at the very first.

The teacher should assist the child in developing both the sense of mental placement and mental reflection on the action done. Suzuki calls it 'preparation' in Book I. He asks for rests between notes to allow time for preparation. This training of the mind becomes more critical as new finger patterns, shifting and vibrato are studied, since all of these cause changes in the basic frame of the hand as learned by the child at the beginning. Suzuki introduces new finger patterns slowly so that the student may gain the feel of each new one before learning the next. Suzuki realizes the problems children face as the hand moves more and more over the fingerboard, but states that it is better to start learning one basic position well than it is to start with many fluctuations of position. All new hand positions may then be related to the first one.

Although the first goal of intonation practice is to develop accuracy as the fingers are first brought down, we should not overlook the importance of the ability to make small adjustments in pitch. This kind of ability should be developed with 'performance' practice, a period in which the student plays straight through a piece or section without stopping. He should try to adjust out-of-tune notes as he plays. (The vibrato is helpful for making small quick adjustments.) It is good practice for the advanced student to play on strings that have gone out of tune so that he may get further experience adjusting his fingers to produce correct pitches.

Suzuki feels that the students with the best intonation should play the harmony parts since they are more difficult to hear. It is a mark of status in Suzuki programs to be allowed to play 2nd violin, the harmony part.

Vibrato

The acquisition of a beautiful expressive vibrato, subject to the artistic demands of the player, should be the goal of every student. It has been said that the vibrato is an intensely personal thing, an expression or extension of the soul or personality of the player. There is nothing wrong with this statement except that for some it carries the inference that one cannot or should not teach vibrato. If a child has serious obstacles to his vibrato production, should not every assistance be given to him to allow his expressiveness to see the light of day? Teachers everywhere can point to students who acquired a fine vibrato without being taught, but everyone also agrees that these students are the exception. Should these few be the only students to acquire a beautiful vibrato?

Acquiring a fine vibrato may take a very long time. Vibrato study should be spread over a number of years as needed. If it is presented in this fashion, "Now we must learn vibrato," it may well be a traumatic experience for the child who cannot do it easily. Rather the vibrato should be taught slowly and carefully along with other material. Preliminary exercises may be done for five minutes a day for months. The teacher should start these early before the child tries to vibrate, before the child psychologically "needs" vibrato. There should be no sense of urgency conveyed to the student. The child should be told again and again that different students take different periods of time to acquire a vibrato. He should be convinced that he *can* acquire a good vibrato.

Children are often heard to remark to one another, "I learned vibrato last year". This shows a basic misconception of the problem. Even after a good vibrato is acquired, the student should work on its further development every day. His goal should be to possess the most expressive vibrato he can produce. This means that he must be able to control it without question, its speed, its breadth, its intensity, and its use. The vibrato should not move automatically as though it were being controlled by some outside agent.

Listening to one's vibrato is of paramount importance in the acquisition of a fine vibrato. If the student doesn't develop the habit of listening to the sound he produces, in other words, doesn't develop a discriminating ear, all physical exercises for vibrato production will be of little avail. This power of discrimination can be developed.

The student should realize from the beginning that the vibrato is used to heighten expression, to enhance the tone. How does vibrato heighten expression? The dictionary describes vibrato as a pulsating or tremulous effect imparted to a musical tone by slight rapid variations in pitch. The variations in pitch must be heard! The student may see his hand or arm moving for vibrato but no change of pitch is heard. Current musical taste puts limits on the width and speed of these variations in pitch but there remains within these limits a great deal of room for self-expression depending upon the style of the music to be performed. The student should listen to recordings of great artists to see how they implement the vibrato for expressive performances of different literature.

Beginners without direction usually try to initiate a vibrato in one of the following ways: 1) They move the wrist back and forth with a slow tortuous action. (The result is usually a large unwieldy arm vibrato.) 2) They try a finger vibrato, jerking the finger back and forth or moving it awkwardly in circles. Both of these attempts at vibrato are the result of the violin being clutched in the left hand.

The Hand Position

Even if a student is not clutching the violin in the left hand, and is holding it principally at the chin, the shift of hand position for vibrato, however slight, can be traumatic for the student. It seems to, and perhaps does at first, jeopardize his placement of the left hand. It is as though all of his previous playing had no relationship to this new hold. The parent observer often cannot understand why this is so difficult—the student doesn't look as though his position had changed radically. Actually it has. He may feel as though he has lost complete control.

The following exercise is helpful to point out the fact that up to this time the left hand had three contact points (thumb, base of 1st finger, and finger down on the string) with the violin. For a free vibrato, the hold must change to two contact points (the thumb, and finger down on the string). This change from three contact points to two is one of the biggest growth changes the student can and will make.

Exercise: (It is helpful to close the eyes during this exercise so that all the attention can be brought to bear on the feelings in the left hand.)

(a) Hold the violin firmly between chin and shoulder. Put the left hand in playing position with the fingers poised over the strings. The hand should touch the sides of the violin neck in two places, at the ball of the thumb, and at the base of the first finger. Since it is difficult to touch the sides 'in the air' so to speak, some teachers recommend that the violin be cradled lightly in the left hand, that is, some of the weight of the neck and peg box should rest lightly on the bones of the thumb and base of the first finger.

(b) Put 3rd finger down lightly on the A string. Then put the finger down firmly but not with excessive pressure. Notice the three points of contact and the pressures felt as the finger is put down. As the finger presses the string down, both the thumb and the base of the first finger press into the neck. This is the normal reaction at this point in the student's development.

(c) Release the finger pressure and leave the finger resting lightly on the string. Notice the decrease of pressure at the contact points of thumb and first finger.

(d) Now move the first finger slightly away from the neck. Again put the third finger down firmly. Try not to touch the violin with the base of first finger. The thumb must provide all the counterpressure to the finger. At this awkward point, some students move their thumbs under the violin to support it from below, and others allow the thumbs to slip up until the violin rests in the hand. Try to keep the thumb in the same place, with the ball of the thumb in contact with the neck. Excessive pressure on the fingertip will cause an equally excessive pressure with the thumb.

The first finger should not move far from the neck.

The student should repeat this many times a day, using different fingers. It is important that the finger pressure be only that necessary to produce a clear tone. Any extra pressure is not only wasted energy, but tends to tighten the hand by requiring an equally excessive counterpressure from the thumb. As the student begins to become more comfortable with this change of contact from three points to two, he is ready for vibrato action. While he must not push into the neck with the first finger, he should keep the finger very close to the neck, even touching lightly. There should be only the slightest difference in the position of the hand vibrating or playing fast passage-work. Once he releases the first finger from pushing into the neck, the student becomes more sensitive to the contact point of the thumb and the direction in which counterpressure is applied. This solo role is new for the thumb. It may be some time before the student feels comfortable with this hold.

The Motion of the Hand

At the same time the student is learning this new left hand position, he should be learning the basic hand vibrato motion, the roll of the hand back and forth in the wrist socket. Hand vibrato is generally taught first. Some of the 'natural' beginners, however, may experiment and quickly acquire an arm vibrato that looks and sounds good. This should be accepted as a good thing. Hand vibrato can be taught much later and very gradually as a means to extend the student's range of ex-

pression. Likewise, those who acquire a fine hand vibrato may be taught an arm vibrato much later to enlarge their range of expressiveness.

The hand vibrato may be divided into two component parts for study purposes: the roll of the hand, and the bending of the fingers. These will be presented separately but could be practiced during the same period, although not together at first.

It is difficult for most students to move the hand back and forth with a rapid, smooth, and relaxed action. The student trying this for the first time often finds the hand jerking spasmodically. The hand should be moved slowly until he develops control. The following exercises are given to assist in the development of the correct hand motion. For some students many or all may be unnecessary. For other students, the teacher may have to add to this list.

The E string has been chosen for the first placement of the fingers because the least weight on the fingertip is required to produce a clear tone. Admittedly, it may be a more difficult position for the hand, since the fingers are so close to the edge of the neck, but the advantage of light weight fingering far outweighs this disadvantage. Strong finger pressure prohibits the correct development of many vibratos.

1. Student places left arm on desk or table top, and taps top with his fingers. The impulse for the motion should come from the back of the hand, not from the fingers. This should be done with a smooth flowing action, not a spring action. The table top keeps the hand from going too far forward, and prepares the student to vibrate away from the fingertip. A beat should be established. At first, the student taps twice to the beat. As he gains facility and is able to move more rapidly without spasmodic jerks, he may increase the speed to three taps per beat, then four, etc.

2. The student duplicates the above motion in the air, with his hand held normally in front of him. The hand should not move forward, but rather from a straight position back, similar to the motion on the table top.

3. The student holds the hand in playing position, but much closer to the body. The hand should then be rolled back and forth.

4. The student holds the hand in playing position, but holds the left thumb with the right hand. Care should be taken that the hand roll is initiated by the hand and not by the fingers and that the hand moves back and forth, and not in circles.

5. If the fingers tend to move too much, the hand may be closed to emphasize the hand roll.

6. Student holds a pencil in the right hand, pointing to the left. He places the ball of his left thumb on the pencil. Holding the first finger next to the pencil, he rolls the hand back and forth.

7. Student holds violin in guitar position. He places the ball of his left thumb on the neck. Holding the 1st finger near the neck, he rolls his hand.

8. Student holds violin in guitar position. Student places one finger at a time lightly on the E string, and rolls hand allowing finger to slide back and forth on the string. Finger should not press into string, nor should the finger initiate the motion.

9. Student puts violin in playing position, supporting the body with the right hand. The left hand is put in playing position. The fingers are not put down but kept at side of neck. Student rolls hand back and forth.

10. Student puts violin in playing position, supporting the violin with the right hand. The left hand is put in playing position with the 3rd finger touching the E string lightly. The hand is rolled back and forth. The finger is allowed to slide back and forth.

11. Student puts violin in playing position and leans against wall or rests violin on music stand for support. Left hand is put in playing position with the 3rd finger touching the string lightly.

The hand is rolled back and forth. The finger is allowed to slide along the string.

12. As Ex. 11 above, only this time the student keeps the 3rd finger in one place, leaning with a little weight on the fingertip. As this is repeated, more weight can be added gradually to the tip of the finger. The finger should bend at the first joint as weight is applied.

13. The student repeats Ex. 12, drawing long bows. The fingertip should have just enough weight to produce a clear tone.

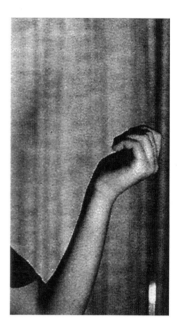

The hand should move back

Supporting the violin . . .

The vibrato action should not be too wide nor too fast at this time. The oscillations should be smooth and regular, not jerky.

At the same time he is practicing the above exercises, the student should be developing his two-contact hold for use with the vibrato.

14. Student puts violin in playing position with a firm hold at chin. Left hand is put in position with the 3rd finger touching on the E lightly. As a long up bow is drawn, the vibrato is started with the finger allowed to slide back and forth. The motion should be quite narrow. As the bow moves, the student adds weight gradually to the fingertip and keeps it in one place. The finger should begin to bend at the first joint. The student can hear a clear tone emerge as the finger weight becomes sufficient. No external support should be used to hold the violin. The thumb should remain in the proper position. This exercise can be repeated many times, with more weight on the fingertip as facility is developed.

15. The student moves the hand into third position so that the hand rests against the body of the instrument. The 3rd finger is put down and the hand is made to vibrate. This is played with the bow. It is good practice for the hand roll with a finger down. Second or third finger can be used easily. The first finger should be disengaged from the side of the neck.

16. This exercise is difficult for the teacher. It is based on the "patterning" technique used for brain-damaged children. The exercise is intended to give the student a sound image for his vibrato and a feel of the muscular motion.

   a) The teacher, standing in front of the student assists in holding the violin with his right hand, also holding the student's thumb in place at the neck.

   b) With the left hand, the teacher activates a hand vibrato, moving the student's hand back and forth. The student does not press on the fingertip. The teacher holds the finger in place with his ring finger as he oscillates the student's hand. The student draws the bow as this is being done.

   c) After keeping the hand moving for a while, the teacher tells the student that he is now going to let him 'take over'. He then withdraws his left hand, keeping the right hand in place.

   d) The student tries to vibrate with the same width and speed he has just witnessed.

Some children respond remarkably quickly to this patterning and succeed in imitating the vibrato very well. It is difficult for them if they press too much on the fingertip.

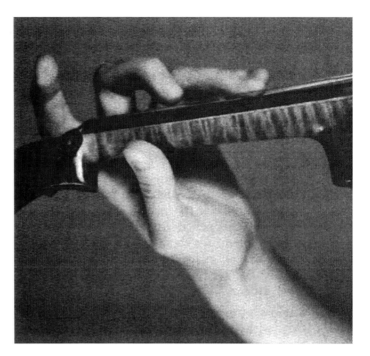

Vibrato motion backward . . .

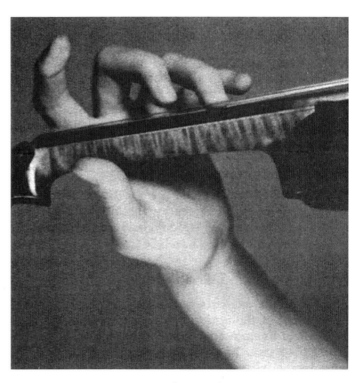

. . . and forward

17. The following exercise is like Ex. 16 except that the teacher does not support the violin with the right hand. The teacher needs to have some support for his own left hand as he moves the student's hand, so he may lean against the scroll with his right hand.

Parents who have learned to do this motion have found it very helpful for their children, since they help them every day. This "patterning" technique can also

153

be used for arm vibrato with the teacher holding the student's arm slightly below the wrist as he moves it back and forth.

Finger Flexibility

The following two exercises are intended to help the student with finger flexibility, although many students will begin to flex their fingers as they add weight to the fingertip in the earlier exercises.

1. Student holds pencil in right hand in front of him, pointing to the left. He places the ball of his left thumb on the pencil. He then places 3rd finger on the pencil up against the right hand support, then rolls the hand back and forth. The finger has no place to slide, so it flexes as the hand rolls. This should be practiced with the other fingers in order.

2. Student puts violin and left hand in playing position, with 3rd finger on the E string lightly. He then reaches over and places his right hand against the 3rd finger, holding it in place. The hand is then rolled back and forth with the finger bending at the first joint. This should be practiced with the other fingers in order.

After a vibrato is functioning well, the following exercises may be practiced:

1. First, play 4 long bows on the note A on the E string, 3rd finger. Second, move the 2nd finger to the same note and play another four long bows. Third, move the 1st finger up to the A and draw four long bows. Try to make the same kind of sound throughout. After some facility has been achieved, try the same exercise on the A, then D, then G strings.

2. Play 4 long bows on the note A on the E string, 3rd finger. Then move the 3rd to the A string to play another 4 long bows. Continue in this manner on the D and G strings.

Arm Vibrato

All of the exercises above may be used for the development of the arm vibrato, with the student moving the whole forearm as a unit instead of moving the hand from the wrist. In order to isolate the forearm motion, one might tell the student that he was going to 'lock' the wrist for this study. It might be advisable to delay the development of a second vibrato for a long time.

Problems

If the student manages to play a superior vibrato on only one of the fingers, he should be encouraged to practice a great deal with that finger rather than ignore it and move to one of the other fingers. This will mean that he is training the hand roll and the hand hold both to a superior degree. This basic training eventually will help him with the other fingers.

Practicing vibrato in third position, resting the hand on the violin.

Practicing finger flexibility.

Practicing finger flexibility.

As the vibrato becomes 'usable' in pieces, the teacher should encourage its use only on long notes. Chorus from Judas Maccabeus in Book II is very popular with students just acquiring a vibrato. Gounod's Ave Maria is one of the best supplementary pieces for the use of vibrato. On occasion, we've used popular songs like "Somewhere My Love" for vibrato training.

If the student tends to a wild, excessive vibrato, it is effective to have him start a long note with no vibrato at all, then very gradually add motion until a pitch change is heard. The vibrato should be kept narrow. The student may be surprised to see how little motion is needed, provided the finger is flexible.

The teacher should delay working with the 4th finger until the vibrato is functioning well with the other fingers. The child's 4th finger should be strong enough for vibrato practice. Some children have to resort to arm vibrato for 4th finger.

If the student's vibrato remains too slow, the first step is to narrow it hoping that this will increase the speed. Less weight on the fingertip also may help to add some speed to the vibrato. It is true that there is some tension, or perhaps a better word is exertion, as the fast vibrato is employed. The student with the too slow vibrato may not be exerting himself at all. The teacher should show the student that certain muscles contract in the forearm and upper arm as the vibrato is quickened. This exercise is helpful.

a) The student places the bow at the tip on the E string. 3rd finger is down.

b) The student leans heavily on the bow stick, preparing to play a quick short accented note of great power.

c) As he moves the bow quickly, lifting it into the air, he tightens his hand and gives the note a fast vibrato accent.
As this exercise is repeated, the notes should become longer, and the tension in the hand less.

The student with the vibrato that is too fast should at first attempt to widen it. If this is unsatisfactory, he should be asked to play a very, very slow vibrato, one for which he can count the slow oscillations which should not be uneven. He should be told to relax his hand and forearm as he plays.

Vibrato accents produce striking results. The student should practice playing staccato notes accompanied by an intense and sudden vibrato that slows after the articulation.

Increasing the vibrato speed with a crescendo is very effective as is its opposite, slowing the vibrato with a diminuendo.

It is difficult to acquire a fine vibrato with double stops. This may come only after the single-note vibrato is well established. Many players use much arm vibrato with double stops, particularly with octaves.

Arm vibrato may also be helpful with vibrato on notes in the very high positions, if the arm can be made free of the body of the instrument. Vibrating with quite flat fingers on high notes can be very effective.

One of the most troublesome kinds of vibrato to develop is that used with notes of short duration. Seashore said that Kreisler vibrated on notes as short as a quarter of a second. This does not mean that several rapid oscillations were made on each of these short notes. This is what many students try to do. They rush to shake three or four times on each note. The ear is confused by the rapid changes of pitch. No, the notes of short duration should have fewer changes of pitch and narrower oscillations. Vibrato accents should be especially avoided. The student should practice playing scale passages, at first slurred, slowly with a narrow, slow, continuous vibrato. The vibrato should start instantly as the finger is put down, without accent or burst of speed. Actually, the hand should vibrate continually throughout all the changes of fingers. Or the arm, if the arm vibrato is used. As the student gains control over this continuous relaxed vibrato, he can gradually increase the speed of the fingerings. In the process, he should learn to vibrate with more than one finger down by using overlapping fingering. This will also help him with vibrato on double stops.

It cannot be emphasized too often that the ear must decide about the quality of the vibrato. The hand and arm and fingers should be taught to present a great variety of choices to the discriminating ear.

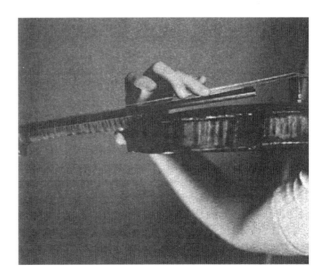

Using flat finger in a high position

Goals of Practice

(The material in the chapter "The Parent as Teacher. Home Practice" was slanted toward the small child dependent upon his parents. This chapter deals with problems of the older student, the student beginning to practice without parental supervision.)

Most teachers are convinced that excellent practice habits are developed by too small a percentage of the students striving to learn to play the violin. One of the biggest obstacles to developing excellent practice habits is at the same time one of the strongest motivating factors stimulating practice, that is, the insatiable desire to learn music to play either for oneself or for others. Even on the conservatory level, the student's better sense is overcome by his desire to get the first movement of the concerto ready to play for Professor X next week at the lesson. He rushes to learn the notes, and then spends hours unlearning his early mistakes. This twentieth-century student knows that his mind is like a computer, that he is the programer, and that he needs to make proper inputs, and yet the need to perform too soon overrides his best intentions.

As we teach more advanced students, we teachers need to adopt a new timetable for them, not one based on our own training. For example, here is an approach suggested for a student in Book VIII.

"You are now approaching the Mozart Concertos. Unfortunately, they are quite a bit more difficult than the music of this present book. It's not Suzuki's fault. It's the composers'. They just didn't decide consciously to write a piece for grade 6½ B. There are technical gaps in the literature due to different styles in different musical periods. I'm going to give you the most difficult passages in the Mozart A Major Concerto now. I'm giving them to you in small segments. I will show you exactly how I want these practiced. You may want to practice the first one until you can play it well, but I'm asking you not to do that but to practice all of them just a few times each day. Work like the building contractor who is building a number of houses at the same time and puts a few bricks on each house every day. Remember that you are not only learning these passages but developing your technique as well. If we complete Book VIII and you're still not quite ready to study the Mozart straight through, we'll review some literature and study some new easier pieces that will enlarge your repertoire. Don't feel any pressure to learn the Mozart to play it for me. I do want to hear how you are practicing the various passages. You can do this at lessons along with performing the easier music you'll be studying."

We talk about freeing the Suzuki student from dependence on his mother so that he can practice independently. The supervision should be gradually withdrawn, but that doesn't necessarily mean the student is ready to determine what and how he should practice. I think the teacher should continue to give specific instructions. If the teacher explains the "why" of his instructions along with the "how," gradually the student will begin to anticipate what to do because he knows the "why".

The student should understand the general goals of practicing new literature. They are as follows:

First: To be able to play the piece one is practicing.

Second: To be able to play similar passages or identical fragments that occur in other works.

Third: To become better acquainted with the bow and fingerboard.

Fourth: To develop better mental control over physical movements.

Mental anticipation of motions to be made and mental reflection on motions made are valuable tools for the student. They serve all of the above goals.

It is extremely important for the mind to be actively engaged as one practices. The following suggestions might be kept at hand as one prepares to practice.

1. Don't dwell too long on one problem.
2. Constantly check your mental awareness. If you have not been paying attention, try moving to another problem.
3. Mix practice objectives frequently. For example, intonation, then bowing, then coordination, etc.
4. Keep constant attention on the quality of tone you are producing.
5. Analyze difficulties before practicing certain problems. Break each problem into component parts.
6. Start with small fragments. Repeat them enough so that you can build speed if facility is part of the problem. Add to the fragments as you feel secure with each.
7. Review for a certain period daily. Try to develop your interpretive powers with the review pieces.
8. Save a period for 'performance' practice. Play straight through the piece, without stops. Make rapid adjustments as necessary. Imagine an audience.
9. Give complete attention to tone for a certain period daily.
10. Remember to use mental placement and mental reflection as often as practicable.

A teacher should prepare check-off lists for his advanced students, lists similar to Suzuki's Progress Reports for parents. These lists should remind the teacher of all the phases of technique the student should be learning at that time so that none are neglected. Here is a sample list for the left hand:

1. Vertical movements of fingers, that is, putting down and raising the fingers.
2. Horizontal movement of fingers, that is, sliding them up and down half steps.
3. Crossing strings. Reaching across strings with the fingers.
4. Shifting
5. Vibrato
6. Intonation
7. Fingering in different positions
8. Double stops
9. Trills
10. Harmonics
11. Glissando

Relaxation

Tension remains the chief obstacle to the development of a fine technique on the violin. From the very beginning, teachers are continually trying to produce the right kind of relaxation in the child's shoulders, hands and arms. Muscles do need to be developed for strength, but these same muscles should not exert more force than necessary, nor should muscles be used that are unnecessary.

The teacher first encounters tension in the child when he teaches him to hold the violin between chin and shoulder. Suzuki teaches the children to move at games while they are holding the violin to relax them and to free muscles that might otherwise be tense. As the left hand is brought up to the neck of the violin, the child will often clutch the neck with great tension. The teacher must constantly check to stop this before it becomes a habit. The child is taught to hold the bow firmly. This is often construed by the student to mean that it's all right to hold the bow with great tension.

Experienced teachers watch constantly for evidences of tension. They try to get the children to relax in many ways, by placing their hands on the children's shoulders, by bending and massaging fingers of both hands, by checking for excessive finger pressure on the strings, and by asking the children to 'feel' the teacher's arms and hands as he plays, to feel their lack of tension.

Suzuki says, "There are four points where we should relax the bow arm, four points at which we should not be stiff. We should teach students to be free and relaxed at these points: 1) shoulder 2) elbow 3) wrist 4) knuckles. Take special care of points three and four. Too many students are stiff in the wrist or knuckles."

Again Suzuki says to teachers, as written in his booklet for the annual teachers' meeting in the spring of 1976: "We must teach the children the proper kind of relaxation. We can borrow the advice that Oriental teachers give to students of the martial arts of sword and karate. From early times, martial arts teachers have explained how to be relaxed and yet centered, ready for instantaneous action. They say, 'Stand to your full height. Exhale a tiny bit and stop your breath.' This will result in putting strength in your center of gravity. At lessons, if we ask students who focus strength in their arms or shoulders to put strength in the area of their center of gravity instead, we find that their shoulders and arms naturally relax. Please do not forget this teaching technique. It can be very useful."

Practitioners of Ki (Coordination of Mind and Body) speak of the center of gravity Suzuki refers to above as the 'one point', a point in the person's lower abdomen several inches below the navel. Putting strength in the area of the center of gravity doesn't mean to tense the abdomen, but merely to think of the center of one's being as being located in the 'one point'. Violin teachers taking Suzuki's advice in this matter find that the students who can do this do relax their arms and shoulders.

Another one of the basic rules of Ki that has helped many violinists to relax is the rule, "Keep weight underside". This has excellent results in combating upward tensions. The instructions before playing might be like these: "Stand straight. Put your violin in playing position. Before you play, think all of your weight down, think of the underside of your feet. Holding the violin in position, think of the underside of both of your elbows. Now, play the violin, concentrating on playing the music. If your mind wanders, your posture will suffer."

This rule also helps the student to comprehend Suzuki's ideas of elbow action. If the child thinks of the underside of his elbow, he feels his elbow as a natural weight without tension. Doubters are always surprised when they try to lift the child's elbow after he has thought of its underside. The elbow seems much heavier than when the child is not thinking about it, or is thinking of the top side of his arm.

Mr. Yoshihiko Hirata, a Ki instructor who as a child was a violin student in Suzuki's Talent Education program in Japan, has given a number of demonstrations in America on the application of Ki to violin instruction. Readers desirous of literature on this subject are urged to write one of the following:

WESTERN STATES KI SOCIETY
c/o Aikido Institute of America
3302 W. Jefferson Blvd.
Los Angeles, CA 90018

NORTHWEST KI SOCIETY
c/o Mr. Yoshihiko Hirata
11713 - 38th N. E.
Seattle, Washington 98125

Memorization

Throughout this book there are many references to memory aids, the principal aid being that of listening. Small children who've heard the recordings many times seem to play effortlessly insofar as memory is concerned. The following suggestions are made primarily for the adolescent or older student who suddenly finds that he can no longer perform without fear of forgetting. He is bewildered by his sudden loss of childlike infallibility. Teachers should be prepared to help the student at this point.

First, it is helpful if the student knows something about the structure of the piece. He can follow it through with his mind. It is particularly helpful to point out to the child the places where similar passages differ. It is also helpful to test the children in group lessons, provided it is done in a spirit of fun.

A proven aid to the more advanced student is the visual one. If he has looked at the music long enough, studying the notes, he should be able to 'see' it as he plays. Soloists have been known to admit that they 'see' the music as they play, that they turn the pages mentally as the music unfolds. Music can be studied visually during the time in bed before the student goes to sleep. The mind's retention is very high at this time.

Writers on yoga state that the mind is constantly 'speaking' thoughts, that we are constantly 'talking to ourselves' when we think. Meditators using principles of yoga are able to stop this automatic self-conversation when they recite continually within themselves a mantra, a neutral sound of not more than two syllables. The meditator practicing yoga recognizes that the mind is constantly filled with sound and substitutes the mantra for thoughts spoken inwardly.

The performer feels that he is giving sufficient attention to his music if he listens to himself play, but a far different effect is felt if the performer sings along to himself internally as he plays. This is not true singing, this internal singing, yet it is an internal sound that helps exclude verbalized thoughts much as does the mantra. This is what the zen masters speak of as they say "When you eat, you eat." They mean that one should think of eating as one eats. Also, as the Ki instructor advises, "When you play the violin, you think about playing the violin." Why not sing along with oneself, experiencing only the flow of the music? Not only will this be immeasurably helpful in excluding distracting thoughts, but one will be more likely to give the music 'breath and spirit,' without which, Suzuki says, music does not live. The performer singing along with himself as he performs should continue to sing the accompaniment parts in all of the rests. He doesn't need to count rests, because he is continually absorbed in the flow of the music.

Stage Fright

Stage fright is notably absent in most young Suzuki children. Most of them seem to be positively enthusiastic about playing either in groups or as soloists in recitals. Parents are particularly grateful for this aspect of the Suzuki training. Their children not only willingly and eagerly look forward to playing for Suzuki programs, but also play without coercion for school, family, and friends.

Suzuki believes children should enjoy playing the violin and should have regular opportunities for performance. He encourages the teacher to allow the child to perform frequently in lessons. He feels performance should be a regular part of the child's home practice. Group lessons, teacher's recitals, and home concerts for the father all add performance opportunities.

There is a marvelous by-product of the child's performances for others. The child realizes that by his violin playing he can actually provide enjoyment for others. This adds a new dimension to his practice—he is working to make someone happier. His playing does not become so self-centered. It takes on a social aspect. This doesn't need verbal explanation. It should be a natural thing.

All of these performances should be true performances. The child should not stop if he makes a mistake but should develop the valuable habit of being able to recover after an error. Kreisler is quoted as having said, "When I make an error, then I feel I must play even better for the audience."

Unfortunately not all children are so enthusiastic about solo performance. Even group performance seems to be a frightening thing for some children. Suzuki doesn't advocate forcing children to play. He believes that if they are brought again and again to watch group lessons that eventually they'll want to join in. One mother reported bringing a five-year-old boy one whole year before he ventured up to play with the others. Now he stands up with the rest without a trace of discomfort. His mother points him out to new mothers whose children are reluctant to leave their mothers at group lessons.

Adolescents who suddenly become afflicted with stage fright are often as surprised by the change in their feelings toward performance as are the parents. Some of this uneasiness may be attributed to fear of memory lapses, in which case every effort must be made to help them in this regard. Simulated performances at home are most effective for these children. It is important that they should go through all the motions of a live performance, including wearing the proper clothes. When they do perform in public, they should have ample time for warm-up. Warm-up time varies considerably with different individuals. Some like to arrive at the last minute.

Everything should be suggested to reinforce a positive viewpoint. Too many children sit around and imagine bad performances, with their making all kinds of mistakes. They should sit down and practice imagining themselves playing fine performances!

These children should have ample training in developing the ability to pick up after they've made a mistake, so that fears of mistakes are minimized. "To err may be human", said one teacher to a fearful student, "but I'm going to train you to be able to go right on after the mistake. After all, when the people in an audience hear a mistake, they hope ardently that the performer won't be upset."

One of the best attitudes to inculcate in students was mentioned above with regard to smaller children, that is, the attitude that one is playing to make others happy, to brighten their lives, and to give them a deep enjoyment of music itself.

Reading Music

Suzuki mentions that reading should be taught as the child reaches the Vivaldi A Minor Concerto, depending on the child's age. Many Western children, having started as 'older' beginners, need to be able to read before they are into Book IV, since they have opportunities of playing in school orchestras and will need to develop the ability to read music with facility.

When we speak of reading music, we should clarify our position by stating what kind of reading we're talking about: 1) the kind of reading in which time is allowed for the student to decipher passages, or 2) the kind of reading in which he plays straight through, with no break in the tempo. In the first kind the student stops, works it out, and goes on. Later he may be able to play the piece without faltering rhythmically. The second kind is called sight-reading. He should be trained for both kinds. Many children never practice pure sight-reading. When they first encounter sight-reading in an audition, they stumble hopelessly. The memory of the first failure lessens their chance of success on later occasions.

There is some question whether sight-reading should be included in auditions. Teachers wishing a compromise, and knowing that the student should have the ability to play the music fairly quickly, have suggested that each student be given the music twenty minutes before his audition. Nevertheless, sight-reading is included in many auditions and the student should be prepared for it. The best way to prepare for it is to do it regularly, that is, keep the beat going no matter how many notes are lost along the way. At first this should be practiced with music quite below the technical level of the student.

Students should also be given practice in the 'figure-it-out' kind of reading. If they know the basic notational symbols, they should be encouraged to try to see if they can read the music, taking their time to figure out problems.

The teacher should give very specific instructions regarding proper posture for reading music, both for sitting and standing. Students should develop the ability to read music on either side of the scroll. This is very helpful in orchestral playing. Suzuki's formula for posture for the beginner, "Nose, string, elbow, foot", can be expanded to "Nose, string, elbow, foot, music, conductor."

The position of the student's chair needs to be considered. If the chair is pointed directly toward the music, the violin will be in the wrong position from the outset, since the violin will be on the left. In order to compensate for misplaced chairs, some students pull their left shoulders to the right in front of them. Others hold the violin out to the left, and turn their faces away from the violin toward the music. In group lessons, children should be given the opportunity of playing in every available orchestral seating position.

Students should know the symbols of musical notation before they actually use them. Fortunately, there are a number of fine workbooks for beginning readers. Even though the child becomes well acquainted with notation, at the outset he should be presented only a few problems in actual performance. Many teachers have found it advisable to separate rhythmic and pitch problems, preferring to present pitch symbols with only a very few different symbols of rhythmic notation. Teachers should use great ingenuity in repeating a limited vocabulary of symbols with every kind of variation. This was suggested by Suzuki to Tanaka for teaching math to first graders. "Give them a little to learn and repeat it many, many times to develop their facility." Too many teachers add new problems too soon with the result that the children cannot read at sight because they do not recognize the symbols automatically. In the chapter entitled 'Group Lessons' there are a number of games to make this repetition attractive and fun for the children.

Ensemble playing is of great value in training the rhythmic sense. This kind of activity falls naturally into the group lessons.

In conclusion, another principle should be mentioned. THE CHILDREN SHOULD READ MUSIC EVERY DAY.

Supplementary Literature

As the student begins his study of the last three Suzuki books, his rate of learning new material slows down radically because of the length and difficulty of the pieces. This is often at the very time he needs a boost to his morale. The instructor may want to use some additional material at this time, both for technical development and for the entertainment of the student and his family.

The following list of pieces contains my own suggestions as well as pieces that have been used successfully by experienced Suzuki teachers, Japanese and Western. Some of these pieces are intended for students currently in the last three Suzuki books. Others may be used as a bridge between Book X and works such as the concertos of Bruch and Mendelssohn. Still others are useful to know for 'popular' programs. Obviously, this is only a partial list of the great amount of suitable literature. The vast sonata literature after Handel has not been included because of the dependence upon a fine pianist as collaborator.

Anderson: Fiddle-Faddle
Bach: Arioso
Bach: Concerto in E
Bach: Sonatas for Klavier and Violin
  (selected movements)
Bach: Sonatas and Partitas for Solo Violin
  (selected movements)
Bartok: 44 Duets
Bartok: Rumanian Folk Dances
Bohm: Perpetual Motion
Beethoven: Romances
Corelli: 12 Sonatas (selected movements)

Dvorak: Sonatina
Falla-Kreisler: Dance from "La Vida Breve"
Gounod: Ave Maria
Granados-Kreisler: Spanish Dance
Handel: Sonata No. 6 in E
Hubay: Hejre Kati
Kreisler: La Gitana
Kreisler: Liebeslied
Kreisler: Rondino on a Theme of Beethoven
Kreisler: Schon Rosmarin
Massenet: Meditation from "Thais"
Monti: Czardas
Mozart: Concerto In G Major
Mozart: Rondo
Nardini: Concerto in E Minor
Nero: Suite for Hot Fiddle (In the Blue)
Novacek: Perpetual Motion
Ponce: Estrellita
Pugnani-Kreisler: Praeludium and Allegro
Schubert-Freidberg: Rondo
Schubert: Sonatinas
Schumann: Prophetic Bird
Telemann: Concertos for Four Violins
Vitali: Chaconne
Vivaldi: Concerto in B Minor for Four
  Violins
Vivaldi: Sonatas
Wieniawski: Romance (from D Minor
  Concerto)

U. of Tenn. tour group in Caracas, Venezuela.